Partnership and Profit in Medieval Islam

PRINCETON STUDIES ON THE NEAR EAST

Partnership and Profit in Medieval Islam

ABRAHAM L. UDOVITCH

PRINCETON UNIVERSITY PRESS
PRINCETON, NEW JERSEY
1970

L.C. Card No.: 78-104097
ISBN: 0-691-03084-7

Publication of this book has been
aided by the Department of Near Eastern Studies of Princeton University
and by the Whitney Darrow Publication Reserve Fund
of Princeton University Press

This book has been composed in Linotype Granjon
Printed in the United States of America by
Princeton University Press, Princeton, New Jersey

To My Parents

Benjamin and Minnie Udovitch

Tu mich ohn in dein kleyd fun graytkeit

un loz mich a grayten in weg.

Preface

Parts of Chapters III and VII of this book, in somewhat revised form, appeared as articles in *The Journal of the American Oriental Society* and *The Journal of Social and Economic History of the Orient*, and as a contribution to *Logic in Classical Islamic Culture*, edited by G. E. von Grunebaum.

The system of transliteration for Arabic words corresponds to that used by the Library of Congress with the single difference that articles preceding "sun letters" are transliterated as pronounced.

In the course of the preparation of this study, I have incurred obligations of gratitude to numerous friends and associates. I would like to single out for special thanks my colleagues Professors J. Neusner of Brown University, Jeanette Wakin of Columbia University, J. Lassner of Wayne State University, and Jeanette Mirsky, Norman Itzkowitz, and L. Carl Brown, all of Princeton, who have read and made valuable suggestions on all or part of this study.

Finally, I would like to express my profound thanks to four of my masters in the field of medieval and Near Eastern studies: to the late Professor Joseph Schacht, from whose generous and penetrating comments the manuscript has greatly benefited, and whose towering contributions to the understanding of Islamic law have put all future students of the subject in his permanent debt; to Professor S. D. Goitein, who initiated me into the mysteries and fascinations of Geniza studies, the results of which are reflected on many of the following pages; to Professor Franz Rosenthal, whose embodiment of the finest and most uncompromising traditions of humanistic scholarship remain an enduring model to all those who have been privileged to work with him; and to Professor Robert S. Lopez, whose guidance and inspiration in my work and life extend far beyond the confines of this book.

Princeton
March 1970

Contents

Partnership and Profit in Medieval Islam

I

Introduction

Commercial Law and Economic History

From the point of view of economic history, the ideal way to study any institution of commercial law would be to compare the information contained in legal codes and treatises with the material relating to its application in economic life as manifested by actual contracts, letters, and business records found in archives and other repositories. In the case of the early centuries of the Islamic period, available sources unfortunately preclude such a procedure. Theoretical legal texts exist in abundance, but any corresponding documentary material is for all practical purposes non-extant. In order to determine the framework in which the trade and commerce of the early Islamic period was carried on—a trade known to have been active and important—we must of necessity rely on legal treatises for most of our information, while trying wherever possible to call upon whatever meager help other literary sources may provide.

In the absence of documentary and similar sources, the possibility of investigating the quantitative aspects of trade is all but eliminated. However, in those areas of trade which have been described as qualitative, such as the variety of goods exchanged, the specialization of the merchant class, and the complexity of business methods,[1] legal and other literary sources provide a great deal of valuable information. It is with the institutions of partnership and *commenda* in the early Islamic period, two of the qualitative components of trade, that this study will be concerned.

Pooling resources, whether in the form of cash, goods, skills, or a combination of these, is one of the indispensable components of any extended commercial activity. In Islamic law, the partnership and *commenda* contracts are the two basic

[1] R. S. Lopez, in *The Cambridge Economic History of Europe*, Cambridge, 1952, 2:258.

legal instruments by which this can be accomplished. Joseph Kohler, an eminent legal historian of the early part of this century, has asserted that the decline of Islamic commercial hegemony in the Middle Ages was due in a large part to the limitations placed by Islamic law on the development of associative relationships.[2] Whether the role of commercial legal institutions was as decisive in the economic history of the medieval Near East as Kohler suggested is open to discussion; there can be no question, however, that the institutions of Islamic commercial law are factors to be considered before any judgment can be made concerning the economic growth and decline of the medieval Muslim world.

Historians of the commercial law of the medieval West generally agree that legal techniques not only reflected but also influenced economic practices.[3] If we assume at least the same for the medieval Muslim world, then, in spite of the absence of archival documents, a thorough investigation of the major institutions of Islamic commercial law will not only be a chapter of "Handelsrechtsgeschichte," but may also serve as an indicator of the level and complexity of those fields of economic activity in which the institution was applicable.

Islamic Law and Practice

From the outset, one confronts the rather complex question of the nature of the *sharīʿa* (Islamic sacred law) and the *fiqh* (Islamic jurisprudence),[4] and the corollary problem of the propriety of using Muslim legal treatises as a source for the investigation of economic and social institutions. Any assumed harmony between medieval Islamic law and the actual practice of that period has been brought into serious question, and even completely denied by several eminent Islamists.

Beginning with the mid-nineteenth century, translations of a number of *fiqh* manuals into European languages made

[2] Joseph Kohler and Leopold Wenger, *Allgemeine Rechtsgeschichte, Orientalisches Recht und Recht der Griechen und Römer*, Berlin, 1914, p. 98.

[3] R. S. Lopez and I. W. Raymond, *Medieval Trade in the Mediterranean World*, pp. 156–235.

[4] For a full definition of these terms, cf. S. Vesey-Fitzgerald in *Law in the Middle East*, 1:86–87.

Islamic legal material available for the first time to Western legal historians and comparative legal scholars. Some of these translations were of questionable accuracy,[5] and the non-Arabist legal scholars treating the material were unable to compensate for this deficiency by referring back to the original sources. In addition, these scholars approached the corpus of Islamic religious law on the assumption that it was a determining factor in the actual practices of the Muslim world, and attempted to impose some consistency within the material by applying their own concepts of legal classification to it. Two of the leading orientalists of the day, C. S. Hurgronje and I. Goldziher, reacted to what they considered to be a misconception and abuse of *fiqh* material by attempting to provide an analysis of the *fiqh* in its Islamic historical context.[6]

Fiqh in their view is not, strictly speaking, law, and any attempt to treat it as such would inevitably be misleading. It is, rather, a religious doctrine of duties (*Pflichtenlehre*) claiming jurisdiction over every aspect of human life. The most important problems of civil, ritual, and criminal law are, in this respect, on the same level as formulae of greeting and amenities of table manners. Those aspects of life which the law encompasses in other societies and cultures form only one part of the *fiqh* and, therefore, according to this view, any purely legal approach to *fiqh* would lead to misunderstanding.[7]

Furthermore, the *fiqh* had very little to do with actual practice. It was only of theoretical significance and was developed by the religious scholars according to the paradigm of what they considered to be a golden age, namely, the period of the first four caliphs. The religious-legal scholars saw their

[5] Cf. Hurgronje's review of one of these translations in his *Verspreide Geschriften*, Bonn and Leipzig, 1923, 2:59ff; also *Selected Works of C. Snouck Hurgronje*, eds. J. Schacht and G.-H. Bousquet, Leiden, 1957, pp. 214–215.

[6] Most of Hurgronje's writings on the subject can now be found in his *Selected Works*; for Goldziher's views, cf. his *Vorlesungen über den Islam*, Heidelberg, 1910, Chap. 2, his article in *Encyclopaedia of Islam* (*EI*), 1st ed., *s.v. fikh*, and his polemical article, "Muhammedanisches Recht in Theorie und Wirklichkeit," *Zeitschrift für vergleichende Rechtswissenschaft* 8 (1889): 406–423.

[7] Cf. Hurgronje, *Selected Works*, pp. 49, 256–258.

task as that of creating an ideal doctrine of how things ought to be; and the fact that things were not as they ought to be can be amply documented by the numerous references to transgressions of the law.[8] The law was destined for the ideal society and did not take into account the needs of a corrupt world. As Hurgronje summed it up: ". . . all classes of the Muslim community have exhibited in practice an indifference to the sacred law in all its fulness, quite equal to the reverence with which they regard it in theory."[9] By implication, he also ruled out the use of legal material as a source for any study except that of the development of Islamic theoretical legal doctrine as one of the important elements of Muslim intellectual life.[10]

The works of Goldziher and Hurgronje on the nature and origins of Islamic law and jurisprudence were a great advance in their own day both in indicating how this material should be approached and in showing that the conventional Muslim view concealed rather than revealed the truth. Their view of the origins and formative period of Muslim law and jurisprudence has since been revised by the detailed research of J. Schacht.[11] However, the judgment of these scholars on the relationship of law to practice and on the validity of legal material as an acceptable source for the social and economic history of Islam, while somewhat modified, has not been subject to any systematic reappraisal. Even though a significant amount of new material bearing on this problem has come to light in the past fifty years, it has not been systematically collected and studied with this problem in mind. An investigation of this nature would, of course, be a subject deserving of a separate study; but, in view of its importance to the present discussion, some of the more relevant material and ideas toward such a re-evaluation deserve mention here.

That the separation between *fiqh* and life was not absolute is conceded by all. In every generation there were groups of pious men whose entire lives were guided by the prescriptions

[8] Cf. Goldziher, "Muhammedanisches Recht . . . ," pp. 408–418.
[9] Hurgronje, *Selected Works*, p. 290.
[10] *Ibid.*, p. 263.
[11] Cf. J. Schacht, *Origins of Muhammadan Jurisprudence*, Oxford, 1950.

of the sacred law. On a broader level, certain segments of the *fiqh* actually had wide application, especially those dealing with ritual and family law. It has become increasingly clear that this distinction between the ideal law and the profane practice did not apply with equal force to all segments of the *fiqh*. G. Bergsträsser was, I believe, the first one to point out that the adherence of Muslim peoples to the various aspects of the *fiqh* varied greatly according to time and place, and that the study of Islamic law and history was not yet at an advanced enough stage to pronounce the final word on the problem of law and practice.[12]

He did, however, distinguish three broad categories: (1) Ritual, family, and inheritance law, which, notwithstanding occasional deviations based on custom, adhered closest to the *fiqh*; (2) Constitutional, criminal, and fiscal law, which diverged farthest and, in some cases, completely from the *fiqh*; and (3) Commercial law, which falls somewhere between the two above extremes.[13] This evaluation of the position of Islamic commercial law *vis à vis* practice stands in sharp contrast to its earlier appraisal by Hurgronje: "Islamic commercial law remained for the most part a dead letter; the great Ghazzālī, 'the reviver of religion,' said in the eleventh century of our era that anyone conducting commerce in accordance with the law was looked upon as ridiculous by all other merchants."[14]

While recognizing the ideal character of Islamic law, one cannot state *a priori* that any given institution had no relationship whatsoever to practice. This is especially so in the area of *fiqh* termed *muʿāmalāt*—pecuniary transactions. Most of the material covered by these laws, for example the contracts of partnership and *commenda*, does not involve any religious or moral principle. No religious or ethical value is attached to them. In the earliest legal texts especially, there is no

[12] J. Schacht, ed., *G. Bergsträssers Grundzüge des Islamischen Rechts*, Berlin, 1935, p. 3.

[13] Schacht, *Grundzüge*, pp. 119–122; Schacht, *Law in the Middle East*, 1:77; R. Brunschvig, "Considérations sociologiques sur le droit musulman," *Studia Islamica*, 3:61–62.

[14] Hurgronje, *Selected Works*, p. 260.

reason not to consider them as a reflection and partial description of institutions as they existed at that time.

One must also bear in mind that, while the *commenda* was apparently a commercial form original with the Arabs, an institution like partnership was not an innovation of, or in any way peculiar to, Islamic law. It was known and practiced in the Near East at least since the Babylonians.[15] It was known and discussed in the Talmud,[16] and it is treated in the *Corpus Iuris Civilis* of Justinian.[17] It appears almost certain that various forms of business association were practiced by Meccan merchants in the period immediately preceding Muḥammad.[18] Gaonic *responsa* of the ninth and tenth centuries amply testify to the use of both partnership and *commendas* by Jewish merchants living under Muslim suzerainty.[19] Partnership and *commenda* alike were known, accepted legal commercial institutions in the medieval Muslim world; in the absence of contrary evidence, we are justified in assuming they were extensively employed in trade.[20]

Although the published Arabic papyri contain, as far as I know, no example of a commercial partnership or of a *commenda* agreement,[21] they do contain examples of other types

[15] Cf. W. Eilers, *Gesellschaftsformen im altbabylonischen Recht*, Leipzig, 1931.

[16] E.g., *Babylonian Talmud, Baba Meṣī'a*, Chapter 5.

[17] Cf. *Institutes*, trans. J. B. Moyle, Oxford, 1906, pp. 148–150; *Digest 17. 2, Pro Socio*, ed. and trans. C. H. Monro, Cambridge, 1902.

[18] Cf. H. Lammens, *La Mecque à la veille de l'hégire*, Beirut, 1924, pp. 116ff.

[19] Cf. S. Asaf, ed., *Gaonic Responsa*, Jerusalem, 1928; *idem*, *Gaonica*, Jerusalem, 1933. For a slightly later period, we have the documentary evidence of the Cairo Geniza, cf. S. D. Goitein, "Commercial and Family Partnerships in the Countries of Medieval Islam," *Islamic Studies* 3 (1964): 315ff., and *idem*, *A Mediterranean Society, The Jewish Communities of the Arab World as Portrayed in the Documents of the Cairo Geniza, Economic Foundations*, California, 1967, 1:169–179.

[20] Cf. Ghazzālī, *Iḥyā 'ulūm ad-dīn*, Cairo, 1957, 2:66ff., where the contracts of partnership and *commenda* are mentioned among the six commercial contracts, the knowledge of which Ghazzālī considers indispensable to any businessman.

[21] The word partnership (*shari*ḳ*a*) occurs in the papyri only once. This reference is in connection with some income from a partnership investment,

of business contracts mentioned in the *fiqh*.[22] The formal similarity of papyri documents from different places and different times indicates beyond a doubt that they followed a uniform legal content.[23] Papyri evidence also indicates that in many cases a contract was written in several copies;[24] this parallels the instructions contained in some of the earliest *fiqh* works.[25] If, then, as the papyri evidence suggests, various types of contracts generally followed the prescriptions of the relevant sections of the *fiqh*, we can expect the same to be true of partnership and related contracts.

The extent to which Islamic law made an accommodation with customary commercial practice is evidenced by the very existence of an entire genre of legal writings known as the *shurūṭ* (legal formulae) literature. From a very early period, Islamic legal theory, diverging from an explicit Qur'ānic ruling, denied the validity of documentary evidence and restricted legal proof to the oral testimony of witnesses.[26] In spite of this, religious lawyers took cognizance of the indispensability of written contracts to commerce by composing formularies. These were intended to serve as handbooks for notaries, and provide the forms for a great variety of practical needs. They had only to be witnessed to be legally valid.[27]

---

and no details concerning the contract are given. Cf. A. Dietrich, *Arabische Papyri aus der Hamburger Staats- und Universitätsbibliothek*, Leipzig, 1937, p. 51, l. 10.

[22] E.g., *kitāb al-kirā'* (lease contract); cf. A. Grohmann, *Einführung und Chrestomathie zur arabischen Papyruskunde*, Prague, 1955, p. 108; and for *kitāb ar-rahn* (pledge contract); cf. p. 121.

[23] Cf. *ibid.*, p. 113.

[24] *Ibid.*, p. 134.

[25] E.g., Shaybānī, *Aṣl, Kitāb ask-sharika* fol. 61b, ll. 5–6; Ṭaḥāwī, *Kitāb ash-shuf'a*, ed. J. Schacht, p. 39, ll. 20–24.

[26] Cf. Emile Tyan, *Le notariat et le régime de la preuve par écrit dans la pratique du droit musulman*, 2nd ed., Beirut, n.d., pp. 5ff.; Schacht, *Law in the Middle East*, 1:35. For the most recent and comprehensive discussion of the place of written documents in Islamic law, cf. Jeanette Wakin, *Islamic Law in Practice: Two Chapters from Taḥāwī's Kitāb al-shurūṭ al-kabīr*, unpublished doctoral dissertation, Columbia University, 1968.

[27] Cf. Ṭaḥāwī, *Kitāb adhkār al-ḥuqūq war-ruhūn, Sitzungsberichte der Heidelberger Akademie der Wissenschaften, Philosophisch-historische Klasse*, ed. J. Schacht, 1926/7, p. 7.

The earliest extant *shurūṭ* works are those of Ṭaḥāwī (d. 321/933).[28] This genre of legal literature, however, goes back to the "founding fathers" of the Ḥanafī school,[29] Abū Ḥanīfa (d. 150/767),[30] Abū Yūsuf (d. 182/798),[31] and Shaybānī (d. 187/803).[32] Indeed, the "Book of Partnership" of Shaybānī's *Kitāb al-aṣl*, the earliest legal compilation of the Ḥanafī school, begins with a suggested formula for writing a partnership contract.[33] Formulae for various types of specialized partnerships are cited throughout the book, forming an integral part of the legal exposition of partnership.[34] The inclusion of contract formulae within the very body of the early *fiqh* texts is one very significant manifestation of the degree to which customary commercial practice was assimilated into, and is reflected by, the theoretical legal works.

In most areas of business law, the *fiqh* allowed considerable leeway to traders and investors and, on the whole, probably provided adequate legal instruments for the commercial needs of the early Islamic period. Islamic law did, however, place some serious restrictions and limitations on the freedom of commercial activity. It is undoubtedly against the prohibitions which grew out of these restrictions that the transgressions of

[28] C. Brockelmann, *Geschichte der arabischen Litteratur* (*GAL*), 2 vols., 1:181–182 (173–4); *Supp.*, Leiden, 1937–1943, 1:243–244. Only two fragments of Ṭaḥāwī's most detailed treatise on *shurūṭ* (*Al-jāmi' al-kabīr fish-shurūṭ*) have been published: the *Kitāb adhkār al-ḥuqūq war-ruhūn* (cf. the preceding note), and the *Kitāb ash-shuf'a*, also edited by Schacht in the same series as the former, 1929/30. Two other large fragments of the work are found in Istanbul: *Shehid Ali Pasha* 881 and 882. In addition, Ṭaḥāwī composed two other *shurūṭ* works: *Kitāb ash-shurūṭ al-awsaṭ*, and *Kitāb ash-shurūṭ aṣ-ṣaghīr*. Three complete copies of the latter are preserved in Istanbul: *Murad Mollah* 997 and 998, and *Bayazit* 18905. These include a brief treatment of the *shurūṭ* for partnership and *commenda*.

[29] Cf. Ṭaḥāwī, *Kitāb adhkār al-ḥuqūq war-ruhūn*, 1926–1927, p. 18. Extracts of Shaybānī's treatment of *shurūṭ* are preserved in Sarakhsī, 30 vols., Cairo, 1324/1906–1331/1912, *Mabsūṭ*, 30:167–209.

[30] Brockelmann, *GAL*, 1:176–177 (168–169); *Supp.*, 1:284–287.

[31] Brockelmann, *GAL*, 1:177 (171); *Supp.*, 1:288.

[32] Brockelmann, *GAL*, 1:178–180 (171–172); *Supp.*, 1:288–291.

[33] Shaybānī, *Aṣl*, *Kitāb ash-sharika* fol. 57b, ll. 3–8.

[34] E.g., credit partnership, *ibid.*, fol. 57b, ll. 12–15; work partnership, *ibid.*, fol. 57b. l. 20–fol. 58; l. 1. For the *commenda shurūṭ*, cf. Shaybānī, *Aṣl*, *Muḍāraba*, fol. 140b.

merchants, which Ghazzālī and others complained about,[35] took place. In this respect, we can agree with Schacht's statement that "the hostile references to the practice in treatises of Islamic law are one of our main sources for its investigation."[36]

The restrictions in the area of trade and exchange, as well as in other areas of life, placed certain aspects of practice on an inevitable collision course with legal theory. This situation gave rise to a special branch of legal writings, the *ḥiyal* (legal devices) literature, in which the lawyers attempted to narrow down the area in which actions would be in violation of the law by making them conform to the law formally while in reality circumventing it.[37]

"They (*ḥiyal*) can be described in short as the use of legal means for achieving extra-legal ends—ends that could not be achieved directly with the means provided by the *sharī'ah,* whether or not such ends might in themselves be illegal. The 'legal devices' enabled persons who would otherwise have had to break the law, or under the pressure of circumstances would have had to act against its provisions, to arrive at the desired result while actually conforming to the letter of the law."[38] Thus, for example, a number of devices were developed to circumvent the taking or giving of interest, and others to permit capital in the form of commodities to serve as investments in partnership and *commenda* contracts.[39]

Of the three extant *ḥiyal* works, only those of Shaybānī and al-Khaṣṣāf, both of the Ḥanafī school, are of interest in connection with commercial practice.[40] The work of Shaybānī dates from the end of the second Islamic century, and that of al-Khaṣṣāf from the third or fourth century.[41] The origins of

35 Cf. Hurgronje, *Selected Works*, p. 260.

36 Schacht in *Law in the Middle East*, 1:80.

37 Cf. J. Schacht, "Die arabische *ḥijal*-Literatur," *Der Islam* 15 (1926): 211ff.

38 Schacht in *Law in the Middle East*, 1:78.

39 Cf. Shaybānī, *Kitāb al-makhārij fil-ḥiyal*, ed. J. Schacht, Leipzig, 1930, p. 58.

40 On the nature of the *ḥiyal* work of the Shāfi'ī al-Qazwīnī, cf. Schacht, *Der Islam* 15 (1926): 213, n. 4.

41 Concerning the date of al-Khaṣṣāf's *Kitāb al-ḥiyal wal-makhārij*, cf. Schacht in *Law in the Middle East*: 1:79.

ḥiyal, like those of *shuruṭ*, go back to Abū Ḥanīfa, who was purported to be a great master in devising them, and to Abū Yūsuf, who is reported to have composed a work on *ḥiyal*.[42]

In using the *ḥiyal* works as an indicator of actual practice, one must exercise a measure of caution in attempting to discern those devices which were of obvious importance for practice and those which were merely exercises in cleverness and legal gymnastics. Taken as a whole, the *ḥiyal* literature represents the pressure points of daily practice on legal theory and can serve, in the field of commercial law especially, as a valuable guide to the practices current in the medieval Muslim world.

Sources

A number of studies of Islamic law have been based on legal manuals chosen more or less arbitrarily. Indeed, there can be no objection to this method if one wishes simply to investigate the various prescriptions of Muslim positive law. This would not be the case, however, in a historically oriented study. I have, therefore, based the following discussion primarily on the earliest compilations of Islamic law dating from the late eighth and early ninth centuries A.D.[43]

Classical Islamic law, as we know it today, was created during the first two centuries of the Islamic era. The raw material from which it was formed was of varied provenance. It was to a large degree non-Islamic, but all was subjected in one degree or another to an Islamicizing process. By the end of the second Islamic century, all the major Islamic positive legal institutions were already formulated, as were its legal theory and jurisprudence. "Islamic law, which until the early 'Abbāsid period had been adaptable and growing, from then

[42] Abū Yūsuf's treatise on *ḥiyal* has not survived; however, there is a manuscript in the Egyptian National Library identical with Shaybānī's *ḥiyal* book, but attributed to Abū Yūsuf. Cf. Chafik T. Chehata, *Théorie générale de l'obligation*, Cairo, 1936, 1:3.

[43] Reference is frequently made, especially in the case of Ḥanafī law, to later sources. In almost all such cases, however, the material cited from these later texts dates back to, or is implicit in, the legal discussions of the earliest period.

onwards became increasingly rigid and set in its final mold. . . . It was not altogether immutable, but the changes which did take place were concerned more with legal theory and the systematic superstructure than with positive law. . . . Taken as a whole, however, Islamic law reflects and fits the social and economic conditions of the early 'Abbāsid period, but has become more and more out of touch with later developments of state and society."[44]

The legal compilations of the eighth and ninth centuries antedate the rigidity and artificiality imposed by the complete triumph of prophetic traditions as the foremost source for Muslim law. They retain a measure of flexibility due to the extensive use of *ra'y* (independent personal judgment) and its specific manifestations in the Ḥanafī and Mālikī schools of *istiḥsān* (juristic preference) and *istiṣlāh* (regard for the public interest).[45] The exercise of these prerogatives was often connected with a concern on the part of the lawyers for the practical needs of daily life. The chapters on partnership and *commenda* contain numerous instances in which systematic legal reasoning is suspended because of the "custom of the merchants" or "because of the needs of merchants." Other applications of juristic preference, although not coupled with these phrases, reveal a clear tendency toward allowing a greater freedom of trade practice.[46] In the later legal treatises, this leniency, which often provides valuable indications of actual practice, is replaced by imitation and rigidity.

Some creative and original legal work continued until the beginning of the fourth century of the Islamic era, at which time "the door of independent reasoning" was closed. After this date, all future legal activity was relegated to commentary, explanation, and interpretation of the existing legal doctrine. Even the *fatāwā* (*responsa*) literature, in which one would expect to find reflections of contemporary problems, generally

[44] Schacht, *Law in the Middle East*, 1:76–77.

[45] Cf. J. Schacht, *An Introduction to Islamic Law*, Oxford, 1959, 1964, pp. 60–61.

[46] E.g., Shaybānī, *Aṣl, Kitāb ash-sharika* fol. 62, l. 20–fol. 62b, l. 1; Sarakhsī, *Mabsūṭ*, 11:180–181; *Kāsānī*, 7 vols., Cairo, 1328/1910, 6:68.

contains only extracts and quotations from earlier legal works. There are exceptions; however, these are almost exclusively *fatāwā* works of the very late Middle Ages or early pre-modern times.

In Muslim law the tendency is to concentrate on specific cases. This led in the course of time to a continual increase in the volume of its subject matter.[47] One may often find a more detailed elaboration of a given institution in the later systematic legal works, but one could rarely expect to find any significant change or development either in its theory or content.[48] Shaybānī's compilations, for example, contain a complete exposition of the state of Ḥanafī law as it existed at his time. This corpus was transmitted intact to following generations of jurists. The resolution of new cases was but in the nature of a complementary activity. The corpus of Ḥanafī law was already constituted. Even before the closing of the "gate of independent reasoning," it was only a case of applying analogy to solutions already admitted or opting for one of a number of solutions in controversy.[49]

The treatment of partnership and *commenda* in Islamic legal treatises remained essentially the same from the time of Shaybānī to that of the Ottoman *Majallah*. The extent to which its application in practice passed through any major changes in the course of the thousand intervening years cannot be determined without other literary or documentary evidence. By focusing primarily on the legal sources and legal material emanating from the eighth and ninth centuries—a period in which Islamic legal theory and practice were least divergent—I hope to be able to describe the institution of partnership as it existed in the law and, to a large extent, in the practice of that period.

[47] Cf. Hurgronje, *Selected Works*, p. 52.

[48] *Ibid.*, p. 54: "A survey of the works on *fiqh* up to the year A.D. 1000 shows that by then each school had discussed and answered practically all questions of any importance."

[49] Chehata, *Théorie générale de l'obligation*, p. 51; for a discussion of the succeeding layers of new cases from the point of view of legal doctrine and presentation, cf. G. Bergsträsser, "Zur Methode der *fiqh*-Forschung," *Islamica* 4 (1931): 291.

SOURCES

The following are the most important primary sources used in this study:

Ḥanafī

(1) The *Kitāb ash-sharika* ("Book of Partnership") of Shaybānī's great legal compilation *Kitāb al-aṣl.* This work is the earliest detailed exposition of *Ḥanafī* law, and only one small section of it has thus far been published.[50] My translations of, and references to, the *Kitāb al-aṣl* are based on the manuscript of the *Dār al-Kutub al-Miṣriyya, Fiqh Ḥanafī* 34, folios 57b–77b.

(2) The *Kitāb al-muḍāraba* ("Book of *Commenda*") of Shaybānī's *Kitāb al-aṣl*, from the manuscript of the *Dār al-Kutub al-Miṣriyya, Fiqh Ḥanafī* 491, folios 42–198.

(3) *Kitāb al mabsūṭ* of Sarakhsī (d. 483/1090).[51] This thirty-volume compendium is a commentary on the *Kitāb al-kāfī fil-fiqh* (unpublished) of al-Marwazī (d. 334/945),[52] which is in turn based on the legal writings of Shaybānī.[53] The *Mabsūṭ* contains a good deal of earlier material unavailable in other sources, and its "Book of Partnership"[54] and "Book of *Commenda*"[55] represent the most extensive treatment of the subjects in Ḥanafī law.

(4) *Badā'i' aṣ-ṣanā'i' fī tartīb ash-sharā'i'* of Kāsānī (d. 587/1191).[56] This work is a commentary on the *Kitāb tuḥfat al-fuqahā'* of Kāsānī's father-in-law and teacher, 'Alā' ad-dīn al-Manṣūr Muḥammad b. Aḥmad as-Samarqandī (d. 538/1144)[57] and is characterized by a highly systematic and well-organized arrangement (*tartīb*) of the legal subject matter.[58]

[50] *Kitāb al-buyū' was-salam*, ed. Sh. Shaḥāta, Cairo, 1954.

[51] Brockelmann, *GAL*, 1:460 (373); *Supp.*, 1:638.

[52] Brockelmann, *GAL*, 1:182 (174); *Supp.*, 1:294.

[53] Cf. Nicolas P. Aghnides, *Mohammedan Theories of Finance*, 2nd impression, Lahore, 1961, p. 177.

[54] Sarakhsī, *Mabsūṭ*, 11:151–220.

[55] *Ibid.*, 22:17–187.

[56] Brockelmann, *GAL*, 1:465 (375–376); *Supp.*, 1:643.

[57] Brockelmann, *GAL*, 1:462 (374); *Supp.*, 1:640, where his death date is erroneously given as 508/1114.

[58] Cf. Aghnides, *Mohammedan Theories of Finance*, p. 178.

Mālikī

(1) *Al-muwaṭṭa'*, of Mālik b. Anas (d. 179/795),[59] the founder of the Mālikī school of Muslim Law. The *Muwaṭṭa'* is a collection of traditions arranged according to relevant legal chapters and is the earliest extant work of Islamic law. Its aim is "to codify and systematize the customary law of Madina" and "give a survey of law and jurisprudence according to the *ijmā'* (consensus) and *sunnah* (traditional practice) of Madina."[60] While it includes a fairly substantial treatment of the *commenda* contract, it does not contain a section on partnership.

(2) *Al-mudawwana al-kubrā,* compiled by Saḥnūn (d. 240/854).[61] It consists of questions by Saḥnūn and answers by his teacher 'Abd ar-Raḥmān b. al-Qāsim (d. 191-806),[62] who studied with Mālik for a period of twenty years. These answers often literally repeat Mālik's own views on the various points of law.

Shāfi'ī

(1) *Kitāb al-umm* of Shāfi'ī (d. 204/820),[63] the founder of the Shāfi'ī school. In this work, as in many subsequent Shāfi'ī legal compendia, the discussion of partnership and *commenda* is rather skimpy, not to say perfunctory, and is only of marginal interest with respect to medieval Near Eastern mercantile practice.

The partnership law of the Ḥanbalī school is not included in this study, because no systematic treatises of this school exist for the early period.[64] The same applies to the Ẓāhirī school. The other minor legal schools which flourished briefly in the early centuries of the Islamic era, such as those of Al-Awzā'ī and Ibn Abī Laylā, have left insufficient literary remains, making it impossible to reconstruct their doctrine on partnership.

59 Brockelmann, *GAL*, 1:184–186 (175–76); *Supp.*, 1:297–299.

60 Schacht, *EI*, 1st ed., 3:206–207.

61 *Supp.*, 1:299–300. His death is erroneously given as 280 A.H. in Brockelmann, *GAL*, 1:186 (177).

62 Brockelmann, *GAL*, 1:186 (176–177); *Supp.*, 1:299.

63 Brockelmann, *GAL*, 1:188–190 (178–179); *Supp.*, 1:303–305.

64 Cf. Brockelmann, *GAL*, 1:193 (182).

II

Proprietary Partnership (*Sharikat al-milk*)

The Ḥanafī and Mālikī schools of Islamic law divide the institution of partnership into two broad categories: *sharikat al-milk*[1]—proprietary partnership, and *sharikat al-ʿaqd*[2]—contractual or commercial partnership. Briefly stated, proprietary partnership is concerned exclusively with joint ownership of property. Joint ownership is, in fact, its only qualification, and no joint exploitation of property is involved. In commercial partnership, joint ownership is not an element necessary for the establishment of the partnership; the emphasis is rather on the joint exploitation of capital and the joint participation in profits and losses. Joint ownership is a consequence, and not a prerequisite, of the formation of a contractual partnership.[3]

Proprietary Partnership in the Formative Period

Ḥanafī

The classification of partnership into proprietary and contractual types is not formulated in the earliest Ḥanafī and Mālikī texts.[4] As far as I can determine, the earliest occurrence of this classification is in the legal manual, *Al-mukhtaṣar*

[1] For the Ḥanafīs, cf. Sarakhsī, *Mabsūṭ*, Cairo, 1324/1906–1331/1912, 11:151; *Kāsānī*, 7 vols., Cairo, 1328/1910, 6:56; Marghīnānī, *Hedaya*, trans. Charles Hamilton, 4 vols., London, 1791, 2:296. The term also appears with the plural of *milk*, *sharikat al-amlāk*. The Mālikī term is *sharikat al-māl*; cf. D. Santillana, *Istituzioni di Diritto Musulmano Malichita*, 2 vols., Rome, 1925–1938, 2:286, and references there. The sources to which Santillana refers are quite late, the earliest being the *Mukhtaṣar* of Khalīl b. Isḥāq (d. 767/1365). It is sufficiently clear from Santillana's description that the *sharikat al-māl* of the Mālikīs is identical with the *sharikat al-milk* of the Ḥanafīs.

[2] In Ḥanafī texts it is also used with the plural of *ʿaqd*, *sharikat al-ʿuqūd*; cf. Ḥanafī sources in note 1. The Mālikīs also use the term *sharikat at-tijārah* (trade partnership) to designate this type of partnership; cf. Santillana, *Istituzioni*, p. 287.

[3] This statement does not apply to the Shāfiʿī theory of partnership, discussed later in this chapter.

[4] It is not found in any of the published legal works of Shaybānī or Abū Yūsuf, nor in the early Mālikī works such as the *Muwaṭṭa*' and the *Mudawwana*.

("The Abridgement"), composed by the Ḥanafī jurist Aḥmad b. Muḥammad al-Qudūrī (362/972–428/1037).[5] As the title suggests, the treatment of the legal topics in this book is rather brief and concise. The entire section on partnership covers slightly more than one and one half pages and is introduced as follows:

> There are two categories of partnership: proprietary partnership and contractual partnership.
>
> A proprietary partnership can occur when two people inherit or purchase anything together. Neither of them is permitted to dispose of the other's portion, except with his permission. Each of them is as a stranger in regard to the portion of his colleague.[6]

Whether it was actually al-Qudūrī who first formulated this classification cannot be stated with certainty. Any definite statement on this point will have to await the publication or consultation of the extant, but unpublished, legal works composed by the several prominent Ḥanafī jurists in the course of the more than two centuries that intervened between Shaybānī and al-Qudūrī.[7]

Whatever the exact date after Shaybānī and Mālik that this classification appeared, it is not to be viewed as anything substantially new or as an extension of the concept of partnership beyond that which already existed in the earliest legal works. The notions of common ownership and joint commercial endeavor conveyed by the terms proprietary and contractual partnership, respectively, are already to be found in the writings of Shaybānī and Abū Yūsuf, as well as of some early Mālikī authorities.

It is especially important to emphasize this point in connection with proprietary partnership, since it is not explicitly mentioned in any of the early legal works. The material in the chapters on partnership of the *Kitāb al-aṣl* or the *Mudawwana*,

[5] Cf. C. Brockelmann, *Geschichte der arabischen Litteratur* (*GAL*), 2 vols., 1:183 (175), *Supp.*, 3 vols., Leiden, 1937–1943, 1:295–296.

[6] *Mukhtaṣar al-Qudūrī*, Istanbul, 1319/1901, p. 53.

[7] Cf. Brockelmann, *GAL*, 1:180–183 (173–174), *Supp.* 1:291–295.

for example, is concerned almost exclusively with the commercial applications of partnership. A cursory reading of these texts might lead one to conclude that joint ownership was not comprised by the earliest jurists' conception of partnership. A close look, however, reveals that the term *sharika* was in fact used in designating situations involving only joint ownership. And while these cases receive only scant attention (as is also true even of the later legal works in which proprietary partnership is explicitly treated) and are of minor significance for trade and commerce, they do have some importance in the early Islamic theory of partnership.

Evidence that the early Ḥanafī lawyers considered joint ownership as falling within the definition of partnership is to be found in some of the minor legal writings of Shaybānī and Abū Yūsuf. In his *Kitāb al-amālī*, Shaybānī discusses the case of a man who purchased twenty dirhams (silver coins) for the price of one dinar (gold coin).[8] After the sale was completed, the purchaser found that some of the dirhams were either counterfeit or below standard quality. The purchaser was then to return the substandard dirhams and exchange them for coins of better quality. Under certain circumstances, however, instead of exchanging them, he was to return them and "he becomes a partner in the dinar that he paid proportional to the number of dirhams he returned."[9] This is not only Shaybānī's opinion but, with some minor differences, also that of the other two "founding fathers" of the Ḥanafī school, Abū Yūsuf and Abū Ḥanīfa.

The legal reasoning underlying this opinion is not of immediate concern here. The significant point is the use of the term *sharīk* (partner) to designate the purchaser's relationship to the seller. The purchaser has a claim on the dinar he paid proportional to the number of dirhams he returned. If, for example, he returned five counterfeit dirhams, he would be to that extent, namely, one quarter, a co-owner of the dinar in question. There is no contractual relationship between the purchaser and the seller, since the minimum requirement

[8] Shaybānī, *Kitāb al-amālī*, Hyderabad, 1360/1941, pp. 17–19.
[9] *Ibid.*, 18, 1. 3.

of a contract, offer and acceptance,[10] did not take place. Furthermore, there is no indication that beyond common ownership there is any joint exploitation involved in this relationship. This is a clear-cut case of inadvertent or compulsory partnership[11] in which nothing beyond joint ownership is in question. Indeed, in this particular instance, the term *sharīk* (partner) may be translated as "joint owner." This situation is one that in the later terminology would be designated as a proprietary partnership.

Another similar case, going back to Abū Yūsuf, is cited by the thirteenth century Ḥanafī writer al-Kāsānī.[12] According to Ḥanafī law, commodities do not constitute a valid form of capital for partnership investment.[13] In this case, two people, either in ignorance or contravention of the law, undertook to enter into a commercial partnership, the capital of which was to consist of a certain quantity of wheat contributed by each or of wheat contributed by one and barley by the other. After this agreement was concluded, the grain was intermingled. The problem was to decide the legal character of this arrangement. In Abū Yūsuf's view, the intended commercial partnership is invalid; and since each party's grain cannot be distinguished, the mixed grain becomes the joint property of the two investors, and the relationship between them is that of a proprietary partnership.

In Shaybānī's *Al-jāmi' aṣ-ṣaghīr* the term *sharīkayn* (two partners) is used to designate the joint owners of a female slave.[14] Slaves were, of course, an important commercial commodity, and common ownership of a slave would not necessarily indicate a proprietary partnership, but could just as well indicate a commercial partnership. In this particular case, however, the context shows the ownership of the slave girl to have

[10] Arabic: *Ījāb wa-qabūl*. Cf. J. Schacht, *Grundzüge*, Berlin, 1935, p. 61; Chafik T. Chehata, *Théorie générale de l'obligation en droit musulman*, Cairo, 1936, 1:117ff.

[11] Cf. Sarakhsī, *Mabsūṭ*, 30 vols., Cairo, 1324/1906-1331/1912, 11:151; S. Mahmasani, "Transactions in the *Sharī'a*," in *Law in the Middle East*, 1:185.

[12] *Kāsānī*, 6:60.

[13] Cf., e.g., *ibid*., p. 59.

[14] Shaybānī, *Al-jāmi' as-saghīr*, Cairo, 1302/1884, p. 55, l. 2.

been not for purposes of trade, but rather for those of personal service.

> A slave girl was owned jointly by two partners. One of them claimed that she was the mother of a child[15] sired by his colleague. His colleague denied this.
>
> The slave girl is to work on alternate days for the partner who denied the charge of paternity, and on the other days is to be suspended from working.[16]

The role of the slave girl here is that of a servant. Her exploitation by her masters, while common, was not joint, since she served each of them on separate days. We have here, as in the preceding examples, an instance of a relationship designated as a partnership which involves only joint ownership.

These cases, dating back to the earliest period of Ḥanafī law, leave no doubt that the concept of partnership included, from the very beginning, the idea of joint ownership as well as that of commercial partnership.[17]

Mālikī

Evidence pointing to the inclusion of joint ownership within the concept of partnership in early Mālikī law is much sparser than that which is found in the Ḥanafī school. Partnership is mentioned only tangentially in Mālik's *Muwaṭṭaʾ* in connection with problems such as the payment of alms tax (*zakāt*), various forms of sale, and the manumission of slaves.

[15] Arabic: *umm walad*, a technical term for a female slave who is mother of a child sired by her master. The birth of the child entitled her to a special status; she could not be sold, and the child, if recognized by its father, was free. These and other limitations on the disposal of an *umm walad*, affected her value and, in the case of joint ownership, could provide grounds for litigation. Cf. *Encyclopaedia of Islam* (*EI*), 1st ed., 4 vols., 4:1012–1015; Juynboll, *Handbuch*, Leiden, 1910, 206, 236; *EI*, 2nd ed., 1:26, 28.

[16] Shaybānī, *Al-jāmiʿ aṣ-ṣaghīr*, p. 55, ll. 2–3.

[17] For additional Ḥanafī examples, cf. Shaybānī, *Al-amālī*, Hyderabad, 1360/1941, pp. 6–10, 39–40; Abū Yūsuf, *Ikhtilāf*, Cairo, 1357/1938, p. 46. In *Aṣl*, *Sharika* fol. 75b, l. 19, Shaybānī refers to "two partners who do not buy and do not sell." This sort of relationship would undoubtedly be designated by later Ḥanafī terminology as a proprietary partnership.

Very few details are given, but from the context of these references the use of the term *sharīk* (partner) seems to include non-commercial joint ownership.[18] In the *Mudawwana* the discussion of partnership is devoted exclusively to the contractual variety. It would appear that the earliest explicit mention of proprietary partnership (*sharikat al-māl*) in Mālikī legal sources occurs in the *Mukhtaṣar* of the fourteenth century Khalīl b. Isḥāq.[19] However, a number of cases attributed to several early Mālikī jurists which treat joint ownership within the framework of partnership are preserved in the monumental legal compilation of al-Wansharīshī (d. 914/1508).[20]

The following example illustrates this point most clearly. Two men were co-owners of a ship. One of them wished to load some of his personal belongings in that part of the ship of which he was proprietor. His colleague objected on the ground that nothing outside the category of commercial freight was to be loaded on the ship. The first party countered this objection by claiming that he had the absolute right to dispose of the space in his own share of the ship as he pleased. This last claim was upheld by Saḥnūn (d. 240/854),[21] the early North African Mālikī authority, famous as the compiler of the *Mudawwana*. He maintained that each co-owner had the right to load his belongings in his own part of the vessel and that

[18] Mālik, *Muwaṭṭa'*, Cairo, 1951, 1:263 and 2:676–677, 772–773; cf. also, Nicolas P. Aghnides, *Mohammedan Theories of Finance*, Lahore, 1961 (reprint), pp. 231ff.

[19] Santillana, *Istituzioni*, 2:286, n. 3.

[20] Aḥmad b. Yaḥyā b. Muḥammad at-Tilimsānī al-Wansharīshī (Brockelmann, *GAL*, 2:320 [248], *Supp.*, 2:348), *Al-mi'yār al-mughrib 'an fatāwī 'ulamā' Ifrīqiya wal-Andalus*, 12 vols., Fes, 1314–1315. The following examples are not based on the original text of al-Wansharīshī, which is inaccessible to me, but on extracts of the work translated into French by E. Amar, *La pierre de touche des fetwas de Ahmad al-Wanscharisi*, 2 vols., *Archives Marocaines*, vols. 12 and 13, Paris, 1908–1909. Immediately following the section on partnership (*De la Société*) in Amar's translation (2:89–102), which undoubtedly corresponds to the *Kitāb ash-sharika* of the original, there is a section entitled *De la Communauté ou Quasi Société* (2:103–109) which deals with problems connected with joint ownership. There is, however, no indication of any special Arabic term that in the *Mi'yār* itself corresponds to this *Quasi Société*.

[21] Brockelmann, *GAL*, *Supp.*, 1:299–300.

neither was obliged to pay any kind of freight charges to his associate.[22]

The implication of Saḥnūn's view is that the nature of the relationship between the two proprietors is that of joint ownership of an indivisible property, rather than that of a commercial or contractual partnership. Theoretically, while one owner may hire out his share of the ship for commercial cargo, the other may use his share for entirely personal and non-commercial purposes. The element of joint exploitation is not essential to their relationship and can, under certain circumstances, be completely excluded. This type of partnership complies exactly with the definition of proprietary partnership as formulated by the later Mālikī jurists and serves as proof for the contention that, like the Ḥanafīs, the early Mālikīs also included joint ownership within the framework of their conception of partnership.[23]

Proprietary Partnership—Its Rules and Applications

W. Heffening, in his article on Islamic partnership, declares that, "*Shirka*[24] originally implied simply that a thing belonged to several persons in common in such a way that each one had ownership in every smallest part of it in proportion to the share allotted to him. . . . The jurists therefore understand primarily by *shirka* common property (*shirkat al-amlāk*) which arises for example through inheritances, gift, or indissoluble combination."[25] Whatever its original implication, the term *shirka*/*sharika* as understood by the earliest Muslim jurists was not primarily common property, but commercial partnership. Only in the Shāfi'ī treatment of partnership does the concept of joint ownership assume any major importance. The discus-

22 E. Amar, *La pierre de touche des fetwas*, p. 106.

23 Another early Mālikī example, although less clear-cut, involving joint ownership of livestock and attributed to al-'Utbī, d. 255/869 (Brockelmann, *GAL*, 1:186 [177], *Supp.* 1:300–301) is found in 2:97, of Amar's extracts.

24 This is an alternate form of vocalization of the word. Both forms of vocalization, *shirka* and *sharika*, are acceptable; cf. Ibn Manẓūr, *Lisān al-'arab*, Beirut, 1956, 10:448.

25 *EI*, 1st ed., 3:380–381.

sions of partnership in all other schools, while covering the topics of joint ownership and common property, are concerned almost entirely with the commercial forms of partnership.

The primary connotation of the term *shirka/sharika* for the Ḥanafī and Mālikī jurists was a contractual partnership involving joint investment and joint sharing of profits and risks. Proprietary partnership appears almost as a peripheral notion. It is not treated extensively anywhere. No more than a few lines are devoted to it in any of the legal compendia. The brief statement on proprietary partnership first found in al-Qudūrī[26] is repeated with only slight elaborations in most succeeding Ḥanafī treatises. As complete a statement as one finds is that of Sarakhsī:

> Proprietary partnership occurs when two people are partners in the possession of property. This can be of two types: (1) A partnership which becomes effective without any action on their part, as, for instance, in the case of inheritance; (2) a partnership which becomes effective through their own actions. This comes about through the acceptance of a purchase or a gift or a bequest.
>
> The rule governing both types is the same; namely, whatever increase or profit accrues is shared by them in proportion to the extent of their ownership. Each of them is in the category of a stranger in regard to any action in the portion of his colleague.[27]

The essence of proprietary partnership is common ownership of property. Theoretically, any kind of property could be subject to this type of common ownership. One would suspect, however, that when it occurred, proprietary partnership usually consisted of property which was difficult to divide or between which it was impossible to distinguish. This would include real property such as houses or ships,[28] as well as animals

[26] Cf. Al-Qudūrī, *Mukhtaṣar*, p. 53.

[27] Sarakhsī, *Mabsūṭ*, 11:151; cf. also, *Kāsānī*, 6:56, 65–66; Marghīnānī, *Hedaya*, 2:296.

[28] For houses, cf. Shaybānī, *Al-amālī*, pp. 6–10; for ships, cf. Amar, *La pierre de touche des fetwas*, p. 106.

and slaves.[29] It would also include different types of cereal grains, such as wheat and barley, which had intentionally or inadvertently been mixed together and would then be impossible to separate.[30]

Proprietary partnership, as Sarakhsī indicates, is divided into voluntary and compulsory categories. The first is brought about as a result of an act of the participants themselves, either through the joint purchase of one specific article or through the joint acceptance of a gift or bequest. It could also occur in a way not indicated by Sarakhsī, namely, the joint seizure of property by Muslims in the course of their conquest of territory governed by non-Muslims.[31]

Compulsory proprietary partnership is brought about by some cause other than the act of the participants or beyond their control, as, for example, through inheritance or the blending of individual properties. The strict rules governing the division of inheritance in Islamic law are such that a situation in which two or more people would fall heir to an indivisible piece of property, such as a house or a garment or a piece of furniture, could be a rather frequent occurrence, thus creating a compulsory proprietary partnership. As far as the blending of individual properties is concerned, this is exemplified by the inadvertent mixture of wheat and barley belonging to different owners or the mixture of any other commodities between which it is difficult, if not impossible, to distinguish.[32]

Both types of proprietary partnership are regulated by the same rule. It is not lawful for either partner to perform any act with respect to the other's share except with the latter's express permission. Their relationship is, as Sarakhsī puts it, "that of strangers," a point well illustrated by the following case:

[29] For slaves, cf. Shaybānī, *Al-jāmi' aṣ-ṣaghīr*, p. 55; for animals, cf. Amar, *La pierre de touche des fetwas*, 2:97; *Kāsānī*, 6:62.

[30] *Kāsānī*, 6:60; also Marghīnānī, *Hedaya*, 2:296.

[31] Marghīnānī, *Hedaya*, 2:296; Santillana, *Istituzioni*, 2:286. Cf. also, Muzanī, *Mukhtaṣar* (on the margin of Shāfi'ī, *Kitāb-al-Umm*), Cairo, 1903, 2:229, where the division of spoils among the early Muslim conquerors is cited as one of the sources for the legality of partnership in Muslim law.

[32] Shaybānī, *Al-amālī*, Hyderabad, 1360/1941, pp. 39–40; *Kāsānī*, 6:60.

> If two are partners only in the possession of a servant, or of a garment, then neither of them can designate an agent to sell it. If either of them does so, it will not be valid for his partner's share. For this is a proprietary partnership, and each of the partners is as a stranger in the other's share and has absolutely no power of disposal in regard to it.[33]

Since joint ownership is the entire basis of the partnership, it follows that any increase or profit is to be divided strictly according to the extent of each partner's ownership. This rule is made explicit in the following passage:

> According to Zufar,[34] it is not permissible for any partner to stipulate a share in the profit higher than his share of the capital. Shāfiʿī concurred with this opinion.
>
> Now, there is no difference of opinion regarding the fact that any increase in a proprietary partnership is distributed in accordance with each one's share of the capital. Thus, in a partnership, the capital of which consists of livestock, any stipulation giving one partner a larger share of the natural increase or of the milk production than his share of ownership is invalid according to all authorities.[35]

We have no documentary sources from the eighth and ninth centuries which would supplement our knowledge of proprietary partnership with details of its application and operation in the daily life of those times. However, the records of the Cairo Geniza dating from the late eleventh and twelfth centuries do offer several examples of an area in which this type of partnership seems to have been particularly prevalent, namely, the ownership of domestic slaves.[36]

At all times, slaves represented a considerable investment and constituted a valuable piece of property.[37] As such, they

[33] *Kāsānī*, 6:69.

[34] Zufar b. Hudhayl, a contemporary of Abū Ḥanīfa, d. 158/774; cf. Ibn Qutlūbughā, *Tāj at-tarājim*, Baghdad, 1962, p. 28.

[35] *Kāsānī*, 6:62.

[36] S. D. Goitein, "Slaves and Slavegirls in the Cairo Geniza Records," *Arabica* 9 (1961):1–20.

[37] For some idea of the price of slaves in the Near East from the tenth

were often the subject of a bequest or gift jointly to several heirs or children or relatives. A document of A.D. 1105 tells of a sale for twenty dinars of a slave who was owned jointly by two brothers.[38] A female slave named "Fidelity" was set free in A.D. 1181 by three sisters whose property she was.[39] Another slave girl, whose name was "Arsenic," was presented by a father to his two daughters as a gift in A.D. 1182.[40]

The complexities to which joint ownership might give rise are illustrated by an undated Geniza fragment involving a black slave girl named "Musk." Half the rights to this slave were inherited by a man from his deceased wife and were given by him to his married son. The rights to the other half belonged to the man's daughter-in-law, who was also his niece and who had herself been given half the slave girl by her mother, who had inherited this portion from her father.[41] Whatever else may be learned from this case, it clearly shows that the duration of joint ownership or proprietary partnership was often quite extensive, in this instance spanning three generations.[42]

The detailed attention devoted to problems resulting from partnership in slaves, which is to be found in almost all early Muslim legal works,[43] would seem to indicate that the social and economic practices current in Muslim society from the eighth century onward paralleled those of the Cairene Jewish middle class of the eleventh and twelfth centuries in that joint ownership of domestic slaves was a common and frequent occurrence. In some texts the treatment of partnership is introduced by the chapter heading "On Partnership and Manu-

---

to thirteenth centuries, cf. A. Mez, *The Renaissance of Islam*, trans. Patna, 1937, pp. 156–169; Goitein, *Arabica*, pp. 10–11.

38 Goitein, *Arabica* 9:8–9.

39 *Ibid.*, p. 11. 40 *Ibid.*, p. 9. 41 *Ibid.*, p. 13.

42 For a similar case of joint ownership dating from the mid-eleventh century and involving a set of scriptural books (an item worth 25 dinars and equaling, in monetary terms at least, the average value of a slave) which passed from uncle to nephews to grandnephews, cf. S. D. Goitein, *Jewish Education in Muslim Countries Based on Records of the Cairo Geniza* (Hebrew), Jerusalem, 1962, pp. 24–25.

43 E.g., Shaybānī, *Aṣl, Sharika*, fol. 72–fol. 73; Saḥnūn, *Mudawwana*, 16 vols., Damascus, n.d., 12:75ff.

mission,"[44] and deals exclusively with the unilateral freeing of a commonly held slave by one of the partners, or of the slave being accorded some special type of privilege without prior consultation and approval of the other partner.[45] The detailed discussion devoted to these problems represents not casuistry and hairsplitting, but is rather a reflection of their practical legal importance.

Proprietary partnership as conceived by the Ḥanafī and Mālikī lawyers had little importance for commercial transactions. There is only one situation discussed in the sources in which proprietary partnership becomes a necessary element for the successful consummation of a commercial partnership. For a partnership to be valid in Ḥanafī law, its investment must be in the form of cash and cannot be in the form of commodities. If two investors whose capital is in the form of commodities wish nevertheless to conclude a valid partnership, they must follow a formula given in the *ḥiyal* (legal devices) books for the purpose of circumventing this restriction. In the case where the goods in the possession of the prospective partners are of equal value, each buys half of the other's goods with half of his own.[46] This exchange establishes a proprietary partnership between the two parties on the basis of which a regular and valid contractual partnership may be negotiated.[47] Although it is in itself not important in terms of trade, proprietary partnership in this case becomes a necessary legal element in expanding the commercial scope of partnership.

44 Abū Yūsuf, *Ikhtilāf*, Cairo, 1357/1938, pp. 93–98; Shāfi'ī, *Kitāb ikhtilāf al-ḥadīth* (on the margin of *Kitāb al-Umm*, vol. 7), pp. 368–372.

45 E.g., one owner may accord the slave the status of a *mukātab*, i.e., the possibility of buying his own freedom for an agreed-upon sum or that of a *mudabbar*, whereby the slave is automatically freed upon his owner's death.

46 If the goods are of unequal value, a slightly different formula is suggested.

47 Shaybānī, *Kitāb al-makhārij fil-ḥiyal*, ed. J. Schacht, Leipzig, 1930, p. 58; al-Khaṣṣāf, *Kitāb al-ḥiyal wal-makhārij*, ed. J. Schacht, Hanover, 1923, p. 67; *Kāsānī*, 6:60; Marghīnānī, *Hidāya*, 2:310–311. In Saḥnūn, *Mudawwana*, 12:54, there is a similar scheme for concluding a partnership in which both investments are in the form of commodities. This device was also adopted by Shāfi'ī law to accomplish the same purpose, cf. Muzānī, *Mukhtaṣar*, Cairo, 1321/1903–1325/1907, 2:230.

Shāfi'ī Partnership

Up to this point, the discussion has been restricted to the Ḥanafī and Mālikī schools of law in which proprietary partnership is a very "junior partner" to the more important and essential concept of commercial or contractual partnership. The structure of Shāfi'ī partnerships reflects quite a different situation; here, a concept akin to proprietary partnership, that of intermingling (*ikhtilāṭ*), is a prerequisite and forms the essential basis of all partnerships. This transforms partnership into a very inflexible institution, excluding all but one type of partnership association.

Shāfi'ī's views on partnership are summarized in the following polemical passage from his *Kitāb al-Umm:*

> Ar-Rabī' said: "Shāfi'ī informed us saying: 'The *mufāwaḍa*[48] partnership is null and void. If the *mufāwaḍa* partnership is not void, then I do not know anything in the world that is void.
>
> 'Only if the two partners take the term *mufāwaḍa* to mean a mingling of the capital, trading with it, and then a division of the profit is there nothing wrong with the arrangement. This is the type of partnership which some of the Easterners designate as *'inān*.[49] If two individuals form such a partnership, stipulating that for them the term *mufāwaḍa* implies the above conditions, then the partnership is valid. And whatever either of them gains from endeavors not connected with the partnership capital, be it through trade, or hire, or a treasure trove, or a gift, or anything else, belongs exclusively to him.

48 A universal partnership. In Ḥanafī law this is an arrangement in which the partnership investment consists of *all* the eligible capital of the partners except their personal and household belongings. Likewise, all expenses except for personal needs are paid out of common funds. In Mālikī law the term *mufāwaḍa* connotes a general mandate partnership, i.e., an arrangement in which each party confers upon his colleague full authority to dispose of their joint capital in any manner intended to benefit their association.

49 A limited investment or partial partnership. An arrangement in which each partner invests a given sum of money and accepts an agreed-upon share of the profit or loss.

'If, however, the two partners declare that the term *mufāwaḍa* implies a partnership in profits from any and all endeavors, those connected with the partnership and those derived from other sources, then the partnership is invalid. If this is not gambling, then I don't know what is!

'What, indeed, would be your opinion to two people who form a partnership with two hundred dirhams, and then one of them finds a treasure? Is this to be shared between them? Or is it permissible that the partners make such an arrangement without even mingling the capital? If a man receives a gift, or hires himself out to do some work and gains money from his labor or gift, can another individual, in your opinion, be partner to his gain? Indeed, less questionable transactions than these have been rejected.' "[50]

The implied answers to all the questions posed in the last paragraph are in the negative. Profit or gain from any common venture can be based only on the cash invested by each partner. Any outside or unknown source of gain is classified in the same category as gambling which, in the *Qur'ān,* is in the same proscribed category as wine drinking.[51]

To make his rejection of the *mufāwaḍa* more effective, Shāfi'ī offers the somewhat extreme examples of extra-partnership income involving the discovery by one of the partners of a treasure trove, or his receiving a gift. Both these sources of wealth have no connection with the partnership and, as such, should not become part of the social capital. Even the early Ḥanafī and Mālikī jurists, who do allow the *mufāwaḍa* partnership, are in agreement with Shāfi'ī on this point, and it is apparently against Ibn Abī Laylā, an Iraqi contemporary of Abū Ḥanīfa, that this remark is directed. Shāfi'ī, however, disagrees not only with those who consider this outside wealth as belonging properly to the common partnership fund—he emphatically rejects the entire concept of an unlimited investment partnership as construed by the other two legal schools and characterizes it as the most legally inadmissible contract

[50] Shāfi'ī, *Umm*, 7 vols., Cairo, 1321/1903–1325/1907, 3:206.
[51] *Qur'ān*, 2:219.

he can conceive of. It is not that the *mufāwaḍa* involves the commitment of the entire eligible capital of each partner that is disturbing to Shāfi'ī; it is rather that the profit and loss of all commercial transactions in which the partners engage, whether jointly or singly, are to be charged to the common partnership fund. For Shāfi'ī, this leaves too wide an area of activity unknown to, and uncontrolled by, the contract, and is thus akin in his eyes to gambling.[52]

Implicit in Shāfi'ī's opposition to this type of partnership is the idea that the right to profit and the liability for losses exist only by virtue of ownership of capital and are in direct proportion to the extent of that ownership. Although Shāfi'ī did not explicitly state his position in this way, his followers interpreted his views as meaning this, and it has become a principle of Shāfi'ī law.[53] This principle was bound to have an inhibiting influence on the formation and effectiveness of commercial partnerships. It meant that there could be no flexibility in the distribution of profits in a partnership agreement, but that this would be determined solely by each partner's share of the total investment. In the division of profits, no premium could thus be placed on such commercially meaningful factors as trading skills, social position, expertise with various commodities, or the amount of time each party devoted to the association's affairs. If adhered to, this restriction would have served as a serious impediment to the free flow of investment capital.

An even more restrictive feature of Shāfi'ī partnership law is its insistence on the intermingling of individual investments. This prerequisite for a valid partnership is expressed in Shāfi'ī's question, the implied answer of which is a negative, "Is it permissible for the partners to make such an agreement

[52] Cf. Schacht, *An Introduction to Islamic Law*, Oxford, 1964, p. 146: "Starting from the Koranic prohibition of a certain game of hazard (*maysir*), Islamic law insists that there must be no doubt concerning the obligations undertaken by the parties to a contract."

[53] E.g., Nawawī, *Minhāj aṭ-ṭālibīn* (printed with commentary of Shirbīnī, *Mughnī al-muḥtāj ilā ma'rifat ma'āni alfāẓ al-minhāj*, Cairo, 1374/1955, 2:215; E. Sachau, *Muhammedanisches Recht nach Schafiitischer Lehre*, Berlin, 1897, pp. 419–420.

(a *mufāwaḍa* partnership) without even mingling the capital?" Later Shāfi'ī writers have spelled out this point clearly and unmistakably:[54] A partnership contract becomes effective only after the complete intermingling of the common capital. The merger of the investments must theoretically be so thorough as to make both partners' individual shares indistinguishable.[55] This means that the capital had to be physically merged as far as possible into one entity in such a way that each contributor had ownership in the smallest unit of it in proportion to the size of his contribution. Before a contractual partnership could begin functioning, a state of joint ownership or proprietary partnership (although this term is never used in Shāfi'ī works) must first have existed.

The centrality of the idea of intermingling and joint ownership for Shāfi'ī partnership was keenly observed and analyzed by the Ḥanafī writer Sarakhsī. In discussing limited investment partnership, he observed the following:

> In our view, limited investment partnership (*'inān*) does not require the intermingling of investments. But according to Zufar, Shāfi'ī holds that mingling is a prerequisite for a valid partnership. In Shāfi'ī's view, proprietary partnership is the underlying principle (*aṣl*) of all partnership, and that contractual partnership must be based upon it.
>
> Shāfi'ī holds that the meaning of the word *sharika* is intermingling and that this is realized only through ownership. An important consideration in every type of contract is the implication of the designation of that contract, as, for example, *ḥawāla* (bill of exchange),[56] or *kafāla* (surety), or *ṣarf* (money-exchange).
>
> If the two investments are mingled in a manner making them indistinguishable from each other, then the partnership becomes effective through ownership, and a contractual part-

[54] Muzanī, *Mukhtaṣar*, 2:230; Nawawī, *Minhāj*, 4 vols., Cairo, 1374/1955, 2:213.

[55] "The intermingling of the two investments so that they will not be distinguishable is to be stipulated." Nawawī, *Minhāj*, 2:213.

[56] Literally, "transfer," i.e., transfer of credit or debts.

nership can be built upon it. If one of the investments is lost before they are intermingled, the loss is borne exclusively by its owner, and any projected contractual partnership cannot become effective because the capital did not undergo the process of intermingling.[57]

With intermingling constituting an absolute requirement for partnership, only investments of a uniform type would be suitable for the formation of a valid partnership; and since all forms of merchandise were ruled out,[58] this left only currency. Furthermore, in order for each partner's contribution to merge indistinguishably with that of his colleague, the currency would have to be of the same denomination and quality.[59]

In a monetary system in which three denominations of currency, gold, silver, and copper,[60] circulated simultaneously, this was a serious restriction. No uniformity prevailed even among coins of the same metal. In many cases, coins several centuries old circulated simultaneously with newly minted ones. There were several sizes and qualities of dinars and dirhams,[61] and almost as many different types of copper coins as there were mints that issued them.[62] The monetary situation in the medieval Islamic world was further complicated by the fact that different currencies predominated in different areas. In Egypt and North Africa the gold dinar served as the coin of the realm, with silver coinage circulating intermittently, whereas in Iraq and the eastern provinces, while gold was always in use, the silver dirham predominated.

In this monetary context, any two pious Shāfiʿī merchants wishing to form a partnership could do so only if they happened to have in their possession at that moment the exactly

57 Sarakhsī, *Mabsūṭ*, 11:152.

58 Nawawī, *Minhāj*, 2:213; Sachau, *Muhammedanisches Recht*, p. 417.

59 Nawawī, *Minhāj*, 2:214, Sachau, *Muhammedanisches Recht*, p. 417.

60 Dinar (gold coin); dirham (silver coin); *fals* (copper coin).

61 Cf. articles of G. C. Miles in *EI*, 2nd ed., *s.v.*, *dīnār* and *dirham* and references there. The legal texts themselves frequently allude to different types of dirhams and dinars and the way these are to be handled within the framework of partnership investment.

62 Cf. *EI*, 2nd ed., *s.v.*, *fals*.

identical type of coins. If, for example, one came with white and the other with black dirhams, they would either have to forego the partnership or else one of them would have to avail himself of the services of a moneychanger, thereby losing out on the changer's commission and on the possibility of an unfavorable rate of exchange.

Intermingling would also make Shāfi'ī partnership a very inefficient instrument for long-distance trade. The requirement of uniform currency would be an impediment to prospective partners from different currency areas. It would also make it impossible to negotiate any partnership by letter, a convenience of which merchants traveling or residing in different cities or countries might wish to avail themselves.[63]

Limited investment partnership is the only type which the rigorous Shāfi'ī view considers permissible. In this arrangement, each partner contributes a certain sum of money to the common fund; this capital must then be intermingled in order for the contract to become effective. The investors may contribute to the partnership equally or in any other proportion they see fit. Each partner's share in the profits or losses is in direct proportion to his share of the total investment. Any stipulation assigning to one of the partners a share in the profits larger than that of his share of the total investment is invalid. No allowance could be made for a partner's special business skills or contacts.

This type of partnership was best suited for the circumstances of local trade where prospective partners would be within easy reach of each other. Living in the same town or working in the same market place would make it more likely that they would be using identical coins, thus making the intermingling of their investments possible. It is also reasonable to expect that since no monetary premium was placed on trading skills, the partnerships would be of a comparatively simple character, involving only few transactions.

The rigid rules governing Shāfi'ī partnership exclude the several other types of partnerships which are permitted and

[63] For an example of "partnership by mail" cf. S. D. Goitein, *Jewish Education in Muslim Countries Based on Records of the Cairo Geniza*, Jerusalem, 1962, pp. 125–126.

thoroughly discussed by the other legal schools. Thus a work partnership in which the investment consists not of money, but of the labor or manual skills of the partners, is ruled out.[64] Also excluded is a credit partnership in which the partners start without any capital, but make their initial joint purchases on credit.[65] The investment capital of neither of the above two partnerships is of the type that could satisfy the Shāfi'ī requirement of intermingling.

To some extent, the limited commercial possibilities of partnership in Shāfi'ī law are compensated for by the institution of the *commenda* (*muḍāraba, qirāḍ*). This is permitted by Shāfi'ī law, as it is by all the other legal schools. The *commenda* could fill the need for a contract suitable for long-distance trade, as well as permit a more flexible distribution of profits. The validity of the *commenda* is not, however, a sufficient explanation for Shāfi'ī's drastic limitation of partnership. Nor does it explain why Shāfi'ī law, unlike any of the other Muslim law schools, places joint ownership at the very foundations of its partnership theory.

The sources for joint ownership as a basis for partnership might be sought in the two legal traditions which are acknowledged to have exercised some degree of influence on Muslim law generally, and on Shāfi'ī in particular, namely, Roman and Jewish law.[66]

Like modern commercial law, Roman law does not consider joint ownership *per se* as constituting *societas* or partnership.[67] For a contract to qualify as *societas*, Roman law re-

[64] Shāfi'ī, *Umm*, 3:206 (bottom); Nawawī, *Minhāj*, 2:212.

[65] Nawawī, *Minhāj*, 2:212.

[66] I. Goldziher, "The Principles of Law in Islam," *The Historians' History of the World*, 8:294–304; J. Schacht, "Foreign Elements in Ancient Islamic Law," *The Journal of Comparative Legislation and International Law*, 3rd ser., 32 (1950):9–17; Schacht, *Origins*, pp. 99–100; S. D. Goitein, "An Introduction to Muslim Law," *Muslim Law in Israel* (Hebrew), Jerusalem, 1957, pp. 8–11. For an attempted refutation of any outside influence on Muslim law, cf. S. Mahamasani, *Falsafat at-tashrī' fil-Islām*, Beirut, 1961, pp. 246–260; English translation by Farhat Ziadeh (with subtitle, *The Philosophy of Jurisprudence in Islam*), Leiden, 1962, pp. 136–145.

[67] W. W. Buckland and Arnold D. McNair, *Roman Law and Common Law*, 2nd ed., Cambridge, 1952, pp. 300–301; W. W. Buckland, *A Text-Book of Roman Law from Augustus to Justinian*, Cambridge, 1932, pp. 506–507.

quires as a minimum the joint exploitation of the common property. The idea of joint ownership constituting *societas* is explicitly excluded by Roman law.

> If there is to be any right to action *pro socio*, there must needs be a partnership in the case; it is not enough that there is property held in common, unless there is partnership. But property can be treated as held in common even without partnership, as for instance where two persons come to own a thing in common without any intention of partnership, as may happen where something is bequeathed to two persons, or, again, if something is purchased by two at the same time, or where people come in for an inheritance or a gift in common, or buy independently from two persons their respective shares, without intending to be partners.[68]

It is interesting that this passage places beyond the pale of partnership exactly those relationships which Ḥanafī law defines as proprietary partnership. It seems fairly obvious that Roman law served as a direct source neither for the Shāfiʿī conception of partnership, in which joint ownership occupies the center of the stage, nor for that of the Ḥanafī and Mālikī schools, in which joint ownership, although in a minor and peripheral role, is still comprehended by the definition of partnership.[69]

The separation of joint ownership from the idea of partnership would appear to be a "non-Semitic" notion, or at least one that is not part of the Near Eastern legal tradition. In Jewish law these two concepts are comprehended by the single term of partnership. While the Jewish law of partnership

[68] *Corpus juris civilis, Digesta* 17:2. 31. This passage is taken from the edition and translation of C. H. Monro, Cambridge, 1902, pp. 19–20.

[69] Roman law did at one time include a form of partnership based primarily on joint ownership. This was the *consortium ercto non cito*; cf. Paolo Frezza, "Il *Consortium Ercto Non Cito* E I Nuovi Frammenti Di Gaio," *Rivista Di Filologia E D'Istruzione Classica*, N.S., 12 (1934):27–46. This form of partnership, however, was archaic long before the time of the Islamic conquests. For the absence of Roman influence in other aspects of Islamic commercial law, cf. Niels J. Andersen, *Studier Over Hovedprincipperne I Den Islamiske Handelsret*, Copenhagen, 1961, p. 116.

differs in many important respects from its Muslim counterpart, it parallels the latter in making no distinction between joint ownership and partnership.[70] Indeed, some of the modern commentators on Jewish partnership law contend that the original significance of the term *shūtafūt* was common ownership and that this concept serves as the basis of the various forms of contractual partnership that developed in Jewish law.[71]

From the few surviving fragments of Pahlavi and Sassanian legal fragments it is abundantly clear that in pre-Islamic Iranian law the common possession of property was a basic principle of partnership. As in Islamic law, the terms for partnership both in the Pahlavi texts and in the Syriac version of a collection of Sassanian legal decisions encompassed, in addition to business associations, the notion of the common ownership of a non-commercial character. It included such cases as the joint ownership of fields, houses, and slaves, the joint inheritance of immovable property, and the unification by a husband of the property of several wives into a single unit. Likewise, the rights and privileges of parties to joint property parallel those outlined for the associates in an Islamic *sharikat al-milk*.[72]

While the detailed comparison of Muslim partnership with

[70] By partnership we refer here only to the contract covered by the Hebrew term *shūtafūt*, and not to the *'isqā* contract. These two are often treated together in medieval Jewish legal codes, e.g., Maimonides, *Mishneh Torah*, Bk. 12, Treatise 4; trans. Isaac Klein, *Code of Maimonides*, Bk. 12, *The Book of Acquisition*, New Haven, 1951, pp. 207–244. For *shūtafūt*, cf. E. E. Hildesheimer, *Das Jüdische Gesellschaftsrecht*, Leipzig, 1930, pp. 1–85; *Jewish Encyclopaedia* (*JE*), 9:545. For *'isqā*, which should be classified as intermediate between partnership and *commenda* and is considered by the Rabbis as a part loan and a part deposit, cf. Hildesheimer, *Gesellschaftsrecht*, pp. 89–131, and A. L. Udovitch, "At the Origins of the Western *Commenda*, *SPECULUM* 37 (1962):199–201.

[71] Hildesheimer, *Gesellschaftsrecht*, p. 1; *JE*, 9:545.

[72] N. V. Peegulevskaya (*sic*), "Economic Relations in Iran During the 4–6 Centuries A.D.," *Journal of the K.R. Cama Oriental Institute*, Bombay, 38 (1956):69–73. The texts themselves are to be found in, E. Sachau, *Syrische Rechtsbücher*, 3 vols., Berlin, 1907–14, 3:142–147, 174–175; and in Chr. Bartholomae, *Zum sasanidischen Recht*, parts 1–5, *Sitzungsberichte der Heidelberger Akademie der Wissenschaften, Philosophisch-Historische Klasse*, 9 (1918), 11 (1920), 13 (1922), 14 (1923).

its counterparts in other legal systems is not strictly within the purview of this study, some of the more striking parallels, especially those between the Shāfi'ī and Jewish treatments of the subject, are worthy of note.

All schools of Muslim law join common ownership and partnership into one legal category; but only in Shāfi'ī law does common ownership serve as the basis for the entire institution. Jewish partnership law is similarly structured; all forms of trading partnerships are based on the merger and joint ownership of the several investments.

As a result of Shāfi'ī's emphasis on joint ownership, he requires the intermingling of investments as a prerequisite to a valid contractual partnership. The almost identical Jewish requirement is found in Maimonides' treatment of partnership:

> If two people wish to form a partnership, how does each one acquire title to the money of the other to become joint owner thereof? If the partnership is entered into with money, then each one brings his money and they put it into one purse and both lift the purse.[73]

Jewish law does not require the identical type of coin from each investor, nor does it rule out investment in the form of commodities as do the Shāfi'īs. But it does insist on a merger of investments, even if it be of a token nature, and even in the case of different types of goods, to establish the joint ownership necessary for a valid partnership contract.

Shāfi'ī is alone among early Muslim legal authorities in rejecting a partnership in which the investment consists not of cash or goods, but of a particular skill or craft. So, too, in Jewish law:

> If artisans enter a partnership in their trade, though each binds himself by a *ḳinyan*,[74] they are not partners.
>
> Thus if two tailors or two weavers agree that whatever each of them takes in should be owned equally by both of them,

[73] *Mishneh Torah*, Bk. 12, Treatise, 4, Ch. 4, para. 1; translation, p. 220.

[74] Literally: acquisition. For the significance of this term in Jewish commercial law, cf. *Jewish Encyclopaedia* (*JE*), 1:394–397.

there is no partnership whatsoever here, because a man cannot transfer to another title to a thing that is not yet in existence.[75]

The basis of Maimonides' opposition to the partnership of artisans, namely, the inability to transfer ownership of a thing not yet in existence, is reminiscent of the objection underlying Shāfi'ī's rejection of the *mufāwaḍa* and other types of partnership because of the element of gambling. Both are bothered by the element of chance and the unknown in regard to the investment capital. While the outcome and profits of any commercial venture are of necessity attended by an element of the unknown, Shāfi'ī as well as Jewish law, because of their requirement of joint ownership as a basis of partnership, insist that no such element be attached to the initial investment of the partnership. The latter, in their view, must be tangible, definite, and known. All other types of investment are excluded.

As indicated, Jewish and Muslim partnership law diverge in many important details. The parallels presented here, however, do suggest a certain relationship. The inclusion of joint ownership within the realm of partnership in Jewish, Sassanian, and Muslim law constitutes what might be termed a legal isogloss, placing the Muslim conception of this institution within the broad tradition of Near Eastern legal ideas. It indicates a probable influence of the earlier traditions on the formation of their Islamic counterpart.

[75] *Maimonides,* Hebrew text, para. 2; trans., p. 220.

III

The Ḥanafī *Mufāwaḍa* Partnership

In Medieval Arabic usage, the term *mufāwaḍa* carried several connotations. Its dictionary meaning simply conveys the notion of mutual consultation, or mutual delegation of authority and jurisdiction, and could be applied in any number of circumstances. Even in the more restricted commercial context, its meaning varied, being used by some as a general term for any kind of commercial association;[1] but in the Ḥanafī and Mālikī schools of law, the term *mufāwaḍa* is employed as a technical designation for a specific form of partnership. The meaning of the term for each of the schools, however, is by no means identical, and the structure of the institutions thus designated varies considerably from one school to the other. For the Mālikīs, *mufāwaḍa* denotes a general type of commercial partnership in which capital and profits are distributed in indefinite shares.[2] For the Ḥanafīs, it has a much more specific meaning.

Commercial partnerships are divided by Ḥanafī law into two types, the *mufāwaḍa*, which is best translated as a universal or unlimited investment partnership, and the *'inān,* which is perhaps best rendered as a limited investment partnership. The emphasis here is on the scope and investment aspects of the contract. This is in distinct contrast to contemporary legal nomenclature regarding partnership in which the determining consideration is the partnership's liability *vis à vis* third parties.

The present-day designations "limited" and "unlimited" for a partnership or company denote the extent of the company's and each of its member's liabilities toward extra-partnership individuals and groups for obligations incurred in the course of the conduct of the company's business. In an unlimited partnership, the company is liable for the complete fulfillment of

[1] Cf. Shaybānī, *Aṣl, Muḍāraba,* fol. 42b, ll. 5–7, and below, Chapter 6. n. 107.

[2] Cf. Chapter 5, section on "Terminology and Classification."

all its obligations, and each partner is liable proportionally to his share in the company's assets, or in accordance with the contractual stipulations governing his share of the profits and losses. Whatever the extent of the partnership's obligation, be it one dollar or a hundred thousand, the partner is responsible for his full share. In a limited partnership there is, as the term implies, a limit to the amount for which the partnership and its members can be held liable. The liability can be limited in several ways, but the basic idea is that it is confined to the assets of the partnership. If, for example, its indebtedness reaches a sum in excess of its capital, the partners cannot be held liable for the difference, nor are any of their extra-partnership assets attachable for payment of their partnership debts.[3]

In Ḥanafī law, and indeed in all of Islamic law, the liability in all partnerships is unlimited.[4] In all Islamic partnerships, the partners are liable in proportion to their share of the total investment. There is no limit whatsoever on the amount of the partnership's liability. Each partner is responsible for his share of the partnership's indebtedness regardless of what it amounts to, or by how much it exceeds the value of his own share of the company's assets.

Liability, therefore, cannot serve, as it does in modern law, as a basis for classifying the different types of Ḥanafī partnerships. It is rather from the perspective of the investment, both its extent and its form, that the different partnership forms are distinguished.[5] In the *'inān*, or limited investment partnership, only that part of his capital which the prospective partner wishes to invest becomes part of the common fund; in the

[3] Cf. H. C. Black, *Black's Law Dictionary*, 3rd ed., St. Paul, 1933, pp. 1103, 1331, 1785.

[4] This fact deserves special emphasis in view of the imprecise terminology used by some of the leading Western authorities on Islamic law in their treatment of partnership. For example, the *'inān* partnership has been described as "*die Gesellschaft mit beschränkter Haftung*" (J. Schacht, ed., *Grundzüge*, Berlin, 1935, p. 75), "*societa ristretta o limitata*" (D. Santillana, *Istituzioni*, 2 vols., Rome, 1925–1938, 2:299), and "limited liability company" (J. Schacht, *An Introduction to Islamic Law*, Oxford, 1959, 1964, p. 156). The nature of the liability in the various forms of Islamic partnership is distinguishable on the basis of jointness and severalty, and not on its limitation or non-limitation.

[5] Cf. *Kāsānī*, 7 vols., Cairo, 1328/1910, 6:56–57.

mufāwaḍa, or universal partnership, all the partners' eligible property is incorporated into the social capital.

Before embarking on a detailed investigation of the *mufāwaḍa* partnership, it would be useful to offer the concise general description of its essential features as given by Qudūrī, an eminent eleventh century Ḥanafī writer.

> A universal partnership can occur when two people of equal wealth, religion, and freedom of action enter into a partnership. It is permissible between two free Muslims, both of age and in possession of their mental faculties. It is not permissible between a freeman and a slave, nor between a minor and one of age, nor between a Muslim and a non-believer. It is contracted with full powers of agency for both partners, and with each partner serving as surety for the other. Except for food and clothing for their respective families, whatever either of them purchases is on the account of the partnership. Both partners are equally liable for any obligation undertaken by either of them in exchange for something valid within the partnership.[6]

Of the four major schools of Muslim law, only the Ḥanafīs recognize the validity of this type of partnership. The Shāfiʿīs and Ḥanbalīs explicitly reject it, and in Mālikī doctrine the *mufāwaḍa* is transformed into an entirely different institution.[7] Its validity within Ḥanafī law is one of the many manifestations of this school's consistently more flexible and lenient attitude in all questions connected with partnership. Ḥanafī law permits a greater variety of partnerships, and, in the course of their operation, imposes far fewer restrictions on the partners' conduct than do any of the other legal schools.

This phenomenon is undoubtedly to be related to the prominence in early Ḥanafī legal thinking of the principles of *ra'y*—independent reasoning, and *istiḥsān*—juristic preference. The connection between these and the development of the *ḥiyal* (legal fiction) literature—a literature which was an almost

[6] Qudūrī, *Mukhtaṣar*, Istanbul, 1319/1901, p. 53; ed. Cairo, 1955, 2:69–71.

[7] For the Shāfiʿīs, cf. *Umm*, 7 vols., Cairo, 1321/1903–1325/1907, 3:206; for the Mālikīs, cf. Saḥnūn, *Mudawwana*, 16 vols., Damascus, n.d., 12:68–69; for the Ḥanbalīs, cf. Ibn Qudāmā, *Al-Mughnī*, Cairo, 1367, 5:25–26.

exclusively Ḥanafī phenomenon, and which was intended to bridge the gap between legal theory and practice in order to expand the area in which commercial and other practices would be within the realm of the *sharī'a*—was already suggested by J. Schacht in his early studies of this legal literary genre.[8] Ḥanafī partnership law provides additional evidence confirming the relationship between *ra'y* and *istiḥsān* and a more lenient attitude toward commercial practice.

In numerous instances, a recognition of the needs of the marketplace is manifested by explicitly justifying the use of juristic preference to suspend strict legal reasoning because of "the custom of the merchants," or "the need of the merchants for it."[9] Indeed, the very legitimacy of a universal partnership is, according to some authorities, based on a modification of strict legal standards by means of the application of juristic preference.

> In our view, this partnership (i.e., *mufāwaḍa*) is permissible on the basis of juristic preference (*istiḥsān*); on the basis of analogy it would not be permissible. The latter, indeed, is the opinion of Shāfi'ī. Mālik said: "I know not what *mufāwaḍa* is." For on the basis of analogy, this form of partnership would comprehend the power of agency (*wakāla*) with respect to an unknown subject and the obligation of surety (*kafāla*) with respect to a thing undefined, and each of these individually is not permissible.
>
> The reason for the exercise of juristic preference is the Prophet's statement: "Enter into partnerships by reciprocity (*fāwiḍū*), for it is most conducive to prosperity." Also, men have had transactions together in this manner with no person forbidding them. For these reasons, analogy is abandoned.[10]

[8] J. Schacht, "Die arabische *ḥijal*-Literatur," *Der Islam* 15 (1926):221–224.

[9] E.g., Sarakhsī, *Mabsūṭ*, 30 vols., Cairo, 1324/1906–1331/1912, 11:80.

[10] al-Marghīnānī, *al-Hidāya*, 4 vols., Cairo, n.d., 3:4. For a somewhat archaic translation of the entire work, cf., *Hedaya, or Guide: A Commentary on the Mussulman Laws*, trans. Charles Hamilton, 4 vols., London, 1791. This passage occurs in volume 2, pp. 297–298.

Derivation of the Term *Mufāwaḍa*

All three essential features of the *mufāwaḍa* partnership—the complete equality of the partners in all respects, the inclusion of all trade activities within its scope, and the mutual agency and surety of the partners—are implied by the different nuances in the meaning of the Arabic term *mufāwaḍa*. These are all neatly summarized in Sarakhsī's speculations concerning the derivation of the term.

> As for the term *mufāwaḍa*, it has been said that it derives from *tafwiḍ* (delegation of authority),[11] for each partner empowers his colleague to act freely with the entire partnership capital.
>
> It has also been said that its derivation is from the idea of dispersal, as it is said: "the water overflowed (*fāḍa*)," meaning that it spread out and dispersed; or "the bounty is spread out (*yastafīḍu*)," meaning, it is distributed widely. Since this contract is based upon the dispersal of authority for all transactions, it was designated as *mufāwaḍa*.
>
> It has further been said that its derivation is from the idea of equality. As the poet said: "A people who are all equal (*fawḍā*), without a leader, do not prosper; And they do not have a leader, if they are led by the ignoramuses among them."[12]
>
> The meaning of *fawḍā* here is equality. And since this contract is based on the equality of investment and profit, it is called *mufāwaḍa*.[13]

Equality in the *Mufāwaḍa* Partnership

Equality of Persons

One of the prerequisites for a valid *mufāwaḍa* partnership is the equality of the partners in all respects. This applies not

[11] Cf. E. W. Lane, *Lexicon*, part 6, London, 1863–1893, p. 2459; R. Dozy, *Supplément aux Dictionnaires Arabes*, 2nd ed., 2 vols., Leiden, 1927, 2:289.

[12] The author of these lines is Al-Afwāh al-Awdī; cf. Abū-l-Faraj al-Iṣbahānī, *Kitāb al-aghānī*, 21 vols., Cairo, 1868–1888, 12:169.

[13] Sarakhsī, *Mabsūṭ*, 11:152.

only to the amount of each one's investment and to the division of profits and losses between them, but also to the personal status of the partners.

A valid *mufāwaḍa* partnership can be contracted only between two free people. "A *mufāwaḍa* is not permissible between a freeman and a slave, nor between two slaves, nor between a freeman and a *mukātab* slave, nor between two *mukātab* slaves."[14] A slave does not possess complete freedom of action in commercial matters. The property of a slave belongs to his master, and as Shaybānī says, "How can he be allowed to be a *mufāwaḍa* partner in something which he does not possess?"[15]

A slave cannot provide surety for another person, nor is he fully responsible for his own actions. A universal partnership between himself and a freeman would create a severe inequality, for the latter would be liable for his own and the slave's actions. It is for this same reason that any such partnership between a minor and one of age, or between two minors, even with the permission of their parents or guardians, is unlawful.

> For the *mufāwaḍa* is based on the idea of mutual surety in which each of the partners provides surety for his colleague. The slave, the *mukātab* slave, and the minor are not of that category of persons who can provide surety, and for this reason any *mufāwaḍa* partnership between them is not permitted. For each of the above does not possess full freedom of action; the master can circumscribe the rights of his slave, as can the guardian those of the minor, and the *mukātab* may be unable to keep up with his payments and thus revert to slave status. What is intended in the *mufāwaḍa* is freedom of action and the seeking of profits. If each of them does not himself possess full freedom of action, then the *mufāwaḍa* is not permissible.[16]

[14] Sarakhsī, *Mabsūṭ*, 11:198; cf. also Shaybānī, *Aṣl*, *Sharika*, fol. 68b, ll. 8 and 12.

[15] Shaybānī, *Aṣl*, *Sharika*, fol. 68b, ll. 9–10.

[16] Sarakhsī, *Mabsūṭ*, 11:198.

If two persons of this category do, nevertheless, conclude a *mufāwaḍa* partnership and commence trading, the association, *ipso facto*, becomes an *'inān* partnership, where the limitations on their rights do not affect the partnership.

There is only one category of slave who, in the opinion of some authorities, is capable of negotiating a valid *mufāwaḍa* partnership. This exception is the *mudabbar* slave, that is, a slave who automatically attains his freedom upon his master's death. According to Abū Yūsuf and Shaybānī, a *mufāwaḍa* contracted between two *mudabbar* slaves is valid.[17] Abū Ḥanīfa takes exception to this view, and it is his opinion that seems to have become accepted Ḥanafī doctrine, since the view permitting this partnership is not repeated in any of the later Ḥanafī sources.

The demand for equality between the associates in a universal partnership extends to religious affiliation as well. The universality of the *mufāwaḍa* partnership, covering, as it does, all commercial transactions of the partners, rules out such associations between a Muslim on the one hand and a Christian, Jew, or Zoroastrian on the other. A *dhimmī*[18] may handle goods, such as pork and wine, which a Muslim may not own, and in the profits of whose sale he can have no share. Certain business arrangements which are permissible for a *dhimmī* may not be so for a Muslim, thus disqualifying the latter from full participation in a "mixed" *mufāwaḍa*. "If the *dhimmī* were to buy wine or pork, would this be lawful for the Muslim partner?" asks Shaybānī, "and if the *dhimmī*, after purchasing these items, sold them, could the Muslim share in the price received?"[19]

Shaybānī and Abū Ḥanīfa answer this question with an unqualified negative. Abū Yūsuf, however, registers a qualified dissent to their opinion, holding that a difference in religious persuasion is not sufficient grounds for invalidating a universal partnership. In his view, the overriding considerations are the

[17] Shaybānī, *Aṣl*, *Sharika*, fol. 68b, ll. 12–14.

[18] Christians, Jews, and other minorities enjoying a protected status in Muslim-dominated lands. Cf. *Encyclopaedia of Islam* (*EI*), 2nd ed., 2:227–231.

[19] Shaybānī, *Aṣl*, *Sharika*, fol. 68b, ll. 3–4.

elements of mutual agency and mutual surety, of which a *dhimmī,* like a Muslim, is capable. Although he permits a *mufāwaḍa* partnership between a Muslim and a *dhimmī,* Abū Yūsuf designates such an arrangement as *makrūh,* that is, not recommendable.[20]

All authorities are agreed that a *mufāwaḍa* partnership between two *dhimmīs* is as valid as one contracted between two free Muslims. It is not necessary that the two or more *dhimmīs* involved be of the same religion, because any impediment that may lie in the way of a commercial association between non-Muslims of different faiths is not the concern of Muslim law.[21]

A *mufāwaḍa* partnership between two Muslims who are adherents of different legal rites is lawful, even though the various legal schools differ as to the legality of Muslims owning certain borderline types of commodities such as date-wine (*nabīdh*).[22]

All authorities unanimously reject an unlimited investment partnership between a Muslim and an apostate from Islam. Apostasy from Islam is punishable by death, which under all circumstances automatically terminates a partnership. Before an apostate is tried, or if he escapes to non-Muslim territory, all his legal rights are suspended, thus preventing any of his actions from having any legal effect. It is for this reason, too, that a *mufāwaḍa* between two apostates is invalid.[23]

A difference in the sex of the prospective partners constitutes

[20] *Ibid.*, fol. 68b, ll. 8–9; Sarakhsī, *Mabsūṭ*, 11:196–197; *Kāsānī*, 6:61. In view of the strong arguments militating against a "mixed" *mufāwaḍa*, Abū Yūsuf's opinion on the matter is especially noteworthy. He does not invoke the principle of *istiḥsān* in support of his view. One might speculate that his more lenient position had some connection with his experience as a *qāḍī*, as a result of which he was more sensitive to practical considerations. On Abū Yūsuf's legal thought, cf. J. Schacht in *Law in the Middle East*, Washington, D.C., 1955, 1:52–53; on Muslim–non-Muslim partnerships, cf. S. D. Goitein, "From the Mediterranean to India," *SPECULUM* 29 (1954):196–197; and *idem.*, *Records from the Cairo Geniza* (guide accompanying exhibition at the Univ. of Pennsylvania), p. 4, nos. 7 and 8, and most recently, *Mediterranean Society*, Berkeley and Los Angeles, 1967, 1:72.

[21] Sarakhsī, *Mabsūṭ*, 11:197.

[22] *Ibid.*

[23] *Kāsānī*, 6:61–62, where other factors are also considered.

a barrier to a valid *mufāwaḍa*; this contract is lawful only between two freemen or women of the same faith.

Equality of Investment, Profit, and Loss

Complete equality in all financial matters is the *sine qua non* of the unlimited investment partnership; any deviation from this rule, whether in respect to each partner's contribution to the joint capital, or to the share of profits and losses assigned to him, immediately renders the *mufāwaḍa* invalid. Thus, whether the partners invest equal amounts of capital but agree on an unequal distribution of the profits, or whether, conversely, they invest unequal amounts while contracting to divide the profits equally, the partnership is not, according to Ḥanafī law, considered a *mufāwaḍa*.[24]

> Two people contracted a *mufāwaḍa* partnership and we wrote a contract between them in which we stated: (a) That by this contract they have become partners in all things, both large and small; (b) That this is a *mufāwaḍa* partnership; (c) That their common capital amounts to such and such and that each has contributed half of it and is entitled to half the profit; (d) That each partner can trade in any manner he sees fit. If they negotiate a partnership on this basis, they are indeed *mufāwaḍa* partners. This is according to what we have explained, namely, that the consideration of equality is the pillar of the *mufāwaḍa* partnership. The partners' equality in the investment and the profit, as well as the fact that the partnership includes all things, both large and small, must be mentioned in the contract. If one of the partners retains for himself the ownership of some capital which is eligible for the partnership, then, because of the breach of equality, the contract will not constitute a *mufāwaḍa* partnership. However, if the property retained by one of the partners is in the form of goods, or is a debt owed him

24 Shaybānī, *Aṣl*, *Sharika*, fol. 68b, ll. 15–17. The only dissenting view is that of Ibn Abī Laylā (cf. Abū Yūsuf, *Ikhtilāf*, Cairo, 1357/1938, p. 93), who holds that a slight inequality in the investment does not invalidate the *mufāwaḍa* contract. Ibn Abī Laylā's construction of the term *mufāwaḍa* probably differed from that of the Ḥanafīs.

> by another person, then the partnership between them is a *mufāwaḍa*. This is so, because goods and debts are not a suitable form of partnership investment; they are comparable to the personal circumstances of each partner with respect to wife and children, which are exempt from the considerations of equality in a *mufāwaḍa* partnership.[25]

Equality of the parties to an unlimited investment partnership constitutes, in Sarakhsī's words, "the pillar of the *mufāwaḍa* contract." Coordinated with this stipulation is the requirement that all of the partners' eligible capital be included in the partnership. "An *'inān* partnership is one in which the communality is specified, whereas a *mufāwaḍa* is one in which the communality comprehends all things."[26] The non-fulfillment of either of these conditions renders the contract invalid. A situation in which each party contributes equally to the common fund, but in which the respective shares, or the share of only one of them comprehends less than all his eligible capital, does not qualify as a *mufāwaḍa*; nor does the reverse situation in which the parties, while investing all their eligible property, do not contribute equally.

The requirements both of equality and of comprehensiveness stop short of the family hearth. Inequality in personal and household property is no barrier to a valid *mufāwaḍa* partnership. Neither the number of wives, concubines, or children, nor the house furnishings and wardrobes of the prospective partners' families enter into the determination of equality. This also applies to any acquisitions in these areas that either partner may make in the course of the operation of the partnership.

The eligibility of property as an investment in a partnership is a further qualification to the equality and comprehensiveness required by the *mufāwaḍa*. The most eligible of all property is ready cash, and that is the primary import of the phrase "property suitable for partnership." Assets in the form of merchandise and debts are deemed unsuitable for partnership investment. The exclusion of goods and merchandise

[25] Sarakhsī, *Mabsūṭ*, 11:177.

[26] Ṭaḥāwī, *Kitāb ash-shurūṭ aṣ-ṣaghīr*, ms. Istanbul, *Bayazit* 18905, fol. 95, ll. 16–17.

from figuring in the formation of partnerships is discussed in detail below; the exclusion of debts owed to either of the partners is based on the rule that only *māl ḥāḍir*—present money, money which is actually on hand at the time the partnership is to go into effect—is eligible for investment.

> If one of the partners possesses property which is suitable for investment in partnership, and he does not invest it in the partnership, then it is not a *mufāwaḍa* because this precludes full equality. If, however, inequality exists with respect to property which is not suitable for partnership investment, such as goods, real estate, and debts, then the *mufāwaḍa* is valid. The same holds true of inequality in absent money. The presence or absence of property with which one cannot contract a partnership is of no consequence. Any inequality in this type of property is in the same category as inequality in the number of wives and children of each partner.[27]

Equality of "capital suitable for partnership" must also be maintained even after the unlimited investment partnership is already in effect. The balance of equality can be upset in a number of ways. If, during the operation of the partnership, one of the partners collects a debt owed to him prior to the contracting of the partnership, and if this payment is in a form suitable for partnership investment, i.e., cash, then the equality is breached, and the *mufāwaḍa* invalidated. Two conditions must be fulfilled before an individual partner's extra-partnership income can disrupt the *mufāwaḍa*: (a) It must be in the form of cash; (b) He must actually take possession of it. If either of these is not fulfilled, no breach of investment equality is considered to have occurred, and the *mufāwaḍa* continues in full force. These rules apply to all cases of extra-partnership income accruing exclusively to one of the partners, be it from a gift, bequest, inheritance, or any other source.[28]

It may be recalled that a prominent argument in Shāfiʿī's denunciation of the *mufāwaḍa* was that this association per-

[27] *Kāsānī*, 6:61.

[28] *Ibid.*, p. 78.

mitted one partner to derive unjustified and undeserved benefit from the extra-partnership income of the other.[29] As can be seen, this particular objection of Shāfi'ī does not apply to the Ḥanafīs. All the major Ḥanafī authorities are unanimous in assigning the ownership of extra-partnership income exclusively to the partner to whom it accrues. The lone dissenter, and against whom Shāfi'ī's polemic is apparently directed, was Abū Ḥanīfa's contemporary Ibn Abī Laylā. His view was that any property inherited by either of the partners in the course of the operation of the *mufāwaḍa* was to be incorporated into the common fund.[30] This would appear to be a rather extreme position, and it is difficult to evaluate on the basis of our sparse knowledge of Ibn Abī Laylā's legal system. From the little that we do know,[31] it would seem that in his conception of the *mufāwaḍa* partnership, the comprehensiveness of the contract took precedence over the preservation of strict investment equality.

The requirement for equality of persons and of investment is best summed up by Shaybānī himself:

> A *mufāwaḍa* can only be contracted by two free Muslims who are both of age, or between two *dhimmīs*. It cannot be contracted between a Muslim and a *dhimmī*. A *mufāwaḍa* can only be contracted if the capital of each partner is equal. If one of the partners comes into an inheritance, or receives a gift in the form of goods, it belongs exclusively to that partner and it does not invalidate the *mufāwaḍa*. If, however, he inherits or receives dirhams or dinars, the *mufāwaḍa* is invalidated.[32]

Investment Form and Formation of Joint Capital

The admissibility of different types of property as investments in commercial associations, including all forms of contractual partnership, is governed in Ḥanafī law by the same rules. No special rules regulate the kinds of capital which may serve as a basis for one or another type of partnership.

[29] Shāfi'ī, *Umm*, 3:206. [30] Abū Yūsuf, *Ikhtilāf*, p. 97.
[31] Cf. Abū Yūsuf, *Ikhtilāf*, p. 93.
[32] Shaybānī, *Al-jāmi' aṣ-ṣaghīr*, Cairo, 1302/1884, p. 101 (top).

The ensuing discussion, therefore, is in its general aspects equally applicable to the *'inān* and *mufāwaḍa* partnerships. The particular requirements of the latter do, however, affect the formation of the joint capital, and these will be considered here in detail.

Copper Coins—Fulūs

Ḥanafī law insists that some form of acceptable currency be used in the conduct of all commercial transactions. Because of their intrinsic value, gold and silver coins are considered the most acceptable of currencies. Ḥanafī authorities are in unanimous agreement concerning the validity of dinars and dirhams, in whatever shape or form, for all commercial operations, including the formation of partnership investment.

This is not the case, however, as far as *fulūs* (copper coins, singular: *fals*) are concerned. The *fals* was a token coin and was never recognized as legal tender comparable to gold and silver currency. The wide margin between the intrinsic and the face value of copper coins, and the fact that their value and acceptance varied widely from place to place, caused uneasiness among the lawyers and cast doubt on the validity of their use for partnership and other investments.

> As for *fulūs*, if they are non-circulating, then neither a partnership nor a *commenda* can be formed with them, because they are in the same category as goods. According to the well-known statement attributed to Abū Ḥanīfa and Abū Yūsuf, this holds true even if they are in circulation. According to Muḥammad (i.e., Shaybānī), it is permissible to use them for investment.
>
> The discussion concerning *fulūs* revolves around a basic issue. According to Abū Ḥanīfa and Abū Yūsuf, circulating *fulūs* are in no circumstances to be considered as currency. This is so, because they can, on the whole, be particularized by specification. *Fulūs* can be sold in transactions between two parties, so that according to the two above-mentioned authorities, the sale of one *fals* for two would be permissible. Since *fulūs* are objects which, on the whole, can be particu-

larized in contracts of exchange and hence are not an absolute type of currency, they are, just like all other goods, unsuitable to form the capital of a partnership.

> According to Muḥammad, the property of currency attaches to circulating *fulūs*, and they are to be considered as an absolute currency. For this reason, he refused to permit the sale of one *fals* for two. They are, in his view, suitable for partnership investment like all other absolute currencies, viz., dirhams and dinars.[33]

Unlike gold and silver coinage, copper coinage was a completely fiduciary currency; that is, its acceptance and circulation as a means of exchange at a value greatly in excess of its intrinsic worth was based entirely on the trust and confidence of those who used it. All three Ḥanafī authorities agree that copper coins that were for some reason not acceptable, or not in use (*kāsid*) in a given locality, are not eligible for partnership investment. At issue in this dispute is whether any circulating token currency—in this case, copper coins—can be considered as legal tender. Abū Ḥanīfa and Abū Yūsuf deny copper coins the status of currency "because, on the whole, they can be particularized by specification"; that is, they are not completely interchangeable as are standard gold or silver coins, but resemble commodities in that each individual copper coin or type of coin may differ in value and acceptance from time to time and place to place. Specifically in relation to partnership, these two authorities are concerned lest the fluctuation in value and unpredictable acceptability of copper coins lead to uncertainty about the amount of each partner's investment. This interpretation of their view is given by Sarakhsī:

> Muḥammad (i.e., Shaybānī), may God have mercy on him, holds that as long as they (*fulūs*) are in circulation, they are in the category of currency. The other two (Abū Ḥanīfa and Abū Yūsuf) hold that the circulation of *fulūs* is merely a convention among people, and that this changes from time to time. If we permit a partnership with them, this will lead

[33] *Kāsānī*, 6:59–60.

> to uncertainty as to the amount of each partner's capital at the time of the division of profit. This can come about if the particular *fulūs* become unacceptable and people start using another type. For at the time of the division of the profit, the amount of each one's capital is determined by consideration of its monetary value and not by the consideration of the number of coins; and the monetary value of *fulūs* fluctuates in relation to their acceptance and non-acceptance.[34]

Abū Ḥanīfa's and Abū Yūsuf's opposition to the use of copper coins in partnership was probably based on an observable fact of monetary life of the eighth and ninth centuries. The minting of copper coins was highly decentralized and was entrusted to local authorities. There was no single standard governing the size, shape, or weight of the coins. This proliferation had two main results: first, the geographic area in which the copper coins of a particular mint were accepted as a means of exchange was fairly small; and second, there was no effective control of the quantity of the petty coins in circulation.[35] An oversupply of petty coins, or a change in their weight or metallic content, could easily lead to the situation envisaged by Abū Ḥanīfa and Abū Yūsuf. The copper coins used to form a partnership one day could be worthless, or close to it, the very next day. The transfer of such partnership capital from one locality to another—an action often dictated by the needs of commerce—could have the same effect.

Shaybānī, undoubtedly aware of the difficulties to which the free circulation of copper coins were subject, nevertheless considered them "in the category of currency as long as they are in circulation," and permitted their use for partnership investment. The fact remained that, in spite of their fluctuation in value, copper coins served in all localities as the accepted and chief means of petty exchange and continued to be minted in apparently abundant quantities.

[34] Sarakhsī, *Mabsūṭ*, 11:160.

[35] Cf. article *Fals*, *EI*, 2nd ed., 2:768–769; also A. L. Udovitch, *The Copper Coinage of the 'Abbāsids*, American Numismatic Society Summer Seminar, 1961, pp. 18–24 (unpublished); C. Cipolla, *Money, Prices and Civilization in the Mediterranean World*, Princeton, 1956, pp. 27–35.

A proper understanding of the controversy concerning the status of copper coins in commerce can, I believe, best be achieved by viewing it in the context of the various factors affecting their circulation as described in the preceding paragraphs. The divergent views of Abū Ḥanīfa and Abū Yūsuf, on the one hand, and Shaybānī, on the other, emanate from an emphasis on different aspects of the problem as they observed it. To the former, the fluctuating value and restricted circulation of copper coinage were paramount, and they therefore excluded it from use as an investment in any commercial association. For Shaybānī, the circulation and acceptance of copper coins, no matter how geographically circumscribed, was an established fact of economic life outweighing all other considerations. He therefore holds that "a partnership with *fulūs* is in the same category as one with dinars or dirhams."[36]

Gold and Silver Coins—Dinars and Dirhams

All Muslim legal authorities are in full agreement concerning the acceptability of gold and silver coins for partnership investment. The legal problems which do arise in connection with these denominations are, as in the case of copper coins, a result of the monetary situation prevailing in the medieval Islamic world. In most Islamic countries, gold dinars and silver dirhams circulated simultaneously. While dinars were, generally speaking, of a single standard weight and fineness over large areas, dirhams varied considerably in both these respects. The simultaneous circulation of different types of gold and silver coins resulted in the establishment of an exchange rate between them which, although it might shift from time to time, was known and accepted in the marketplace at all times.[37]

In terms of the formation of partnership capital, this posed two sets of problems: first, that of a "mixed investment" involving dinars and dirhams; and second, that of a "mixed invest-

[36] Shaybānī, *Aṣl, Sharika*, fol. 62, l. 14.

[37] Cf. A. Grohmann, *Einführung und Chrestomathie zur arabischen Papyruskunde*, Prague, 1955, 1:190–214; A. Ehrenkreuz, "Studies in the Monetary History of the Near East in the Middle Ages," Part 1, *Journal of the Economic and Social History of the Orient* (*JESHO*), 2 (1959):128–161; Part 2, *ibid.* 6 (1963):243–277.

ment" involving different types of dirhams. Both these types of mixed investment are permitted by Ḥanafī law for all partnerships. The chief concern of the lawyers in such cases is the determination of the value of each partner's investment, so that at the partnership's conclusion, the profits and losses can be properly assigned. Different types of coins from the two investors would make it impossible to reckon the investment simply by the number or weight of the coins. The possibility of a fluctuation in the value of one or both types of coins made it imperative to devise rules by which the value of each partner's investment could be determined at the various stages of the partnership. This was especially important for the *mufāwaḍa* partnership in which the equality of each partner's capital was a prerequisite.

> If the capital of one of the partners consists of one thousand white dirhams, and the capital of the other of one thousand black dirhams,[38] then it is permissible for both *mufāwaḍa* and *'inān* partnerships. If the exchange rate of the white is higher, or if the exchange rate of the black is higher, that is, if the exchange rate of either is higher than the other, then a *mufāwaḍa* partnership is not permitted between them. Any partnership they conclude in these circumstances will be an *'inān* partnership. The *mufāwaḍa* partnership will be nullified because the investment of one is greater than that of the other and a *mufāwaḍa* partnership is not permissible in such circumstances. If the two investments are of equal value on the day the partnership occurs, but one of them rises in value before any purchase is made, then the *mufāwaḍa* is invalidated. If this rise occurs after separate purchases are made with both capitals, then the *mufāwaḍa* is not invalidated. If the rise in value of one of the investments occurs before a purchase is made, then the partnership is invalid; if it occurs after both capitals are used to make a purchase, then the partnership is permissible, and each partner will be indebted

[38] For the black dirhams, cf. Grohmann, *Einführung*, pp. 203–204, and P. Balog, *The Coinage of the Mamluk Sultans of Syria and Egypt*, N.Y., 1969, pp. 40, 45, 55, 146, 253. I have been unable to find any information concerning the white dirhams.

to his colleague to the extent of half the latter's investment. Likewise, if the capital of one consists of one hundred dinars whose value equals the one thousand dirhams of the other, this is similar to the first case above, and is permissible. If, in the course of trade, either of them uses his capital to purchase merchandise for his colleague, then they are to share in the profit and loss according to the value of their respective capital on the day on which the purchase occurs. As for the *mufāwaḍa*, it binds both parties in all cases, so that if they make a joint purchase with the capital of only one of them, it is binding on both of them. If they make a purchase with both capitals, or if the purchase is made by only one of them with the other's permission, then the partnership becomes effective. This is so even if they do not intermingle the capital, for the purchase is equivalent to the intermingling of the capital.

If either the dinars or the dirhams exceed each other in value, an *'inān* partnership, but not a *mufāwaḍa* partnership, is permissible. If the partners divide up and separate, then each one is to deduct his capital, or the equivalent of the value of his capital on the day in which they divide up, from the common fund.[39]

In discussing the use of dirhams of different types for partnership investment, the legal sources usually refer, as examples, to white and black dirhams. The same rules, however, apply to the numerous other kinds of dirhams in circulation. In addition to black and white dirhams, Kāsānī distinguishes between whole (*ṣaḥāḥ*) and broken (*mukassara*) dirhams,[40] and Shaybānī, between freshly minted and circulating dirhams.[41] In short, any currency which is in itself suitable for partnership investment can, in combination with any other currencies of the same qualification, form the capital of a partnership contract.[42]

[39] Shaybānī, *Aṣl, Sharika*, fol. 61b, l. 11–fol. 62, l. 4.
[40] *Kāsānī*, 6:60–61.
[41] Shaybānī, *Amālī*, Hyderabad, 1360/1941, pp. 12–13.
[42] Sarakhsī, *Mabsūṭ*, 11:178.

The foremost difficulty created by mixed investments for all types of partnership is that of determining each partner's proportional share of the capital, in order, at the proper time, to be able to calculate his share of the profit and liability. Sarakhsī proposes the following sliding rule for this purpose.

> In short, for the purposes of the contractual provision of profit, one considers the value of each one's capital at the time the partnership is contracted. For the distribution of the ownership of goods purchased with the partnership capital, one considers the value of each one's investment at the time of purchase. For the determination of the profit on their respective shares, or on the share of only one of them, one considers the value of the investment at the time of division; because one cannot determine the profit before the investment is deducted.[43]

Sarakhsī's formula is intended to compensate for any possible fluctuation in the value of the currencies of which each partner's investment is composed, while at the same time assuring stability in the distribution of profit and loss for the duration of the partnership contract. The formula envisages a two-stage procedure for settlement of the financial accounts at the partnership's termination. At that time, one would not simply divide the entire common fund in accordance with the stipulated share assigned to each partner; rather, each partner would withdraw the amount of his investment, either in the form in which he originally contributed it, or in its monetary equivalent based on the exchange rate on the day of division. Only after this was accomplished, would the remainder, which constitutes the profit, be divided according to the proportions agreed upon when the partnership was contracted. If the contract stipulated that each partner's share of the profit was to be based on his share of the total investment, this share would be determined by the value of each currency on the day the partnership was contracted. Thus any fluctuation in the value of either currency making up the partnership investment, while affecting the absolute amount of profit, would not affect each

[43] *Ibid.*, p. 165.

partner's share in it. If division of the joint property becomes necessary before the partnership's intended conclusion, that is, at a time when the capital was in the form of merchandise and not in cash, then the proportional ownership of the goods would be established on the basis of the value of each partner's currency on the day on which the goods were purchased. In any mixed investment partnership, Sarakhsī's formula provides a method, in all contingencies, for the determination of the amount of each partner's capital and his share of the profit and liability.

Like any other *mufāwaḍa* partnership, one involving a mixed investment must conform to the requirements of investment equality. The decisive consideration in such a case is the value of each partner's currency at the time the initial joint purchase is made. If the requirement for investment equality is satisfied at that moment, then the *mufāwaḍa* is valid. Any change in currency value subsequent to the initial purchase does not affect the validity of the partnership,[44] but is subject, as far as the distribution of capital and profit are concerned, to the rules outlined above.

For Ḥanafī law, the transaction of the initial purchase on behalf of the partnership is the moment when the *mufāwaḍa* partnership becomes truly effective. The role of the first partnership purchase in Ḥanafī law is comparable to that of the intermingling of investments in Shāfiʿī law. For example, it is not necessary that all the conditions making for a valid *mufāwaḍa* be met at the time the contract is negotiated or the partnership agreed upon; it is, however, mandatory that this be the case at the time the first purchase is made on behalf of the partnership.

A requirement for all partnerships is that they be formed only with ready cash (*māl ḥāḍir*) and not with absent cash (*māl ghā'ib*), that is, capital not immediately available for use in the

[44] For a fuller discussion of the effect of fluctuating currency values on the *mufāwaḍa*, cf. Sarakhsī, *Mabsūṭ*, 11:178. It is only by invoking the principle of *istiḥsān* that a mixed investment *mufāwaḍa* is considered valid; by the strict application of analogy, according to Shaybānī, this arrangement would be invalid; cf. Shaybānī, *Al-jāmiʿ āl-kabīr*, Cairo, 1356/1937, p. 268; *Kāsānī*, 6:79.

partnership. The absence of capital committed to partnership investment at the time the contract is negotiated does not invalidate the partnership as long as it is on hand when the initial joint purchase is made. "The presence of the capital is a prerequisite only at the time of purchase, and not at the time the partnership is contracted. For the partnership contract is consummated through a joint purchase and the presence of the capital is a consideration only then."[45]

Up to the time of the joint purchase, the partners share no liability. If, even after the partnership was agreed upon, the capital of one of the partners was lost, stolen, or came to grief in any other manner, the loss is borne solely by the individual owner. If, however, such an untoward occurrence takes place after a joint purchase was made, the loss is borne by both partners jointly.[46]

Before concluding the discussion of mixed partnership investments, one rather remarkable dissenting opinion should be noted. Abū Yūsuf, while agreeing with his Ḥanafī colleagues that dirhams of different types are suitable for investment in the same partnership, objects to distinguishing the coins on the basis of quality.

> Ismāʿīl b. Ḥammād[47] related from Abū Yūsuf: "If one of the two groups of one thousand dirhams making up the investment is superior to the other, it is permissible and the *mufāwaḍa* is valid. This is so, because any consideration of quality in currency of the same metal and denomination is equivalent to usury, and has no legal force. Any consideration of quality is overlooked, and the dirhams are treated as if they were all of one type."[48]

In effect, Abū Yūsuf was demanding that in all commercial dealings, dirhams be exchanged at face value regardless of their

[45] *Kāsānī*, 6:60.

[46] Shaybānī, *Aṣl*, *Sharika*, fol. 58b, ll. 18–21.

[47] The grandson of Abū Ḥanīfa, died 212/827. Cf. Ibn Qutlūbughā, *Tāj at-tarājim fī ṭabaqāt al-ḥanafiyya*, Baghdad, 1962, pp. 17–18.

[48] *Kāsānī*, 6:61; cf. also, Sarakhsī, *Mabsūṭ*, 11:154, where in addition to this quotation, a tradition from the Prophet to the same effect is cited.

silver content. Whatever its merits, this idea was far in advance of its times and was, in the context of medieval Islamic finance and trade, impossible of realization.[49]

Goods ('Urūḍ) *as Partnership Investment*

> As for cash partnership, it has several requirements. One is that the capital consists of absolute currency—currency which, in exchange, can under no circumstances be particularized by specification, namely, dirhams and dinars. This requirement is applicable to both *'inān* and *mufāwaḍa* partnerships.
>
> According to the majority of legal scholars, a partnership in which the investment consists of goods is invalid. Mālik, may God have mercy upon him, said that this (capital in the form of currency) is not a prerequisite, and that a partnership in goods is valid. The correct position is that of the majority; for the element of agency is one of the necessary attributes of partnership, and the type of agency which is comprehended by partnership is not valid with goods, but is valid with dirhams and dinars.
>
> It is not permissible for one person to say to another: "Sell your goods so that their price will be between us." And since agency, which is one of the indispensable features of partnership, is not permissible, partnership itself is also not permissible. It is, however, permissible for one to say to another: "Buy goods with the hundred dirhams belonging to you, on the condition that what you buy be shared between us."

[49] Some doubt has been cast on the assumption that money was given and taken as metal, and not at its face value, in the first three Islamic centuries; cf. Cl. Cahen, "Quelques Problems Concernant l'Expansion Economique Musulmane au Haut Moyen Age," *L'Occidente e l'Islam nell'alto Medioevo, Settimane di Studio del Centro Italiano di Studi sull'alto Medioevo,* 12, 2 vols., Spoleto, 1965, 1:406–407. For evidence supporting the opinion expressed here, cf., my remarks on Cahen's paper, *ibid.*, pp. 488–490, and my review of P. Balog, *The Coinage of the Mamluk Sultans of Egypt and Syria, Journal of the American Oriental Society* (*JAOS*), vol. 90 (1970), forthcoming. For a similar conclusion in the context of medieval European monetary history, cf. H. A. Miskimin, *Money, Prices and Foreign Exchange in Fourteenth Century France,* New Haven, 1963, p. 117.

> Partnership in goods is not permissible because it leads to ignorance regarding the profit at the time of division. For the amount of the investment will consist of the value of the goods and not of the goods themselves, and this value will be unknown except by conjecture and estimate. The amount of profit will therefore be unknown, and this will lead to disputes at the time of division. This will not occur if the investment consists of dinars and dirhams, for these will be the same at the time of division and will not lead to ignorance of the profit at the time of division.[50]

As in the case of investments consisting of different types of dirhams, the chief concern is the difficulty of determining the amount of the investment if it is in the form of goods. At the conclusion of the partnership, the investment would not be in its original form, and calculating its exact value would be a matter of "conjecture and estimate" leading to disputes and recriminations. The problems resulting from investments in the form of goods are the same regardless of the type of partnership involved. This type of investment is equally unacceptable for a limited or unlimited investment partnership.[51]

The only commodities which are, with some qualification, excepted from this ban are gold and silver. In areas where these precious metals in their unminted state served as a customary means of exchange, their employment for the purposes of partnership investment is also permitted.[52]

Given the circumstances of medieval commerce, the enforcement of a ban on investments in the form of goods and merchandise would have constituted a severe handicap, especially for merchants engaged in long-distance trade. Merchants

[50] *Kāsānī*, 6:59.

[51] Cf. Shaybānī, *Aṣl*, *Sharika*, fol. 58b, ll. 1–11; Sarakhsī, *Mabsūṭ*, 11:159–160. Ḥanafī law also excludes goods as an investment form in a *commenda*. Ibn Abī Laylā permits a *commenda* formed with an investment of goods (cf. Abū Yūsuf, *Ikhtilāf*, p. 30). We do not have the latter's view on a parallel case in partnership, but we can be fairly certain that he also permitted goods as an investment in partnership, thus being the only legal authority in Iraq allowing this form of investment without the use of a legal fiction (*ḥīla*).

[52] Sarakhsī, *Mabsūṭ*, 11:159–160.

in a given locality wishing to form a partnership might have all their capital tied up in merchandise which could not be advantageously sold at that place. Details of commercial activity that can be garnered from the Cairo Geniza records and from *fatwās* of the Zirid period in North Africa indicate that this was often the case.[53]

It is in connection with this prohibition that the efficacy of legal fictions (*ḥiyal*) can be observed. To paraphrase a proverb, Islamic law in this case provides the remedy together with the ailment; concurrent with the prohibition against goods as a valid form of partnership investment, the legal sources outline a method of its circumvention.

> I said: "What is your opinion of two men wishing to form a partnership with their possessions, one of whom has merchandise worth five thousand dirhams and the other merchandise worth one thousand dirhams?" He said: "Partnership in goods is not permissible." I said: "What type of legal fiction can they employ which would make them partners in the merchandise they possess?" He said: "Let the owner of the merchandise worth five thousand dirhams purchase five-sixths of his colleague's merchandise with one-sixth of his own. If they do this, they will be partners in accordance with their shares in the investment; the one whose merchandise is worth one thousand dirhams becomes a one-sixth owner of the combined investment, and his colleague becomes an owner of five-sixths of it."[54]

This passage is from Shaybānī's treatise specifically devoted to legal fictions. In later Ḥanafī literature, this particular method of circumvention is incorporated into the very body of the legal codes and is usually presented immediately follow-

[53] Cf. S. D. Goitein, "From the Mediterranean to India," *SPECULUM* 29 (1954):196–197, (n. 20); H. R. Idris, *La Berbérie orientale sous les Zirides, Xe–XIIe siècles*, Paris, 1959, 2:660ff.; also Goitein, *A Mediterranean Society*, pp. 170 and 178.

[54] Shaybānī, *Kitāb al-makhārij fil-ḥiyal*, ed. J. Schacht, Leipzig, 1930, p. 58; cf. also al-Khaṣṣaf, *Kitāb al-ḥiyal wal-makhārij*, ed. Schacht, Hanover, 1923, p. 67.

ing the prohibition.[55] So complete was the assimilation of this legal fiction into the body of Ḥanafī law that in several codes it is given without the designation of *ḥīla* and appears as an accepted feature of positive law.[56]

What is perhaps even more significant in relation to commercial practice is the fact that this legal fiction is included—without being so designated—in the earliest *shurūṭ* (legal formulary) works.[57] These were intended as practical handbooks for scribes and lawyers, and, in addition to the formulae for various types of contracts, they contain thumbnail summaries of the laws pertaining to these contracts. The earliest complete text of this legal literary genre is the *Al-jām'i aṣ-ṣaghīr fish-shurūṭ* of Ṭaḥāwī, the shortest and most concise version of the three formularies he authored. The slightly more than four pages of this work which are devoted to partnership contain only the most essential information concerning this contract. The fact that instructions for drawing up a partnership contract in which the investment of one or both parties consists of goods are included in this brief summary lends support to the assumption that such partnerships were a fairly common occurrence and played an important part in commerce.

The operation of this legal fiction is quite simple, involving only a mutual transference of the ownership of a portion of each prospective partner's goods. It can be adjusted to accommodate either a limited or unlimited investment partnership. In the latter case, each partner's merchandise must be equal in value to that of his colleague; by exchanging half of one's merchandise for half of the other's, they can conclude a valid *mufāwaḍa* partnership. This legal fiction is applicable as well for the formation of a partnership between one party investing cash and another investing goods.[58]

55 E.g., *Kāsānī*, 6:59.

56 E.g., Sarakhsī, *Mabsūṭ*, 11:179.

57 Cf. Ṭaḥāwī, *Kitāb ash-shurūṭ aṣ-ṣaghīr*, ms. Istanbul, *Bayazit* 18905, fol. 95b.

58 Sarakhsī, *Mabsūṭ*, 11:179. In Shāfi'ī law this legal fiction (termed *makhraj*—way of escape) is used for the same purpose; cf. Muzānī, *Mukhtaṣar*, vols. 1–4, Cairo, 1321/1903–1325/1907, 2:230.

Labor as Partnership Investment

In Ḥanafī law labor is considered as valid a form of investment as is currency, and is acceptable for the formation of both a limited and unlimited investment partnership. Unlike the *commenda*, in which one party provides the capital and the other the labor, the capital in a work partnership consists primarily of the labor of both partners. The type of labor envisaged is usually a skill in some kind of manufacture such as tailoring, dyeing, weaving, etc.

This partnership is designated in several ways: *sharika fī ʿamal bi-aydihimā*, "a partnership of work with their hands";[59] *ash-sharika bilaʿmal*, "a partnership in work";[60] *sharikat al-abdān*, "a partnership of bodies"; *sharikat aṣ-ṣanāʾiʿ*, "a partnership of crafts"; and *sharikat at-taqabbul*, "a partnership of acceptance."

> A partnership of acceptance is when two craftsmen form a partnership in the acceptance of work such as tailoring, fulling, and the like. It is also designated as the partnership of bodies, because they work with their bodies, and as partnership of crafts, because their craft is their capital.[61]

The division of labor in medieval industry was usually such that the person who did the manufacturing did not necessarily own the raw material upon which he worked or have anything to do with the sale of the finished product. The manufacture and processing of materials was highly specialized.[62] Their

[59] Shaybānī, *Aṣl*, *Sharika*, fol. 57b, 1. 18.

[60] *Kāsānī*, 6:56.

[61] Sarakhsī, *Mabsūṭ*, 11:152. In the ensuing translations all these phrases are translated as work partnership. My translation of *taqabbul* as "acceptance" requires some explanation. Schacht (*Der Islam*, 37 [1961–62]:275), following Dozy (*Supplément*, 2:304), says regarding this term, "*taqabbala*, a well-known technical term, does not mean 'erhalten, empfangen,' but 'to take a lease, to rent for exploitation.' " In the case of partnership, Schacht's suggested translation would be inappropriate. The contextual meaning of *taqabbala* in connection with partnership is the acceptance by one or both of the partners of some raw material belonging to a third party for the purpose of undergoing some process of manufacture; for example, a tailor accepts cloth belonging to his customer in order to cut and sew it into a garment.

[62] Cf. S. D. Goitein, "The Main Industries of the Mediterranean as Re-

skills were often the only commodity which craftsmen sold. This situation made it possible for craftsmen to form work partnerships without pooling any cash or goods, their sole asset consisting of their particular skills.[63] In this type of partnership, the *taqabbul*, the acceptance of work, assumed a central function, paralleling that of the initial purchase in a cash partnership. Just as the initial purchase on behalf of the partnership gives final effect to the cash partnership, so in a work partnership, the initial acceptance of a job in the name of both partners is the moment at which the association becomes truly effective. It is undoubtedly because of the centrality of the *taqabbul* transaction that, among others, a work partnership was designated as *sharikat at-taqabbul*.[64]

> As for the work partnership, it is valid according to our view. It is not valid according to Shāfiʿī, may God have mercy upon him, in whose view the basic principle of partnership is proprietary partnership, an element which is not found in this particular partnership because of the fact that intermingling of labor is not realizable.
>
> We, however, hold to the permissibility of this partnership on the basis of the element of agency (*wakāla*). Just as the appointment of either partner as an agent for the acceptance of work will be valid, so too will this partnership be valid. People have been conducting their affairs through this form of partnership and through a credit partnership without disapproval since the time of the Messenger of God, may God bless him and keep him, up to our very own day. This is the basis for the permissibility of the partnership.

---

flected in the Records of the Cairo Geniza," *JESHO* 4 (1961):168–197. Goitein counted two hundred and sixty-five different arts and crafts and asserts that "industry itself was divided up into highly specialized branches"; cf. also, *Mediterranean Society*, pp. 99–116.

[63] Cf. Saḥnūn, *Mudawwana*, 12:43: "Ibn Qāsim said: There are types of work which do not require any capital investment, and there is no objection to people forming a partnership with the work of their hands."

[64] In the section on partnership in Sarakhsī's *Mabsūṭ*, 11:151–220, this designation is the most frequently used for a work partnership. Cf. also, Shaybānī, *Amālī*, pp. 44–45.

The right to profit in a partnership derives in some cases from the money invested and in others from the work invested. The latter case is exemplified by the *commenda* in which the investor is entitled to his portion of the profit by virtue of his money, and the agent by virtue of his work. This contract (the *commenda*) is a partnership of hire. Like hire, it does not obligate the agent; like a partnership, it does not require the setting of a time limit. If, therefore, a partnership contract between two people with money is valid, such a contract is similarly valid with an investment of work; for the right to profit is secured by either of the two investment types. This holds true, in our opinion, whether or not each partner's craft is the same.

Zufar, may God have mercy on him, held that when the work is the same, such as a partnership between two fullers or between two dyers, the contract is permissible; if each one's work is different, such as a partnership between a fuller and a dyer, then the contract is not permissible. In the latter case, each of them is incapable of doing the work his colleague accepts because it would not be of his craft. A difference between the crafts of each partner makes it impossible to realize the intended aim of the partnership. We, however, hold to the permissibility of this partnership on the basis of the element of agency. The appointment of a person as an agent for the acceptance of work is valid on the part of one who is himself able to do the work involved, as well as from one who is unable to do so. The person accepting the work is not specifically obliged to execute it with his own hand; he need only help in the work and see to its execution. Each of the prospective partners is not incapable of carrying this out, and the contract is therefore valid.

This type of partnership can be in the form of an *'inān* or, with the proper combination of conditions, a *mufāwaḍa* partnership. That is, in the case of the *mufāwada*, each one is liable, by virtue of the mutual surety (*kafāla*) implied in this contract, for any obligation incurred by his colleague. In the case of an *'inān* partnership, each one is fully liable only for the obligations personally incurred by himself, as is the case in agency.[65]

It is on the basis of three arguments that Sarakhsī justifies the work partnership. Two of these, agency as a basis for partnership and the equation of labor with money as a source of profit, are theoretical, and one, that of continuous usage since the time of Muḥammad, is an historical argument.

The concept of agency is the very cornerstone of contractual partnership in Ḥanafī law. Its function is equivalent to that of joint ownership in Shāfiʿī partnership law. Any commercial transaction for which the appointment of an agent is valid is also valid for the formation of a partnership.[66] Since a craftsman may appoint another to accept work on his behalf, a partnership in which two craftsmen contract to share the income of their work in any mutually agreed upon manner is also legitimate.

By analogy to the *commenda* contract, Sarakhsī establishes investment in the form of labor as a valid basis for profit in a partnership on the same level as the investment of money. In a *commenda*, one party's claim to profit is based on his work, and that of the other on his money; the right to profit in a partnership, therefore, is equally secured by either of these two investment forms.

In addition to the two theoretical arguments in support of the legitimacy of a work partnership, Sarakhsī, for some reason, feels it appropriate or necessary to adduce a third argument based on historical usage. From the time of Muḥammad, and probably even earlier, people have practiced this form of partnership without criticism or rebuke. The implication here is that if there were anything legally objectionable in a work partnership, the Prophet would have outlawed its use. Sarakhsī's statement constitutes a surprising and possibly unintentional admission of the reception of non-Islamic institu-

[65] Sarakhsī, *Mabsūṭ*, 11:155.

[66] Cf. Sarakhsī, *Mabsūṭ*, 11:152. Ibn ʿArafa defines agency as follows: "Agency arises where one person authorizes another to replace him in the exercise of civil rights." Quoted in F. H. Ruxton, *Mālikī Law*, London, 1916, p. 201. For a brief survey concerning the rules of agency, cf. *Mālikī Law*, pp. 201–204; Schacht, *An Introduction to Islamic Law*, pp. 119–120.

tions into Islamic law, since historical usage and custom when not supported by a statement or precedent attributed to the Prophet do not constitute an acceptable source of Muslim law (*uṣūl al-fiqh*). In the course of his treatment of partnership, Sarakhsī frequently cites the customs and needs of merchants to bolster his argument, but he does not, in the "Book of Partnership" at least, designate this factor, as he does in this instance, as a basis or source (*aṣl*) for legitimacy. In most cases, his appeal to custom is either an ancillary argument or one invoked to justify a practice for which no basis can be found in the application of strict legal reasoning. There are, thus, two noteworthy aspects to Sarakhsī's use of this line of argumentation. First, its very invocation is surprising in view of the fact that he had already firmly established the validity of the work partnership on the basis of two solid theoretical legal arguments. Second, the designation of its continuous practice as a source for the legitimacy of the work partnership is unusual, since custom is not a recognized source of the *fiqh*.

The nature of work as a partnership investment presents a number of problems, some paralleling those connected with a cash partnership and others peculiar only to a work partnership. In a cash partnership, the investment of different types of currency on the part of each partner is permitted because the value of each one's investment at any given stage of the partnership is easily determined. The parallel problem in a work partnership, that of an association between two craftsmen of varying trades, is also allowed, but on very different grounds. The value of different types of work is not subject to the same accurate determination as is that of different currencies. This kind of work partnership is valid, according to Sarakhsī, because the element of agency is realizable in such a relationship. Irrespective of the kind or amount of work each one contributes, the distribution of profit and loss follows the shares agreed upon at the formation of the partnership.[67]

> If one of the partners in a work partnership is absent, or sick, or does not work while his colleague is working, the profit

[67] Cf. Sarakhsī, *Mabsūṭ*, 11:159.

is still to be shared between them according to what they agreed upon. This is similar to what is recounted concerning a man who came to the Messenger of God, may God bless him and keep him, and said: "While I am working in the market place, my partner is praying in the mosque." The Messenger of God, may God bless him and keep him, replied: "Perhaps your business success[68] derives from him." The meaning of this is that the claim to reward derives from the acceptance of the work and not necessarily from its direct personal execution; in this case, the acceptance was on behalf of both partners, even if the work itself was carried out by only one of them.[69]

It is the acceptance of work, either jointly by both partners or by one of them in the name of the partnership that, according to Sarakhsī, provides the basis for the communality in the work partnership. The distribution of profits and losses need not bear any relationship to the distribution of the actual labor.

It should be noted, though, that underlying the entire Ḥanafī discussion of the work partnership is the assumption that, regardless of the kind and amount of work each partner does, both are to participate to some extent in the partnership work. While undoubtedly concurring with the Prophet's view concerning the efficacy of prayer for the success of one's business affairs, Ḥanafī jurists nevertheless disqualify a work partnership which provides that one partner spend his entire time praying at the mosque, while his colleague does all the work in the market place.

While labor on the part of both partners is a necessary feature for a valid work partnership, it is not the measure of each partner's investment, and it is superseded as a basis for partnership profit, in Sarakhsī's view, by the act of the acceptance of work. Kāsānī, a Ḥanafī writer who flourished a century after Sarakhsī, refined the implications of this idea and carried it a step further by stating: "The reward in this work

[68] Arabic: *baraka*, which literally translated means "blessing"; contextually, here, its means God's blessing or bounty in relation to one's worldly pursuits.

[69] Sarakhsī, *Mabsūṭ*, 11:157–158.

partnership derives from the liability for the work undertaken, and not from the execution of the work itself."[70] As a result of Kāsānī's insight, we are finally provided with a method of measuring the investment in a work partnership. Paradoxically enough, this is expressed not in the amount or quality of work invested, but in the degree of liability undertaken by each partner. In a *mufāwaḍa* work partnership, the requirement of investment equality would not, therefore, extend to the amount of labor each partner contributes, but would be satisfied instead by an equal share of liability undertaken by each.

The flexibility of Ḥanafī partnership law and its attentiveness to the practical needs of commerce are nowhere more clearly reflected than in its treatment of one special form of a work partnership—the association between a craftsman and a stall-owner.

> If an artisan takes another man into his stall with the intention of assigning all the work to the latter on a half profit basis, this arrangement is, by analogy, invalid.[71] This is so, because the investment of the stall-owner consists of intangible property,[72] and intangible properties are not suitable for partnership investment. If it is the stall-owner who accepts the work, the artisan is his hired man on a half profit basis. This last sum, however, is indefinite, and ignorance of the wage invalidates a hire contract. If, on the other hand, the artisan himself accepts the work, he becomes a lessee of the stall to the extent of one half the proceeds of his work. This sum, again, is unknown, and the lease contract is, therefore, invalid. By exercising juristic preference (*istiḥsān*), he (referring to Shaybānī) permitted this arrange-

[70] *Kāsānī*, 6:76–77: For my translation of *ḍamān* as "liability," cf. Schacht, *Grundzüge*, p. 64.

[71] The analogy here refers to a case considered in the text immediately preceding this quotation. It involves a partnership in which *A* invests 2,000 dirhams and *B* 1,000 dirhams, with the profit to be shared equally and all the work to be done by *A*. This is invalid, because *B* has no basis for claiming any of the profit in excess of his one-third share of the joint capital.

[72] Arabic: *manfa'a*, also utility, usufruct, as opposed to *'ayn*—tangible property. Cf. S. Mahmasani, in *Law in the Middle East*, 1:180.

ment because of its continuous use in the affairs of men without any disapproving voice being raised against it. Objecting to transactions which are in common use among the people is in itself a type of offense. In order to avoid this offense, this contract is permissible. For there is no explicit text (*naṣṣ*) nullifying it, and the people have a need for this contract. For example, if an artisan arrives in a certain town, its inhabitants will not know him and will not entrust him with their merchandise. They will, however, entrust their merchandise to the stall-owner, whom they do know. As a rule, the stall-owner will not gratuitously provide the likes of this service to the artisan. The validation of this contract achieves the desired ends of all parties concerned. The artisan receives compensation for his labor; the people derive the benefits of his services; and the stall-owner receives compensation for the use of his stall. The contract is permissible. The stall-owner is entitled to a share of the profit because he has taken the artisan into his stall and given him some help with his merchandise. He may perhaps help in some aspect of the work, as for example, a tailor who accepts cloth, oversees its cutting, and then hands the material over for completion of the tailoring to another artisan on the basis of half profit. For these reasons, the stall-owner is entitled to a share of the profit.

The basis for the permissibility of this contract is like that underlying the permissibility of the *salam*[73] contract; for in relation to this contract, the requirements of the law yielded[74] in face of the people's need for it.[75]

All the numerous, weighty legal considerations militating against the validity of this particular form of work partnership are overruled solely on the grounds of practical necessity. By

[73] A form of sale in which the price is paid in advance and the delivery of the merchandise is delayed to a specified later date. Cf. Schacht, *Grundzüge*, p. 71.

[74] The Arabic verb *rakhkhaṣa* is used here in the same sense as the noun *rukhṣa*—"special dispensation"; cf. N. J. Coulson, *A History of Islamic Law*, Edinburgh, 1964, p. 44.

[75] Sarakhsī, *Mabsūṭ*, 11:159; cf. also, *Kāsānī*, 6:64.

analogy to a parallel form of cash partnership, the association between the stall-owner and the artisan should be invalid. Furthermore, the stall-owner's contribution consists of intangible property, which is not an acceptable form of partnership investment. The association is disqualified as a hire or lease contract because the remuneration which would correspond to the wage or the rent is not specified. Only by the exercise of juristic preference is this partnership permitted. From Sarakhsī's description of the special circumstances which in this case warrant the suspension of traditional legal considerations, one is left with the strong impression that partnerships between artisans and stall-owners were a common occurrence and that they fulfilled an important, if not indispensable, function in urban economic life. Ḥanafī jurists chose, in this case, to act in accordance with the dictum that discretion is the better part of valor. Rather than insisting on the rigid application of legal norms and risk thereby almost certain violation of an untenable and unenforceable prohibition, they yielded to the prevalent commercial custom and included this contract within the pale of legally sanctioned practice.

While the passage from Sarakhsī quoted above is an unusually candid statement of the concessions which Ḥanafī law was prepared or forced to make to popular business usages, it is by no means unique. Throughout their discussion of partnership (and also of other commercial contracts and practices), Ḥanafī writers, from Shaybānī on, frequently invoke customary practice or the needs of merchants as a justification for their exercise or juristic preference in the face of the occasionally confining effects of systematic legal reasoning. The total effect of this greater leniency was to enlarge the area of legitimacy for transactions and contracts, thereby giving merchants and others a much freer hand in the conduct of their affairs.

While the comparative frequency with which juristic preference is exercised may shed some light on the nature of Ḥanafī legal method, the circumstances in which it is used, and the rationale for its application provide some valuable insights into the attitude and awareness of the Ḥanafī jurists themselves. They did not, as I think this passage amply demonstrates, develop their legal norms in splendid isolation from, or total disregard of, their surroundings. Sarakhsī, for example, does not limit himself to a general appeal to custom and the needs of commerce, but illustrates his argument by outlining the specific circumstances in which the prohibition of a partnership between an artisan and a stall-owner might create great difficulty. It would appear that the jurists' discussion of commercial matters was based on a fairly clear and accurate understanding of the economic realities of their environment,[76] and that they were quite conscious of the likely effects of their promulgations on the conduct of economic life. Without obliterating the distinction between how people actually conduct their affairs and how they should be conducted, the jurists strove, within reasonable limits, to narrow the gulf between the two and, in this case at least, successfully bridged it.

Exclusion of Unskilled and Non-Sedentary Labor

In their discussions of work partnerships, Ḥanafī jurists had in mind primarily associations between skilled workers. The examples illustrating various aspects of this partnership are consistently drawn from the skilled crafts, such as dyeing, fulling, tailoring, etcetera. There seems also to be a predilection for sedentary work—work which can be accomplished by the partners while sitting in their stall and does not involve any roaming and roving about the town or countryside. While these qualifications are not explicitly stated, they emerge both from the context of the discussion of the work partnership and from the specific exclusion of certain categories of work as a basis for it.[77]

[76] In this regard, it is interesting to note that Abū Ḥanīfa himself was a silk merchant and is reported to have carried on his business in partnership with a Baghdādī merchant. Cf. Al-Khaṭīb al-Baghdādī, *Ta'rīkh Baghdād*, 13:324ff.

[77] No single legal rule serves as a basis for the disqualification of the diverse types of unskilled labor as partnership investment. In Ḥanafī treatises, these are as a rule listed in one of the concluding sections of the "Book of Partnership" under the heading, "The Chapter of Invalid Partnership," and, in each case, one or another legal argument is marshalled to justify their ineligibility.

A partnership in hay-cutting, or gathering firewood, wild berries, nuts, or dates is not valid. It is not permissible, for example, for two people to agree to gather brush and firewood on the condition that they share equally, or in some other proportion, in the income derived from its sale.[78] Similarly, no partnership in hunting, fishing, or treasure hunting is allowed. Only if the partners hunt together with the same dog, or fish together with the same net, or stumble upon a treasure while in each other's company can they legitimately share in the gain resulting from their endeavors. Otherwise, whatever each one gathers, traps, or finds, belongs exclusively to him, his colleague having no claims whatsoever to any share of it.[79]

A partnership between two porters, stipulating that they share the wages either may earn from transporting goods on their own backs or on the backs of their respective pack animals, is invalid. A partnership in the fees deriving from hiring out an animal, with one party providing the beast and the other the saddle and accessories, is not permitted. Invalid, as well, is a partnership in which one supplies the animal, while his colleague uses it to wander around selling merchandise on the condition that the sales profits are to be shared between the two of them. By analogy, a ship or a house is also excluded from being used this way in a partnership.[80]

Any partnership involving work on resources or raw material belonging to neither of the partners, or which are part of the public domain, is invalid. This applies to the extraction of minerals from public lands or to the use of sand or clay from this source for the purpose of manufacturing glass or bricks. If, however, the two parties jointly purchased the raw material or jointly leased the land from which it was extracted, the partnership would become permissible. Any initial joint purchase or lease would immediately provide the basis for a valid partnership contract, and the partners could then proceed to process the raw material and share in the profit of its sale in any manner mutually agreed upon.[81]

78 Shaybānī, *Aṣl*, *Sharika*, fol. 76, ll. 7–8; Sarakhsī, *Mabsūṭ*, 11:216.
79 Shaybānī, *Aṣl*, *Sharika*, fol. 76b, ll. 4–15.
80 *Ibid.*, ll. 15–19; fol. 77, ll. 5–13.
81 *Ibid.*, fol. 76, l. 19–fol. 76b, l. 4; Sarakhsī, *Mabsūṭ*, 11:217.

Generally, a partnership concluded and carried out on the basis of any of the disqualified types of work listed above is treated either as a hire or a lease contract. In cases where the partners worked separately, each one's earnings are his own and neither has any claim to any share of his colleague's gain. If they worked together, or if one used equipment belonging to the other, the profits are assigned entirely to one of the partners, while the other is entitled to an equitable wage for his labor or a rental fee for the use of his equipment. The nature of each party's claim in such a case is determined by the particular circumstances of the intended partnership. For example, if two porters agreed to work together on a partnership basis and the pack animal they used belonged to one of them only, the owner of the animal would be entitled to the entire proceeds of their work and in turn be obligated to pay his colleague an equitable wage. In the event that the non-owning partner labored alone, the entire income would be his and he would be required to pay the owner a fee for the use of the animal.[82]

While all Ḥanafī authorities agree that each party is entitled to some degree of restitution for the service he renders, the standard to be applied in determining this wage or fee is a matter of dispute. Abū Yūsuf holds that the associate who is assigned the role of employee is entitled to a wage equal to that customarily paid for similar work,[83] providing that the amount does not exceed half the total income. The same limit is placed on the amount of any rental which either partner might be required to pay the other. Abū Yūsuf is not completely consistent in treating an invalid work partnership as a simple hire contract. By making the amount of restitution due the employee-partner contingent on the total income of the undertaking, and thereby limiting the liability of the employer-partner, he still retains an element characteristic of partnership. Shaybānī is more consistent in this respect. While agreeing with Abū Yūsuf's criterion for arriving at an equitable wage, he rejects the imposition of any ceiling on this amount. He gives no con-

[82] Shaybānī, *Aṣl*, *Sharika*, fol. 77, ll. 5–10.
[83] Arabic: *ajr mithluhu*.

sideration to the financial situation of the employer-partner; the employee-partner, like any other hired worker, is entitled to an equitable wage, no matter what it comes to.[84]

Credit Partnership

The precise role of credit in the context of medieval economic life has been subject to dispute by economic historians. As recently as forty years ago there were those who viewed the Middle Ages as a pre-credit era, an age in which credit transactions, to the extent that they were employed, were of minor economic importance, and whose function was restricted to consumption to the exclusion of production and trade. Accordingly, proponents of this view denied any significant relationship between credit and trade.[85] In an important study of medieval credit, the English economic historian M. M. Postan convincingly demonstrated that this view did not correspond to the economic realities of medieval Europe. On the basis of data found in English medieval archives, he showed that by the thirteenth century credit had already assumed a major role in the trade of Northern Europe.[86] In Southern Europe, especially Italy, this had been the case a century or more earlier.[87] For the medieval Near East, the still unpublished commercial records from the Cairo Geniza show that by the eleventh century credit operations formed an integral, even indispensable, element in the commerce of that area.[88] This date can be pushed back even further. The earliest Muslim legal sources now justify the assertion that by the late eighth century, and possibly earlier, credit arrangements of various types constituted an important feature of both trade and industry.

84 Shaybānī, *Aṣl, Sharika*, fol. 76, l. 10; *Kāsānī*, 6:64.

85 A classic statement of this view can be found in Cary Bücher, *Industrial Evolution*, N.Y., 1901, p. 128: "It may even be doubted whether in medieval trade credit operations can be spoken of at all." Cf. also pp. 129, 145–46.

86 M. M. Postan, "Credit in Medieval Trade," *Economic History Review* 1 (1927):234-261.

87 Cf. G. Luzzatto, *Storia economica d'Italia*, Rome, 1949, 1:383ff.

88 A great deal of material bearing on this problem will be found in the chapter on trade and commerce is S. D. Goitein, *Mediterranean Society*, pp. 197–200. Cf. his "Bankers' Accounts from the Eleventh Century A.D.," *JESHO* 9 (1966):28–66.

Credit fulfilled several important functions in medieval trade. It financed trade by providing capital or goods for those who temporarily or otherwise did not have the means of carrying out trade. It provided an outlet for surplus capital to be utilized in a productive and profitable way. It contributed to the expansion of trade by providing merchants with a means of doing business in an age when the supply of coins was not always adequate. In long-distance trade, it dispensed with the necessity of transporting large sums of money across perilous routes and, in combination with other contracts, it served as a means of sharing the risks of commercial ventures.

While a full study of the role of all the above mentioned aspects of credit in medieval Islamic trade has yet to be undertaken, one fact is certain: the legal instruments necessary for the extensive use of mercantile credit were already available in the earliest Islamic period. Credit arrangements which could both facilitate trade and provide a framework for the use of credit as a means of investment in trade are found in a developed form in some of the earliest Islamic legal works. Buying and selling on credit were accepted and apparently widespread commercial practices, whether a merchant was trading with his own capital or with that entrusted to him by an associate. In the "Book of Partnership" of Shaybānī's *Kitāb al-aṣl,* a provision entitling each party in a partnership to buy and sell on credit is included in the very text of the suggested contract formula. Furthermore, unless otherwise stipulated, neither partner requires the express permission of his colleague for the sale on credit of any of their joint property.[89]

References to the widespread use of credit continue to appear in all subsequent Ḥanafī literature. The eleventh century legal scholar Sarakhsī declares that "selling on credit is an absolute feature of trade"[90] and Kāsānī, approximately a century later, referring to merchants, states that "it is their custom to sell for cash and credit."[91]

[89] For the *mufāwaḍa* partnership, cf. Shaybānī, *Aṣl, Sharika,* fol. 61b; for the *'inān* partnership, cf. fol. 57b; and for the uses of credit by an agent in a *commenda* contract, cf. Sarakhsī, *Mabsūṭ,* 22:38–39.

[90] Sarakhsī, *Mabsūṭ,* 22:38.

[91] *Kāsāni,* 6:68.

The legal treatments of the two most important forms of commercial association, partnership and *commenda*, take the existence and use of credit for granted. Credit sales, both in the shape of deferred payments for goods sold (*al-bay' bit-ta'-khīr*) and advances for future delivery (*salam*), were considered fully legitimate forms of commercial conduct. Indeed, if we are to believe Sarakhsī, credit dealings were almost indispensable to successful and profitable trading. In discussing the rights of the agent or managing partner in a *commenda* contract, Sarakhsī says:

"We hold that selling for credit is part of the practice of merchants, and that it is the most conducive means for the achievement of the investor's goal which is profit. And in most cases, profit can only be achieved by selling for credit and not selling for cash. . . ."[92]

He then adds:

"Proof that selling for credit is an absolute feature of trade is found in His statement, may He be exalted, 'unless it be local trade that ye are conducting amongst you.'[93] This shows that trade can also be long distant,[94] and this latter type of trade cannot come about except by selling on credit."[95]

I have translated the Qur'ānic passage quoted by Sarakhsī as he understood it, and not as it is usually rendered in English translations. The passage reads: *illā an takūna tijāra ḥāḍira tudīrūnuhā baynakum*. Bell translates: "Unless it be present merchandise that ye are circulating amongst you,"[96] and Arberry renders it: "Unless it be merchandise present that you give and take between you."[97] The key phrase here is *tijāra ḥāḍira* (literally: present trade). It is understood by Sarakhsī,

[92] Sarakhsī, *Mabsūṭ*, 22:38.

[93] *Qur'ān*, 2:282; this passage occurs in the context of the well-known verse enjoying believers to record their debts in writing.

[94] Arabic: *ghā'iba*, literally: absent.

[95] Saraksī, *Mabsūṭ*, 22:38.

[96] Richard Bell, *The Qur'ān. Translated, with a critical re-arrangement of the Surahs*, 2 vols., Edinburgh, 1937–39, 1:42.

[97] A. J. Arberry, *The Koran Interpreted*, N.Y., n.d., p. 70.

correctly I believe, to mean local trade, and by *tijāra ghā'iba* (literally: absent trade), which he contrasts to the former, he means long-distance trade. This is not conjecture, but is explicitly stated by Sarakhsī a few lines later. "Trade," he tells us, "is of two types: local (*ḥāḍira*), in a man's own town, and long distance (*ghā'iba*) in another town; and a man cannot directly engage in both these types by himself."[98]

According to Sarakhsī, therefore, not only is long-distance trade impossible without the use of credit, but a credit sale is the surest, if not always the swiftest, method of achieving profit. Why this is so is explained by Sarakhsī in another passage. He states that "a thing is sold on credit for a larger sum that it would be sold for in cash."[99] This statement makes clear only *why* there was a greater profit to be derived from credit transactions, but also *how* it was possible for traders to extend credit, sometimes for a long period, without straining or completely immobilizing their resources. The difference in price between a credit and cash sale also helps explain why the prohibiton against usury, to the extent that it was observed (which was probably considerable), did not exercise any crippling restriction on the conduct of commerce. For, while the difference in the price for which one sells on credit and the price for which one sells for cash does not formally or legally constitute interest, it does fulfill, from the point of view of its economic function, the same role as interest. It provides a return to the creditor for the risks involved in the transaction, and compensates him for the absence of his capital.

Islamic commercial law outlines not only methods of dealing for credit, but also makes provisions for dealing in credit. Instruments of credit such as the *ḥawāla* (transfer of debt, novation) and the *suftaja* (letter of credit) are prime examples of this category of credit.[100] In addition, and what is most relevant to the present discussion, credit could serve as a valid form of commercial investment. Among the various forms of commercial partnership recognized as valid by Ḥanafī law,

[98] Sarakhsī, *Mabsūṭ*, 22:38 (bottom). [99] *Ibid.*, 22:45.

[100] Cf. Schacht, *An Introduction to Islamic Law*, pp. 148–149, and R. Grasshoff, *Das Wachselrecht des Araber*, Berlin, 1899.

the credit partnership constitutes a separate category. It is an arrangement in which the capital of the parties consists not of cash or merchandise, but entirely of credit. It is the only form of partnership for which ready cash (*māl ḥāḍir*) is not required for the validity of the contract. The credit partnership is already found fully developed in the earliest Ḥanafī sources, and its description and elaboration offer interesting clues and insights into its economic function. Concerning it, Sarakhsī says:

> As for the credit partnership, it is also called the partnership of the penniless (*sharikat al-mafālīs*). It comes about when two people form a partnership without any capital in order to buy on credit and then sell. It is designated by this name (*sharikat al-wujūh*) because their capital consists of their good reputations; for credit is extended only to him who has a good reputation among people.[101]

Whether or not Sarakhsī's comments regarding the derivation of the designation for the credit partnership are historically accurate is not important here. The significant point is that the two designations for the credit partnership—*sharikat al-mafālīs*, the partnership of the penniless, and *sharikat al-wujūh*, which with Sarakhsī we may freely translate as the partnership of those with good reputations—reflect the two major functions of credit in trade. The first reflects a situation in which traders without sufficient resources of their own seek financing, one in which the traders hire the capital; the second reflects a situation in which the capital is seeking a profitable investment outlet, one in which the capital hires the trader.

The role of credit as an investment in trade and as a means of financing trade is articulated in a remarkably sophisticated way by Kāsānī in a polemical passage directed against the Shāfiʿī view of partnership. According to Shāfiʿī, the chief function and purpose of the institution of partnership is the augmentation of the capital investment (*namāʾ al-māl*). This can be achieved, in his view, only with a tangible investment such as cash, but not with labor or credit. For this reason,

[101] Sarakhsī, *Mabsūṭ*, 11:152.

among others, Shāfi'ī rejects the validity of both a credit and a work partnership, the latter being an association in which the primary investment is the craft or manufacturing skills of the parties involved.[102] Kāsānī counters Shāfi'ī's objection by arguing that people have been engaging in these two forms of partnership for centuries without rebuke from anyone, and that surely, as the Prophet himself had said, his community would not unanimously agree upon an error. Furthermore, the element of agency (*wakāla*)[103] is operative in these types of partnership, and they are, therefore, valid. The following is what Kāsānī says:

> His (Shāfi'ī's) statement that partnership was considered permissible in order to facilitate the augmentation of capital implies the existence of some original capital to be augmented. We hold that cash partnership was indeed considered permissible in order to facilitate augmentation of capital; but as for work and credit partnerships, these were not considered permissible to facilitate the augmentation of capital, but for the purpose of creating the capital itself. The need for the creation of capital takes precedence over the need for its augmentation.[104]

The credit partnership is thus justified on the grounds of usage, of legal principle, and by virtue of the general economic function of partnership which Kāsānī epitomizes as "a method for augmenting or creating capital."[105]

A credit partnership can be formed on the basis of either a total (*mufāwaḍa*) or partial (*'inān*) investment. In each case, the rights and obligations of the individual partners follow the same rules as those in a cash partnership.[106] Only on the ques-

102 *Shāfi'ī, Kitāb al-umm*, 7 vols., Cairo 1321/1903–1325/1907, 3:206. Re: work partnerships cf. A. L. Udovitch, "Labor Partnerships in Early Islamic Law," *JESHO* 10 (1967):64–80.

103 Cf. J. Schacht, *An Introduction to Islamic Law*, pp. 119–20; in Ḥanafī law, agency is one of the basic legal relationships making partnership possible.

104 *Kāsānī*, 6:57.

105 *Ibid.*, p. 57, l. 25.

106 Shaybānī, *Aṣl, Sharika*, fol. 59b, ll. 15–19; fol. 62, ll. 14–18; fol. 76, ll. 3–5; Sarakhsī, *Mabsūṭ*, 11:179; *Kāsānī*, 6:65, 77.

tion of profit distribution does the credit partnership deviate from the rules governing all other forms of Ḥanafī partnership.

> Two people enter into a trade partnership, and neither of them has any capital. One of them, because of his superior trading skill, stipulates a share of the profit for himself in excess of his share of the liability. The circumstances of the partnership are that they make a purchase on the basis of their credit.
>
> This is not a satisfactory arrangement, because one partner will be enjoying the profit of something for which the other is liable. It is not permissible that one partner receive more profit than does his colleague for a comparable share of the liability. A disparity between each partner's share in the profit and his share of the liability is, however, permitted in all partnerships which are not based on a credit purchase, such as cash and work partnerships.
>
> If, however, two people form a partnership without any capital, on the condition that they buy on credit and share the profits and losses according to their respective shares in the investment, this arrangement is permissible.[107]

In the Ḥanafī law, credit partnership is unique in that the profit must strictly follow the ratio of each partner's share in the investment. The correspondence of liability to investment holds true for all partnerships;[108] in all other forms, however, the division of profit is optional. Within the broadest limits, any ratio stipulated in the contract is to be honored.

To summarize: According to Ḥanafī law, liability in partnership corresponds to investment in all cases; profit follows any ratio stipulated in the contract, except in the case of credit partnership where it, too, follows the investment.

The inclusion in the partnership agreement of any invalid

[107] Shaybānī, *Aṣl, Sharika*, fol. 57b, ll. 9–12; cf. also. Sarakhsī, *Mabsūṭ*, 11:154; *Kāsānī*, 6:77.

[108] This rule is epitomized in a tradition attributed to ʿAlī b. Abī Ṭālib: *ar-ribḥ ʿalā mā ishtaraṭā ʿalayhi wal-waḍīʿa ʿalā al-māl.* "The profit is according to what they have agreed upon, and the liability according to the capital." Cf. Shaybānī, *Aṣl, Sharika*, fol. 61, ll. 19–20.

provision, such as the non-correspondence of profit with liability, does not invalidate the entire agreement. Only the offensive clause is cancelled; the partnership is valid and, regardless of any stipulation to the contrary, the profit is to adhere to each partner's share of the investment.[109]

The credit partnership could be adapted to serve a variety of purposes, those of a single-venture partnership confined to a specific commodity or to a specified time period, as well as those of an unrestricted association.

> If two people without any capital enter into a partnership on the condition that any purchase of fine flour either of them makes is to be their joint property, this is permissible.
>
> It is likewise permissible when two people without any capital enter into a partnership on the condition that whatever either of them purchases at any time is to be their joint property, or on the condition that whatever either of them purchases in the current year or month is to be their common property. This is so, regardless of whether or not any class of merchandise or type of work was specified.[110]

A credit partnership could be restricted either by the scope of the commodities it is to comprehend or by the term in which it is to be effective. Either of these two factors could be adjusted to meet the needs of a variety of commercial situations. One can readily envisage the manifold usefulness of these arrangements, especially for long-distance trade. A traveling merchant, setting out with a caravan or embarking on a voyage, could be assured that half, or some other fraction, of the cost of the shipment he returned with would be covered. This would give the merchant some measure of protection against possible adverse market conditions and provide partial insurance against loss in transit since, once a purchase is made, the loss would be borne by both partners. On the other hand, a sedentary merchant, unwilling or unable to travel to foreign parts himself, could assure himself a share in a normally lucra-

[109] Cf. *Ibid.*, fol. 59b, ll. 15–19; Sarakhsī, *Mabsūṭ*, 11:154.
[110] Shaybānī, *Aṣl*, *Sharika*, fol. 59b, ll. 6–8.

tive import trade without at the same time tying up his capital for long periods.

An all-inclusive, unspecified credit partnership posed theoretical difficulties for Ḥanafī jurists. For them, the legitimacy of credit partnership, as well as all its other forms, is based on the operativeness of the element of agency. Empowering a person with a general mandate, with neither a time limit nor a specific object in mind, is not a valid form of agency. By analogy, an all-inclusive, unspecified credit partnership should be equally invalid. Sarakhsī resolves this difficulty by distinguishing between the purposes of these two transactions. In agency, the purpose is the achievement of a specific task or the acquisition of a specific object. A general, unrestricted mandate is invalid because of the difficulties in which it could involve both parties. In partnership, the sole purpose is the attainment of profit. This end can be achieved through the purchase on credit and resale of any number of commodites in any number of ways. An unrestricted credit partnership is appropriate to the realization of this goal and is, therefore, valid.[111]

Professor Goitein has very kindly made available to me from the Geniza records a document illustrating an actual example of a credit partnership.[112] It dates from A.D. 1125, and involves two partners—one Mūsā b. Bishr and a certain Hiba—who formed a partnership in order to establish a bakery. Both were to contribute equally to the necessary work and to share equally in the profits and losses. The partners apparently had no capital of their own, and their entire venture was financed by a loan of four dinars extended to them by one Ibn ar-Riḍā the Supervisor. Their venture, unfortunately, did not fare too well. As a result, the document in question was drawn up to apportion the liabilities consequent upon their business failure. In comparison with numerous other business transactions recorded in the Geniza documents, the investment in this case is rather paltry. However, it is not the quantitative but the

111 Cf. Sarakhsī, *Mabsūṭ*, 11:179.

112 This document is found in the library of the Jewish Theological Seminary of America, E. N. Adler Collection, no. 4011, fol. 57a.

qualitative aspect of this document which is significant here. There is no reason to doubt that similar transactions financing trade and production by means of credit on a larger scale were practised.

This example clearly demonstrates that the possibilities outlined in Islamic legal sources for the alliance of credit with trade did find their way into commercial practice. Any assertion that medieval credit was used for consumption only, and not for production, is quite untenable with reference to the medieval Near East.

The Contract

Islamic law contains no general theory of contracts. Only by combining and generalizing the rules governing the conduct of various transactions do a number of general rules for the conclusion of a valid and binding contract emerge. Of these, the following four are applicable to all commercial transactions: (1) Consent of the contracting parties; (2) Legal competence of the contracting parties; (3) A subject matter; (4) A consideration. For the purposes of evidence in case of litigation, a fifth condition should be added, namely, the presence of qualified witnesses.[113] No special formula is required, nor need the contract be embodied in any particular form.

"Documents (*ṣakk*, written contracts) fulfill no role whatsoever; there are no transactions for which a written format is prescribed."[114] This single sentence summarizes the status of written agreements from the standpoint of Ḥanafī legal theory. In no commercial transaction under Islamic law is a written instrument a requirement. A written agreement *per se* does not give rise to any obligation, nor does it constitute competent

[113] For a brief and well-presented discussion of contracts in Islamic law, cf. S. Mahmasani, in *Law in the Middle East*, 1:191–198; also, by the same author, *The General Theory of the Law of Obligations and Contracts Under Muhammadan Jurisprudence* (Arabic), Beirut, 1948, 1:8ff.; Schacht, *Grundzüge*, pp. 61–62; O. Spies, "Das Depositum nach islamischem Recht," *Zeitschrift für vergleichende Rechtswissenschaft* 45 (1930):252–264; this last contains a very concise, useful summary of Islamic contract law; also *EI*, 2nd ed., *s.v.* *'aḳd*.

[114] Schacht, *Grundzüge*, p. 113.

evidence in the event of litigation. Theoretically, a written document can acquire legal force only through the verification of its contents by the oral testimony of qualified witnesses. It is the oral testimony which is the decisive factor in determining the existence and nature of an obligation. The existence of documentary evidence constitutes, at best, corroborative evidence only.[115]

Despite their devaluation by legal theory, written documents continued in use, as Sarakhsī puts it, "from the time of the Prophet to our very own day."[116] Aside from Sarakhsī's testimony, there is considerable evidence, both direct and indirect, pointing to the extensive use of written documents in all areas of economic life. The Arabic papyri contain hundreds of examples of sales contracts, tax receipts, etcetera, all duly witnessed and with the names of the witnesses recorded.[117] By the standards of customary popular practice, these documents were considered to have evidential force.[118]

The numerous contracts and other business records preserved in the Cairo Geniza bear eloquent testimony to the importance attached to written documents in the commerce of the medieval Islamic world. For purposes of reference, records of business transactions were preserved for long periods and often accompanied the merchants in their travels from India to Tunis. The elaborate care taken of written contracts is exemplified by the fact that, in several instances, copies of the same

[115] By denying validity to documentary evidence and confining legal proof to oral testimony, Islamic law deviated from an express Qur'anic injunction (2:282) and from prevalent Near Eastern legal practice which, in so many other areas, influenced the development of Muslim legal institutions. As yet, no satisfactory explanation has been offered for this seemingly strange development. Cf. Schacht, *Law in the Middle East*, 1:39; Emile Tyan, *Le notariat et le régime de la preuve par écrit dans la pratique du droit musulman*, 2nd ed., Beirut, n.d., pp. 5–13.

[116] Sarakhsī, *Mabsūṭ*, 30:168.

[117] E.g., A. Grohmann, *Arabic Papyri in the Egyptian Library*, 6 vols., Cairo, 1934–1962.

[118] Grohmann, *Einführung*, pp. 108–113; cf., e.g., *Arabic Papyri in the Egyptian Library*, 1:205, line 1 (a sale contract): "this document has evidential force, and Idrīs b. Ja'far wrote it with his own hand." Cf. also, A. Merx, *Paléographie Hebraique et Arabe*, Leiden, 1894, p. 14.

contract were dispatched by two or three different routes in order to ensure the safe arrival of at least one at the desired destination.[119]

Even though not every business transaction may have been recorded in some written form,[120] one can conclude with reasonable certainty that transactions of any importance were as a matter of course accompanied by written documents.

Islamic legal theory, while persisting in its neglect of written documents, took cognizance, at a very early stage, of their indispensability and widespread use by creating a special branch of practical law, the *'ilm ash-shurūṭ*, devoted exclusively to notarial science. Practitioners of this legal specialty (*ahl ash-shurūṭ*, *aṣḥāb ash-shurūṭ*) exercised two complementary functions, that of notary public and that of professional witness. As notaries public, they drew up documents for a variety of transactions in accordance with the precepts of the *sharī'a*; as professional witnesses of the documents they drew up, they could provide the oral testimony required to give the written contracts evidential force. In their dual role, they satisfied the practical need for written records and the theoretical insistence on the oral testimony of witnesses.[121]

The extent to which Ḥanafī law recognized the desirability of written contracts is nowhere more strikingly evidenced than in the "Book of Partnership" of the *Kitāb al-aṣl*. Its very first lines contain a suggested formula for a written partnership contract.[122] A written deed is not required for a valid partner-

119 Cf. S. D. Goitein, "From the Mediterranean to India," *SPECULUM* 29 (1954):185–189.

120 Cf., for example, the remark of Rab Sa'adia Gaon (10th century), is one of his *responsa*, to the effect that many people carry on their business affairs without the benefit of witnesses or contracts. From the context, it appears that he is referring to daily buying and selling or to minor investments of short duration. His remark is part of a recommendation for the consistent use of written contracts. Cf. E. E. Hildesheimer, *Rekonstruktion eines Responsums des R. Saadja Gaon zum judischen Gesellschaftsrecht*, Frankfurt A.M., 1926, pp. 36–37.

121 Cf. E. Tyan, *Le notariat*, pp. 10–12; Schacht, in *Law in the Middle East*, 1:79. For the most recent and comprehensive discussion of this problem, cf. Jeanette Wakin, *Islamic Law in Practice: Two Chapters From Ṭaḥāwī's Kitāb al-shurūṭ al-kabīr*, dissertation, Columbia University, 1968.

122 Shaybānī, *Aṣl*, *Sharika*, fol. 57b, ll. 3–8 (lines 1–2 contain the standard opening pious phrases and the title).

ship; yet it is clear that whenever Shaybānī refers to the formation of a partnership, he envisages its accomplishment primarily by means of a written agreement. This is illustrated by the introductory sentence of the "Book of Partnership": "If one man wishes to take on another as a partner in a limited investment partnership for the purposes of a specific trade, and they both wish to have a written agreement drawn up between them, then they are to write. . . . "[123] It is true that Shaybānī makes the writing of the contract dependent on the desires of the parties concerned. Nowhere, however, is there a reference to an alternative procedure for the formation of a partnership.

Sarakhsī, who is normally very attentive to the nuances of Shaybānī's text, omits this conditional phrase. "If two men wish to form an unlimited investment partnership, then we write. . . ."[124] A summary formula for a written contract follows, but without any reference to the desires of the parties for a written contract.

The attitude of Ḥanafī law toward the use of written documents was by no means a passive one. Not only did Ḥanafī jurists recognize their usefulness, but they went a step further and actively encouraged their use in all transactions. In the introductory paragraphs to the section on *shurūṭ* of the *Mabsūṭ*,[123] Sarakhsī makes a forceful plea for the consistent employment of written records. He characterizes notarial science as one of the most useful and important branches of knowledge. He points to the precedents of the Prophet's use of written documents both in his business and administrative affairs, and to their continuous use up to his own times.

Sarakhsī stresses the substantial advantages, especially in business affairs, offered by the use of written documents.

> The first of these is the preservation of property; for he (the Prophet) commanded its preservation and enjoined against its dissipation. The second is the prevention of dispute; for a document will serve as a basis for judgment between par-

[123] *Ibid.*, fol. 57b, l. 3.
[124] Sarakhsī, *Mabsūṭ*, 11:177; cf. also, p. 155.
[125] *Ibid.*, 30:167–209.

ties, something to which they can refer in case of dispute. It will be a cause for the allaying of discord. A party to a contract would not deny the rights of his colleague for fear that the latter would produce the document and that the witnesses would testify against him, thereby disgracing him among the people. The third advantage is the prevention of invalid contracts. For the parties concerned may not be aware of those elements which invalidate a contract, so that they can avoid them. However, if the parties go to a scribe for the writing of the document, he would point out to them the invalidating factors. The fourth advantage is the removal of doubt. In the event that the contract extends over a long period, the parties might become uncertain as regards the amount of money involved or the extent of the time limit of the contract. However, if they refer to a written document, there will be no doubt in either party's mind. The same applies to doubts that might arise in the minds of heirs, should any of the original parties to the contract die.[126]

Concerning the particular desirability of drawing up a written instrument to record a partnership contract, Sarakhsī says the following:

> "Partnership is a contract which extends over a period of time, and a written document is necessary in cases of this kind in order to provide a basis for judgment between the parties in the event of any dispute. God, the Exalted, said: 'Oh ye who believed, when ye contract a debt one to the other for a stated term, write it down.'[127] The purpose of a written document is to serve as a security and a precaution; it is necessary, therefore, that it be written in the most binding fashion, so as to prevent any recriminations."[128]

For legal theory, the use of written documents, while highly commendable, nevertheless remained an optional practice.

[126] Sarakhsī, *Mabsūṭ*, 30:167–168. Cf. also, Tyan, *Le notariat*, pp. 59–61, where some of these notarial functions are discussed.

[127] *Qur'ān*, 2:282: this verse, according to the commentators, is not to be interpreted as a binding divine command, but is to be taken, rather as a piece of general advice. Cf. Tyan, *Le notariat*, p. 8, and references there.

[128] Sarakhsī, *Mabsūṭ*, 11:155.

Witnessing, in the manner prescribed by law,[129] continued to be, for evidential purposes, an essential requirement. In practice, no doubt, this order of importance was reversed; documents were an almost essential accompaniment of every transaction of importance, and the witnessing a formality to make them fully valid.[130]

The absence of formalism is one of the characteristic features of Islamic contract law. Whether a contract is embodied in writing or whether it is negotiated in some other way, no special words need be spoken and no specific forms or technicalities observed as a prerequisite to its validity. "In contracts effect is given to intention and meaning, and not to words and phrases."[131] This applies, of course, to all business contracts, including the various forms of partnerships. Some difficulties, however, arise in connection with the *mufāwaḍa* partnership. Because of its extraordinary comprehensiveness, some jurists held that it could be validly contracted only with the express use of the term "*mufāwaḍa*."

> Al-Ḥasan[132] related from Abū Ḥanīfa that universal partnership cannot be contracted except with the term "*mufāwaḍa*." If the term "*mufāwaḍa*" is not employed, the arrangement is to be construed as a general limited investment partnership; for limited investment partnership can take the form of a general or specific association.[133] This statement is to be understood as follows: Most people are not aware of the rules governing the universal partnership. Therefore, the consent[134] of the parties concerned to its rules

129 To qualify, a witness must meet the rather stringent moral standards of *'adāla*—trustworthiness, probity; cf. Schacht, *Grundzüge*, p. 36; Tyan, *Le notariat*, pp. 11–12.

130 Schacht, in *Law in the Middle East*, 1:79.

131 *Majalla*, Article 3; quoted by Mahmasani in *Law in the Middle East*, 1:198.

132 Probably Al-Ḥasan b. Ziyād al-Lu'lu'ī, d. 204/819; cf. Ibn Qutlūbughā, *Tāj at-tarājim*, p. 22.

133 *'inān 'āmm*—general *'inān* partnership, comprehending a variety of business operations; *'inān khāṣṣ*—specific *'inān* partnership, limited to a single purchase and resale.

134 Consent is the first and most essential condition to the conclusion of a valid contract.

cannot be effective until they know them. The express use of the term "*mufāwaḍa*" becomes a substitute for all this.[135] If the parties of the contract are aware of its rules and if the meaning of the unlimited investment partnership is spelled out, the contract between them is valid even if the term itself is not used. For the primary consideration in a contract is the intended meaning, and not the phrasing.[136]

Abū Ḥanīfa's statement, which, if taken at its face value, would establish one minor formal requirement for a valid *mufāwaḍa* contract, is interpreted in a manner which removes even this modicum of formalism. The non-formalism of Islamic contract law is thus extended to include this distinctive form of partnership as well.[137]

The earliest formulae for partnership contracts are found in Shaybānī's *Kitāb al-aṣl.* Formulae intended specifically for *mufāwaḍa*, work, and credit partnership contracts are, to the best of my knowledge, not found in any other Ḥanafī work emanating from the formative period of Islamic law.[138]

Following is the translation of the suggested formula for a general *mufāwaḍa* partnership:

"This is a document stating the agreement upon which[139] *X* the son of *Y* and *A* the son of *B* have entered into a partnership. They entered the partnership in a God-fearing man-

135 I.e., the phrase "*mufāwaḍa*" in the contract takes the place of a detailed enumeration of the unlimited investment partnership rules.

136 Sarakhsī, *Mabsūṭ*, 11:154.

137 Cf. *Kāsānī*, 6:62; Schacht, *Grundzüge*, p. 25.

138 The traditionist An-Nasā'i (d. 303/915, cf. C. Brockelmann, *Geschichte der arabischen Litteratur* (*GAL*), 1:170 [162]), himself a Shāfi'ī, gives the text of a *mufāwaḍa* contract in his *Sunan* (ed. Cairo, 1930, 7:56–57) under the heading: "A *Mufāwaḍa* Partnership Between Four People According to the legal Schools Which Allow It." This contract, however, does not meet all the Ḥanafī requirements for a valid *mufāwaḍa*. While it stipulates equality of investment and profit sharing, it makes no mention of the inclusion of all the partners' eligible capital.

139 The phrase *hādhā mā* (literally: this is what) is the most frequently used introductory formula in Arabic contracts. It introduces what Grohmann has termed the objective style contract, one in which the parties are referred to, as in this case, in the third person. This is in contrast to the subjective style contracts, in which the partners, as it were, address each other using the first and second person singular. Cf. Grohmann, *Einführung*, pp. 115–116.

ner and with mutual fidelity.[140] They have become partners in all things, acquisitions, and skills,[141] in a universal partnership. They may sell for cash or credit, and they may buy for cash or credit; and each of them may operate in these matters according to his judgment.[142] Their capital is such and such, belonging equally to both of them, and all of it is in their possession.[143] Whatever benefit God, the Exalted, grants them is to be shared equally between them; whatever loss or setback overtakes them is to be borne by them in equal shares. They have entered into a partnership on this basis in the month so and so of the year so and so."[144]

140 Sarakhsī, commenting on these two phrases, says: "This contract is a contract of fidelity, the aim of which is the attainment of profit; and this is attained by the fear of God and mutual fidelity" (*Mabsūṭ*, 11:156). Fidelity, faithfulness, or trust (Arabic: *amāna*) is a property attaching to a number of different contractual relationships, such as partnership, *commenda*, deposit, etcetera. When something is entrusted to a person in *amāna*, he is not liable for loss, except in case of some trespass or violation; e.g., if the joint capital was in the care of one of the partners and all or part was lost in transit or as a result of a legitimate, but unfortunate, business transaction, that partner would not be obligated to restore the loss. If, however, the money was lost in an activity outside the realm of acceptable business conduct, such as gambling, then the partner responsible would be liable for the restoration of the entire amount of his colleague's share of the lost capital. Cf. Schacht, *Grundzüge*, p. 64.

141 Arabic: *nayl wa-ḳays*. This phrase is apparently an idiomatic expression or technical term signifying the comprehensive nature of the *mufāwaḍa*, indicating the inclusion of all eligible capital and all business activities of the partners. Another phrase used in a similar way is: *fī ḳull qalīl wa-ḳathīr*—"in all things, large and small"; cf. Shaybānī, *Aṣl*, *Sharika*, fol. 61b, l. 6.

142 Sarakhsī remarks that, in his view, the very nature of the partnership contract automatically confers on both partners the privileges mentioned in this sentence. He adds, however, that there are some jurists for whom these privileges are not implicit in the partnership unless explicitly spelled out in the contract. To avoid any complications, therefore, this sentence should be included in the written contract. Cf. Sarakhsī, *Mabsūṭ*, 11:156.

143 This last phrase is mentioned because of the requirement that all capital be on hand, i.e., *māl ḥāḍir*; cf. *ibid.*

144 Shaybānī, *Aṣl*, *Sharika*, fol. 61b, ll. 1–5. A very brief summary of this contract is also found in Sarakhsī, *Mabsūṭ*, 11:177. The formulae for the labor and credit partnerships occur in *Aṣl*, *Sharika*, fol. 57b, l. 20–fol. 58, l. 1 and fol. 57b, ll. 12–16, respectively. These contracts are in the nature of suggested model texts and can be adjusted for either a *mufāwaḍa* or *ʿinān* partnership. As we might expect, the feature distinguishing these last two contract formulae is the specification of the nature of the partners' in-

The form of this contract is simple and direct; its contents are brief and concise, covering only the most essential elements of the transaction. These include: (1) The nature or subject of the transaction (partnership); (2) The names of the contracting parties; (3) The consideration, that is, the amount of each one's investment or, in the case of a non-cash partnership, the nature of the investment; (4) Distribution of profit; (5) Distribution of liability; (6) Work on the part of both parties; (7) Right of each one to deal on credit and to conduct business according to his best judgment; and (8) The date. One can assume that any other conditions, such as a time limit and the like, could be added at the discretion of the partners.

The formulae for these contracts occur in the context of Shaybānī's over-all treatment of partnership law. Their unceremonious brevity leads one to suspect that they were intended not as samples of contracts actually in use, but as skeletal outlines containing only those essential elements without which a written contract would have been inadequate even for the limited degree of usefulness accorded it by Ḥanafī legal theory.

This is confirmed, to some extent, by comparing Shaybānī's text with the partnership contract in Ṭaḥāwī's notarial handbook *Kitāb aṣ-ṣaghīr fish-shurūṭ*, where the contract follows the same general outline, but is much more elaborate.[145] For example, the type and quality of the money are indicated, and the rights and obligations of the parties are enumerated in greater detail. The difference between the two formulae is probably to be explained by the different purposes of the two treatises. Ṭaḥāwī's work was not intended as a legal code, but as a specialized, practical manual for the use of notaries presenting sample formulae for all major categories of contracts. All the notary would have to do is copy out the formula for the desired contract and merely fill in the names, amounts,

---

vestment; in the first case it is the labor of their hands, and in the second, their credit purchases.

145 Ṭaḥāwī's contract is for an *'inān* partnership. Its text is discussed in the following chapter.

and dates. It is much more likely, therefore, that the contract formulae of Ṭaḥāwī represent a closer approximation of the contracts that were actually in use than do the summary-like formulae found in the *Kitāb al-aṣl*.[146]

Ṭaḥāwī's treatise contains no example of a *mufāwaḍa* contract. This handbook is a short version of his much larger *Al-jāmi' al-kabīr fish-shurūṭ*, of which the section of partnership is not extant. This latter work may have indeed included a sample *mufāwaḍa* contract. In his shorter compilation, Ṭaḥawī gives only one sample partnership contract, that of a limited investment partnership, and includes in it only those provisions upon which jurists from all legal schools are in agreement.[147] By his own admission, the exclusion of the *mufāwaḍa* contract was intentional. "We have executed our contract in the form of a limited investment partnership (*'inān*) and excluded the *mufāwaḍa* partnership, because of the differences and disagreements concerning the latter's rules on the part of a number of people of knowledge."[148]

Ṭaḥāwī offers the identical explanation for his exclusion of sample work and credit partnership contracts.[149] The absence of these contracts is again connected with the function his treatise was intended to fulfill. As a concise handbook for notaries and scribes who could be expected to have dealings with adherents of all the legal schools, its sample contract formulae would have to exclude all provisions subject to disagreement and controversy. Ṭaḥāwī does, however, briefly outline the main features of the *mufāwaḍa* and other controversial partnership forms. Consequently, any notary could, with the slight application of his own ingenuity to the model text, devise any needed partnership contract.

146 It should also be noted that the formulae in the *Aṣl* contain no reference to witnessing, whereas those of Ṭaḥāwī do. Cf. Ṭaḥāwī ms. *Bayazit*, 18905, fol. 95, l. 11.

147 The limited investment (*'inān*) partnership is the only partnership form recognized by all the major schools of Islamic law.

148 Ṭaḥāwī, *Kitāb ash-shurūṭ aṣ-ṣaghīr*, fol. 95, ll. 11–12.

149 *Ibid.*, fol. 96, ll. 15–18, re: work partnership; ll. 12–22, re: credit partnership.

Once a written contract is drawn up, a copy is to be deposited in the possession of each partner. This procedure is recommended by Shaybānī in the passage immediately following the text of the *mufāwaḍa* contract formula. "Let each of them write a contract according to this format, and let it be in his possession."[150] Although no such recommendation is explicitly made following the texts of the work and credit partnership contracts, one can be quite certain that this procedure applies to these contracts as well.[151]

Effectiveness of the Contract

Neither the signing of a written agreement nor its oral negotiation before qualified witnesses gives final effect to the partnership. This can only be accomplished through some act. Unlike Shāfiʿī law, Ḥanafī law does not require the physical intermingling of the respective investment capitals. If, however, this should occur, the act of intermingling would constitute the initiation of the partnership. Otherwise, the partnership would not take full effect until one or both of the partners actually began to do business with the joint capital. This requirement applies to all cash and credit partnerships, both the limited investment and universal forms. In a work partnership, it is the initial *taqabbul,* or acceptance of work in the name of the partnership, which fulfills this function.

150 Shaybānī, *Aṣl, Sharika,* fol. 61b, ll. 5–6.

151 Ṭaḥāwī also recommends the drawing up of two copies of a partnership contract and includes a reference to the number of contract copies made at the conclusion of the text of the contract itself (ms. *Bayazit,* 18905, fol. 95, ll. 10–11). Making two copies of an agreement was undoubtedly a standard practice in connection with most categories of contracts. Evidence for this is found in the Arabic papyri (cf. Grohmann, *Einführung,* pp. 124–125) and in the business records of the Geniza (cf. Goitein, *Mediterranean Society,* p. 284). In the "Book of Pre-Emption" of his large work on notarial science, Ṭaḥāwī instructs notaries and scribes as follows: "You should draw up the contract in two copies, and you should note this fact at the conclusion of your contract, saying as follows: "This contract was written in two copies according to the same order and arrangement. Neither copy exceeds the other even by a letter which might alter a rule or remove a meaning. One of the copies is in the possession of *A* the son of *B*, as a security for him and a proof; and one of the copies is in the possession of *X* son of *Y* as a security for him and a proof' " (*Kitāb ash-shufʿa,* p. 39, ll. 20–24). Cf. also, Tyan, *Le notariat,* pp. 55, 73.

Conduct of the *Mufāwaḍa*

The partnership contract contains a clause conferring upon each partner the right to act with the common capital according to his best judgment. In the case of a limited investment partnership, this broad mandate might be modified by the addition of any number of conditions restricting each partner's activities to a certain category of goods, or to a given locality, or to certain types of transactions. In the universal partnership, embracing as it did every facet of commerce, each partner's right to conduct trade according to his best judgment assumed the widest possible scope.

Medieval trade, like its modern counterpart, was not simply a matter of buying and selling. The successful prosecution of commerce involved the judicious employment of a variety of transactions. The business records of the Geniza vividly document the great variety and complexity of the business methods employed by merchants active in the Islamic world in the tenth and eleventh centuries.[152] People had to be hired for care and transportation of merchandise. Circumstances often required that goods be consigned to another person's care, either to be sold or to be retrieved at a later date. Credit might have to be extended and a pledge taken to guarantee payment or, conversely, a pledge given to cover credit purchases for the partnership. Advantage might be gained by concluding partnerships of short duration with third parties or by the investment or acceptance of capital in the form of a *commenda*.

All these contingencies were the normal accompaniments of trade. Any comprehensive legal treatment of Islamic partnership, therefore, would be obliged as a matter of course to define the limits of each partner's rights and duties in relation to the conduct of business and to outline the framework within which the best judgment of each partner might be legitimately exercised.

In Ḥanafī law, these problems are discussed within the general context of partnership as a contract of fidelity (*'aqd*

[152] Cf. Goitein, *Mediterranean Society*, pp. 164–208.

al-amāna). Each partner is considered to be a *amīn*, a trustworthy, faithful party in regard to the money of his colleague, one who cannot be held responsible for any loss occurring in the normal course of trade.[153] "The loss of money while in the possession of a faithful person (*amīn*) is like its loss while in the possession of its very owner."[154] The entire burden of the discussion concerning each partner's rights and duties is to determine those uses to which the joint capital can be put and those relationships with third parties into which the individual partner can enter without exceeding the bounds of *amāna*. Conversely, it is concerned with the definition of *ta'addī*, the trespass or violation of *amāna,* which results in the liability of the violating partner toward his colleague and toward third parties for any losses.[155]

Modern law recognizes the existence of corporate entities independent of, and distinguished from, the individuals which the corporation comprises. Consequently, modern treatises on partnership law are mainly concerned with the relations between the "firm" and third parties. This is not the case either in Roman or Islamic legal literature. "Roman law had no theory of agency by which a partner could automatically have authority to bind his partners. If a *socius* made a contract on firm business, it was, so far as the third party was concerned, a contract with the partner who made it, and there would be no action against other members of the firm. The *socii* would have claims against each other for account, but the third party had nothing to do with this."[156] Consequently, "the title *Pro socio* in the Digest deals almost entirely with the relations between the *socii inter se*."[157]

From the standpoint of the problems with which it is primarily concerned, the treatment of partnership in Islamic law closely resembles that found in Roman law. As in Roman law,

153 Cf. Sarakhsī, *Mabsūṭ*, 11:157; also, cf. above, n. 140.

154 *Ibid.*, p. 177.

155 Cf. Schacht, *Grundzüge*, pp. 64–65.

156 W. W. Buckland and A. D. McNair, *Roman Law and Common Law*, 2nd ed., Cambridge, 1952, p. 301. Cf. also, W. W. Buckland, *A Text-Book of Roman Law from Augustus to Justinian*, 2nd ed., Cambridge, 1932, p. 507.

157 Buckland and McNair, *Roman Law and Common Law*, p. 301.

most of the partnership discussion revolves around the rights and duties of the partners in relation to each other. Even though Islamic law does have a theory of agency,[158] the partners' transactions with third parties are nevertheless viewed, with one major exception, exclusively from the perspective of their relations to each other. In all their dealings, there is no such thing as a corporate entity. Obligations arising from the multifarious commercial activities in which the partnership might be engaged attach primarily to the individual partner involved in any specific transaction, and only secondarily to the partnership. That is, the claim of any third party can be directed only against the partner responsible for the transaction which gave rise to the claim; the latter can, in turn, seek satisfaction from his partners.[159] The same applies in the reverse situation. Any claim of the partnership against a third party can be pressed only by the individual partner involved. Transactions conducted jointly by both partners are also viewed from the same perspective. The claims of third parties, in this event, are to be directed against the individual partners in proportion to their contractually determined shares of the total liability.

The Ḥanafī *mufāwaḍa* partnership constitutes the single exception to the approach outlined in the preceding paragraphs. This institution is the closest approximation found in Islamic law to a corporate entity.[160] Concerning the *mufāwaḍa* partners, Kāsānī declares: "They are in reality two persons, but from the standpoint of the principles of commerce, they are like a single person."[161] If, in this statement,

[158] Arabic: *waḳāla*; cf. Schacht, *Grundzüge*, pp. 29–30. Most Hanafī treatises contain a separate chapter devoted to the theory of agency.

[159] Cf. Santillana, *Istituzioni*, 2:299.

[160] Cf., however, Schacht, *Grundzüge*, p. 74, where it is pointed out that the town quarter (*maḥalla*), under certain circumstances, takes on the characteristics of a corporative organization in connection with the payment of blood-wit for manslaughter.

[161] *Kāsānī*, 6:73: *wa-humā fil-ḥaqīqa shaḳhṣān wa-fī aḥḳām at-tijāra ḳa-shaḳhṣ wāḥid*; also Sarakhsī, *Mabsūṭ*, 11:74: *li'anna al-mutafāwiḍayn fī mā huwa min ṣanī' at-tujjār ḳa-shaḳhṣ wāḥid*; "for the *mufāwaḍa* partners, in matters that are the occupation of merchants, are like one person." Cf. also, Sarakhsī, *Mabsūṭ*, 11:190.

we were to substitute the word law for the word commerce, it would constitute a fairly accurate and acceptable definition of a corporation.[162] All the eligible capital of the partners, as well as all their commercial activities, are comprehended by the *mufāwaḍa* partnership. By virtue of this inclusiveness, each partner is fully liable for the actions and commitments of the other in all commercial matters. The claims of third parties are thus actionable against either partner; and conversely, either partner can press a claim against a third party, regardless of whether or not he was actually involved in the transaction which gave rise to that claim. As far as third parties are concerned, dealing with the individual *mufāwaḍa* partner is equivalent to dealing with the partnership firm. In this respect, the *mufāwaḍa* approaches the modern conception of partnership.

The relationship between the partners themselves, and between the partners and third parties in the various forms of Islamic partnership, can be summarized as follows: In all partnerships, including the *mufāwaḍa*, the liability is unlimited. In all partnerships, except the *mufāwaḍa,* the liability toward third parties is several but not joint; within the partnership, however, the liability is joint. In the *mufāwaḍa* partnership, liability toward third parties is both several and joint.[163] Liability in the *mufāwaḍa*, as well as the rights, privileges, and duties of the partners with respect to each other, is governed by the two fundamental legal principles upon which this partnership is based. The first is mutual agency (*wakāla*), which in Ḥanafī law is the basis of all forms of contractual partnership; within the scope of their joint undertaking, each partner is considered to be an agent of his colleague. The second principle, and the one which is unique to the *mufāwaḍa*, is that of mutual surety (*kafāla*). Not only is the *mufāwaḍa* partner his colleague's agent; he is also the guarantor (*kafīl*) for all his actions connected with the partnership. In some

[162] Cf., for example, the definition of corporation in Black, *Black's Dictionary of Law*, 3rd ed., St. Paul, 1933, p. 438.

[163] Cf. *Black's Dictionary of Law*, p. 1020: "A liability is said to be joint and several when the creditor may sue one or more of the parties to such liability separately, or all of them together at his option."

cases, this surety extends even unto matters not directly related to their business affairs.

The first priority of partnership in the view of Ḥanafī jurists is the attainment of profit by means of commerce and trade.[164] This point is constantly emphasized, and it is in the light of this over-all aim that the extent of each partner's freedom to dispose of the common property is determined. "The disposition of the *mufāwaḍa* partner is effective in all things which redound to the benefit of the partnership capital, regardless of whether or not the nature of his disposition is normally a part of trade."[165] This criterion is individually applied to the several types of transactions which in the normal course of trade the partners were likely to encounter, and the limit of their freedom of disposition in relation to each transaction is defined in some detail.[166] In all cases, two general categories of actions are consistently excluded. Neither partner may use the joint funds to his own private advantage, exclusive of that of the partnership; neither partner has the right of *tabarruʿ*, that is, the right of complete and unfettered ownership over the joint property.[167]

Ibḍāʿ in the *Mufāwaḍa* Partnership

If one of the *mufāwaḍa* partners gives over money or goods belonging to the partnership as a *biḍāʿa* to another person, there is no liability attaching to him *vis à vis* his partner. He is entitled to hand over goods or money as a *biḍāʿa*, as he is entitled to invest them in a *commenda* or to leave them as a deposit. He does not have the right to give a loan

[164] E.g., Sarakhsī, *Mabsūṭ*, 11:179, 198; *Kāsānī*, 6:57.

[165] *Kāsānī*, 6:73–74. For dispositions not normally part of trade, yet acceptable, cf., e.g., Sarakhsī, *Mabsūṭ*, 11:180–181; Shaybānī, *Aṣl Sharika*, fol. 66b.

[166] For example, the subheadings of the "Book of Partnership" in the *Aṣl*: "Chapter Concerning the Deposit of the *Mufāwaḍa* Partner," fol. 65-66b; "Chapter Concerning the Loan of the *Mufāwaḍa* Partner," fol. 66b–67b.

[167] Cf. Schacht, *Grundzüge*, p. 35, where *tabarruʿ* is defined as "das Recht zur Leistung aus eigener Initiative"; cf. also p. 51, where freedom of disposition (*taṣarruf*) is distinguished from *tabarruʿ*. The partner possesses the freedom of disposition within the context of his contractual relationship; he does not, however, possess absolute freedom of action with respect to the joint property as he would were the property entirely his own.

(*qarḍ*). If he does, he is liable for half the sum of the loan, but the *mufāwaḍa* is not thereby invalidated.[168]

This statement summarizes the partners' rights with respect to some of the types of business activities in which each partner might be called upon to engage. Foremost among these is the *biḍā'a* or *ibḍā'*, a transaction for which I have been unable to find a corresponding English term. Bergsträsser has translated it into German as "*Geschäftsführungsauftrag*."[169] It is easier to describe this practice than to define it. It involves a merchant who, unable personally to attend to a business affair, hands over some of his property to another party so that the latter will take care of it for him.[170] Upon completion of his task, the outside party, without receiving any commission, profit, or compensation in any other form,[171] returns the proceeds of the transaction to the merchant whose bidding he has done.

Of all formal contracts, it resembles that of agency most closely. Exactly in what way the *biḍā'a* relationship differs from agency is not made clear. From the context in which it is discussed, it appears to be a less formal type of relationship than that implied by agency, more akin to a favor which one merchant might do for another. It might best be described as a type of quasi-agency.

It may seem somewhat strange that merchants whose entire activity was directed toward making a profit would expend time and energy overseeing transactions from which there was no prospect of gain for themselves. It is not a question here of a casual or occasional favor, but of a recognized commercial practice looming large in the discussion of partnership on the same level as deposit, pledge, and similar contracts. The valuable information concerning the commercial techniques of

[168] Shaybānī, *Aṣl*, *Sharika*, fol. 61b, l. 19–fol. 62, l. 1.

[169] Schacht, *Grundzüge*, p. 75.

[170] This relationship is usually indicated by the phrase, "giving something over as a *biḍā'a*," with this last word in the accusative (*biḍā'atan*); the verb is *abḍa'a*; the owner of the goods is the *mubḍi'*; and the one who receives them the *mustabḍi'*.

[171] Cf. *Kāsānī*, 6:68: "the handling of merchandise in the *biḍā'a* is without compensation."

medieval Islamic trade provided by the Geniza records contributes toward a clearer appreciation of the role of *ibḍāʿ*. The term itself is, to the best of my knowledge, used only once,[172] but a practice corresponding to the *ibḍāʿ* figures prominently in the Geniza documents.

S. D. Goitein has described the practice in question as "informal commercial cooperation" and ascribed to it a central role in the Mediterranean trade of the eleventh century Islamic world. Numerous letters from merchants in southern Iran, Tunis, and Qayrawan addressed to colleagues in Old Cairo are replete with requests for business favors or reports on services rendered. These included a great variety of transactions. A merchant might be requested to take delivery of his correspondent's shipment, supervise its sale, and from the proceeds render payment to specified persons, or purchase local goods and dispatch them safely. Fulfillment of these requests often involved considerable expenditure of time and effort and held out no direct prospect of financial gain. Yet, as far as the Geniza records show, these requests were invariably carried out.

The prevalence of this informal cooperation or quasi-agency would appear to be connected less with mutual trust and friendship among merchants than with their common needs. Itinerant merchants and others engaged in long-distance trade could, in the course of their business careers, fully expect to encounter situations which would call for the cooperation and aid of colleagues in distant parts. A merchant, therefore, would be willing to invest much time and effort on behalf of a colleague, in the expectation that his effort would be reciprocated when the need arose. As one merchant expressed it in a Geniza letter, "you are in my place there, for you know well that I am your support here."[173]

172 Cf. *Fragments from the Cairo Geniza in the Freer Collection*, ed. Richard Gottheil and William H. Worrell, New York, 1927, p. 32, line 7, where the word *abḍaʿū* appears, but is incorrectly translated and understood.

173 Cf. Goitein, *Mediterranean Society*, pp. 164–169. A similar type of arrangement was apparently practiced in Western medieval trade. In discussing the operation of various forms of business association in medieval Europe, an eminent economic historian has the following to say: "It is

Entrusting some aspect of partnership business to an outside party in the form of quasi-agency known as *ibḍāʿ* is within the bounds of fidelity (*amāna*). Should any loss occur, neither the partner responsible for the *ibḍāʿ* (the *mubḍīʿ*) nor the quasi-agent (the *mustabḍīʿ*) bear any special liability. Such a loss is borne by the partnership, as would any other financial setback resulting from transactions personally conducted by either of the partners.

The actions of an individual *mufāwaḍa* partner are binding on his colleague. If a quasi-agent (*mustābḍiʿ*) made a purchase on behalf of the partnership, he can collect its price from either partner regardless of which one actually instructed him to make the purchase. In the event of the partnership's dissolution, any obligation arising from an *ibḍāʿ* commissioned by either of the partners before its dissolution, even if the actual execution of this commission took place after the dissolution but without the *mustābḍiʿ* being aware of this event, is reckoned on the account of the partnership and not on that of the individual partner involved.[174]

Deposits and Pledges in the *Mufāwaḍa*

Ḥanafī writers keep reiterating that the conduct of a partnership is posited on the customary practices of the merchants (*ʿadāt at-tujjār*). For this reason:

> Each partner has the right to deposit goods belonging to the partnership; for depositing is one of the customary practices of merchants. It is also one of the necessities of trade and one which is indispensable to the merchant. He has need of

possible that sometimes (as in the Hanseatic *Sendegeschäft*) the services of 'commissioner,' or even those of permanent 'factor,' were discharged without any apparent remuneration." (M. M. Postan, "Partnership in English Medieval Commerce," *Studi in Onore Di Armando Sapori*, Milan, 1957, 1:532–533.) In a note to this sentence (p. 533, n. 32), Postan comments that the remuneration for this service may have been indirect and that the recipient could at some other time avail himself of similar services on the part of the sender. This type of business relationship seems, however, to have been quite infrequent in the medieval West as compared with the situation in the Muslim world of that time.

174 Cf. Shaybānī, *Aṣl*, *Sharika*, fol. 62, ll. 20ff.

this transaction in many situations which are likely to occur. Since a partner has the right to pay a fee to have a deposit taken care of, he has this right, *a fortiori*, when no compensation is involved.[175]

Deposit is classified as an *amāna* contract and involves no payment of a fee or any other compensation to either party. A party would place money or goods in the custody of the depositary, whose task it was to safeguard them. The ownership of the property and, therefore, the risks remained with the depositor. The depositary could be held liable only in the case of negligence, and all obligations were extinguished with the return of the deposit.[176]

The use to which the depositary could put the deposited property was severely prescribed.[177] It may be due to this legal provision that the deposit contract apparently fulfilled such different functions in the Islamic world as compared with the medieval West. In the West, the depositary not only kept the goods, but also had the right to use them for a variety of commercial purposes. In consideration of this privilege, the deposit was returned to its owner with a premium, and deposit developed into a type of proto-banking.[178] It is not at all clear whether the deposit contract was put to similar uses in the Islamic world. Its function in Islamic law, as well as in earlier near Eastern legal traditions, was restricted to that implied by its title, the deposit and safeguarding of money or goods when circumstances did not permit this to be accomplished by their owner.[179]

175 *Kāsānī*, 6:68.

176 For a thorough treatment of the deposit contract as conceived by all the major Islamic legal schools, cf. O. Spies, "Das Depositum . . . ," *Zeitschrift für vergleichende Rechtswissenschaft*, 45 (1930):241–300; also Schacht, *Grundzüge*, p. 76.

177 Only the Ḥanafīs permit some slight use to be made of the deposited property; the other schools prohibit the depositary from making any use of it. Cf. Spies, *op. cit.*, pp. 273–275.

178 Cf. Robert S. Lopez and I. W. Raymond, *Medieval Trade in the Mediterranean World*, New York, 1955, pp. 212–215.

179 For Jewish law, cf. *JE*, s.v. *Bailments* (2:451–459). The function of deposits in the banking activity reflected in the Geniza documents remains yet to be clarified, i.e., the conditions under which people entrusted funds

Any loss of, or damage to, deposited partnership property is borne by the partnership; no individual liability attaches to the partner who arranged for the deposit. Either partner is entitled to retrieve the deposit, and either one can bring suit against the depositary in case of the latter's negligence.[180]

The use of pledges[181] on behalf of partnership business is governed by the same rules as those of the deposit. Either *mufāwaḍa* partner may independently give a pledge as guarantee of payment for credit extended to the partnership or take a pledge as a security for payment of a debt owed to the company. In either case, both partners are equally bound by the contract.[182]

Loan in the *Mufāwaḍa*

Islamic law distinguishes between two types of loans. One, the *'āriyya*, is a loan for use which transfers the usufruct of property gratis to the borrower. The ownership of the object of the loan remains that of the lender, and the borrower is not liable for any destruction of the loaned property or any diminution of its value except in the event of negligence. "The borrower is entitled to make use of the loan without compensation in accordance with the conditions of the contract or custom. He must meet the maintenance expenses of the property while it is in his possession and must return it in substance at the termination of the loan."[183] The second type of loan, the *qarḍ*, involves the loan of fungible commodities, that is, goods which may be estimated and replaced according to weight, measure, and number. In this case, the borrower undertakes to return the equivalent or likes of that which he has received, but without any premium on the prop-

---

to "bankers" may have been those of a loan or of some special form of investment, and those of a deposit. Cf. Goitein, *Mediterranean Society*, pp. 246ff.

180 Cf. Shaybānī, *Aṣl, Sharika*, fol. 65b, l. 16–fol. 66b, l. 4.

181 Re: the general features of the pledge contract in Ḥanafī law, cf. Schacht, *Grundzüge*, pp. 55–56.

182 Cf. Shaybānī, *Aṣl, Sharika*, fol. 70b, l. 6–fol. 71, l. 3.

183 Mahmasani in *Law in the Middle East*, p. 199; cf. also, Schacht, *Grundzüge*, pp. 76–77, and *EI*, 2nd ed., 1:633.

erty, which would, of course, be construed as interest.[184] The most likely object of a *qarḍ* loan would be currency or some other standard means of exchange. This twofold division corresponds approximately, although not exactly, to the Western distinction between *commodatum*—a loan for use, and *mutuum*—a loan for consumption.[185]

Neither *mufāwaḍa* partner has the right individually to grant a *qarḍ* loan from the common funds. The bonds of mutual agency and surety between the partners extend only to matters connected with trade. Granting this type of loan is not considered a part of trade, but is classified as an act of *tabarru'*, that is, an act which is permissible only with property wholly owned by the person disposing of it. A *qarḍ* loan can be given only with the full agreement of both partners.[186]

> By analogy to the *qarḍ* loan, the *mufāwaḍa* partners should also not be entitled to grant a loan for use (*'āriyya*). If one of the partners does so, and lends out a pack animal belonging to the partnership which collapses under the borrower, then, by analogy, the lender shall be liable for half the value of the animal to his colleague. However, on the grounds of juristic preference, I (Shaybānī) do not hold him liable. . . . Similarly, if he lends out a garment belonging to the partnership, and it is destroyed while in the possession of the borrower, no liability attaches either to the lender or the borrower.[187]

The *mufāwaḍa* partner's right to grant loans for use from the partnership property without incurring any special liability in case of loss or damage is not unqualified. It was intended

[184] Mahmasani in *Law in the Middle East*, pp. 199–200.

[185] Cf. *Black's Dictionary of Law*, p. 1126: "Loan for use (called '*commodatum*' in the civil law) differs from a loan for consumption (called '*mutuum*' in the civil law) in this: that the *commodatum* must be specifically returned; the *mutuum* is to be returned in kind. In the case of a *commodatum*, the property in the thing remains in the lender; in a *mutuum*, the property passes to the borrower." Cf. also, Buckland, *A Text-Book of Roman Law*, pp. 462–473; Santillana, *Istituzioni*, 2:373–397.

[186] Cf. Shaybānī, *Aṣl, Sharika*, fol. 62, l. 20–fol. 62b, l. 1; *Kāsānī*, 6:72.

[187] Shaybānī, *Aṣl, Sharika*, fol. 62b, ll. 1–3.

to apply primarily to what Sarakhsī calls "the accompaniments of trade."[188]

> Granting loans for use is one of the accompaniments of trade from which the merchant finds no escape. If someone with whom he is doing business approaches him, he has no alternative but to lend him a garment to wear or a pillow to recline upon, nor has he an alternative to lending out a balance and scales to some of his neighbors. For he who does not grant loans for use to others, will not receive them when he is in need of them.[189]

Use of partnership property for loans and for other generous purposes was conditioned by custom and by business expediency. In those days, as in our own, the good will of customers, clients, and business associates was very much prized; to nurture this good will by means of small favors was viewed with approval. There was also an element of practical foresight involved; for if no favors were given, none could be expected in return when they might be needed.

The extent of these favors and loans was ultimately determined by custom. Use of the common property by one partner for the giving of a gift is proscribed because it cannot be construed as constituting an integral part of trade. Exceptions are made in the case of bread, fruit, and meat, or in the case of an invitation to a meal extended by a *mufāwaḍa* partner to an outside party, since sharing food with colleagues is "a practice of the merchants."[190] The basis for distinguishing between those favors which an individual partner can dispense while still remaining within the bounds of propriety and those which constitute a violation of fidelity is the prevalent business custom; "the source for knowing the difference between them is common usage."[191]

188 Arabic: *tawābi' at-tijāra.*

189 Sarakhsī, *Mabsūṭ,* 11:180–181; cf. also, Shaybānī, *Aṣl, Sharika,* fol. 66b, l. 5–fol. 67b, l. 21. The savings which might accrue to merchants as a result of such small favors can be appreciated in the light of Albert Dietrich, *Arabische Briefe,* Hamburg, 1955, pp. 130–131, where there is reference to a four-dirham rental fee for the use of a saddle.

190 Sarakhsī, *Mabsūṭ* 11:193; Arabic: *min ṣanī' at-tujjār.*

191 *Ibid.*: *wal-marja' fī ma'rifat al-firq baynahumā ilā al-'urf.*

Just as a partner was entitled, within certain limits, to grant loans for use, so too did he have the right to accept them.[192] In case of any mishap for which the borrower would be liable, that is, negligence or non-adherence to the conditions of the loan contract, the responsibility of the partnership is contingent upon the use to which the borrowed property was put. If it was used for purposes connected with partnership business, then any negligence or breach of contract notwithstanding, the liability attaches to the partnership. If it was put to private use, the borrowing partner is liable for the damages from his own share of the profits.[193]

Purchase, Sale, and Debts of the *Mufāwaḍa* Partners

Any business purchase made by one *mufāwaḍa* partner, be it merchandise, slaves, houses, or whatever, belongs in equal shares to each partner. By analogy, this should also be true of clothing, food, and other household necessities purchased for the consumption of the partners' families; by exercise of juristic preference, the application of analogy is suspended in this case, and the ownership of personal items is assigned exclusively to the purchasing partner.

What is true of partnership purchases applies equally to the proceeds of any sale of the joint property.[194]

In regard to the rights and obligations arising from any purchase or sale in connection with their joint enterprise, the *mufāwaḍa* partners are, from the point of view of third parties, like one individual. The price of a purchase made by one of them is collectable from the other; either partner may cancel a sale or purchase made by the other, and either one may return, because of some flaw (*ʿayb*), merchandise purchased by the other.[195] Any sale or purchase on credit is binding on both partners.[196]

Concerning the payment and collection of debts, Ḥanafī law distinguishes between debts owed by one of the partners and

[192] Cf. Shaybānī, *Aṣl, Sharika*, fol. 67, ll. 1ff.
[193] *Ibid.*, ll. 5–10.
[194] *Ibid.*, fol. 73–fol. 73b; *Kāsānī*, 6:74.
[195] *Kāsānī*, 6:70–71, 75.
[196] Shaybānī, *Aṣl, Sharika*, fol. 74, l. 2.

debts owed to one of the partners.[197] Money owed by one of them can be collected from either, because a commitment made by one partner is binding on the other. This includes all debts[198] except those arising from criminal liability (*jināya*) or from marital obligations, such as the amount due for a bride price (*mahr*). These last two categories of activities are beyond the bounds of the mutual surety comprehended by the *mufāwaḍa* partnership.

Not all the debts owed to one of the partners can be collected by his colleague from the debtor. For example, the proceeds from the sale of property inherited by one of the partners, and consequently not part of the joint capital, can be collected only by the partner concerned.

Expenses of the *Mufāwaḍa* Partners

All expenses connected with the pursuit of trade are to be covered from partnership funds. These include living expenses while traveling on business, fees to cover the hiring of help and equipment for the transportation and handling of merchandise, taxes and customs expenses, as well as various amenities, such as small gifts and dinner invitations to customers and colleagues. These expenses are all borne by the partnership, and, regardless of which of the two partners incurred them, any resulting debt can be collected from either of them.

As already noted, supplies for each partner's household are not considered common property, but are assigned to the private ownership of the partners. Debts incurred by one of the partners for his personal expenses can be collected from his colleague regardless of whether or not these were incurred with the latter's knowledge or permission. At the appointed times in which the income of their joint venture is divided between them, these sums are deducted from the account of the partner involved.[199]

197 *Ibid.*, fol. 73b, ll. 10–13.

198 This also covers debts incurred for personal and family needs. The partners then settle their accounts between themselves.

199 Shaybānī, *Aṣl*, *Sharika*, fol. 69b, l. 9; fol. 70, l. 13; fol. 73, l. 6; fol. 73b, l. 13. It would appear that in actual practice there was no standard procedure for the treatment of personal expenses in partnership, but

For example, if a *mufāwaḍa* partner should engage transportation for a pilgrimage to Mecca, the expenses for the journey would ultimately have to be paid from his private funds. The party supplying the transportation could, however, demand payment at any time from the pilgrim's partner. If the pilgrim combined the fulfillment of his religious duties with the pursuit of business, the cost of the entire trip could legitimately be deducted from partnership funds.[200]

Certain exceptional personal expenses incurred by one partner without his colleague's permission are not subject to the procedures outlined above. Prominent among these, and the case to which most attention is devoted in the legal literature, is the unilateral purchase of a slave girl.

> A *mufāwaḍa* partner is not entitled to purchase a slave girl for purposes of intercourse or general service without the express permission of his partner. A slave girl is a valid object of common ownership, and there is nothing which would require her being owned by one of them to the exclusion of the other. She is to be considered like other objects belonging jointly to both partners. This is unlike the case of food and clothing in which there is a necessity exempting them from the communality of partnership. There is no such necessity in the case of a slave girl, and she is comprehended by this communality.[201]

A slave girl was considered a perfectly valid object of trade, one in which, like all other categories of merchandise, the partners were free to deal. The problem here is the purchase with partnership funds of a slave girl for the very private and personal use of only one of the partners. This practice, which to contemporary eyes might appear as a flagrant abuse of expense

---

that this varied from one contract to another. Cf., e.g., S. D. Goitein, *Jewish Education in Muslim Countries*, Jerusalem, 1962, p. 34, where a partnership contract stipulated that flour, wine, and other daily household necessities should be paid out of partnership funds, whereas housing expenses and tuition for children's education would be paid from each partner's private funds.

200 Shaybānī, *Aṣl*, *Sharika*, fol. 70, ll. 4–8.

201 *Kāsānī*, 6:74.

account privileges, was not seen quite in that light by the early Ḥanafī jurists. One need only recall Pegolotti's advice to European merchants traveling to Cathay: "And if the merchant wishes to take along from Tana any woman with him, he may do so—and if he does not wish to take one, there is no objection; yet if he takes one, he will be regarded as a man of higher condition than if he does not take one."[202] One can also point to instances of merchants' relations with slave girls mentioned in the Geniza documents.[203] From the point of view of Ḥanafī partnership law, the companionship of a slave girl is not seen from the perspective of the increased stature that might accrue to a merchant as a result of such a liaison, but from the standpoint of physical need. The consensus of Ḥanafī opinion is that intercourse with a slave girl is not a need comparable to that for food and clothing.[204] Consequently, the price of a slave girl purchased by one partner for his exclusive gratification cannot be demanded from his colleague, as would be the case if the subject of the purchase were food or other less controversial household necessities.[205]

Investments with Third Parties

The most significant circumstance affecting the *mufāwaḍa* partner's investments with third parties is the fact that all commercial transactions he partakes in are comprehended by the partnership agreement. The comprehensiveness or generality (*'umūm*) of the *mufāwaḍa* partnership precludes any independent business activity on the part of either partner. The *mufāwaḍa* partner may make or accept on his own only those types of investments which are in consonance with this feature of the partnership.

202 Quoted in Lopez and Raymond, *Medieval Trade in the Mediterranean World*, pp. 356–357, from a selection from Pegolotti's fourteenth century trade manual *La pratica della mercatura.*

203 Cf. S. D. Goitein, "From the Mediterranean to India," *SPECULUM* 29 (1954):189, where reference is made to an India merchant who abandoned a slave girl who had borne him a child.

204 For a discussion of this problem by Ḥanafī jurists in a different context, that of the physical needs of an imprisoned person, cf. F. Rosenthal, *The Muslim Concept of Freedom*, Leiden, 1960, p. 64.

205 Shaybānī, *Aṣl*, *Sharika*, fol. 73b, ll. 12–13.

Without the prior consultation of his colleague, the *mufāwaḍa* partner may invest cash or goods in a *commenda,* or accept capital from outside parties as a *commenda.* Any profits or losses resulting from such an enterprise are reckoned to the partnership account and are shared equally by both partners.[206]

The same holds true of a limited investment partnership. A *mufāwaḍa* partner may on his own initiative and without the prior consent or knowledge of his colleague negotiate an *'inān* partnership with a third party. This can be either a single venture partnership (*'inān khāṣṣ*) or a more inclusive type of association (*'inān 'āmm*). In either case, the commitment by one *mufāwaḍa* partner of the joint capital to such an enterprise is binding on his colleague.[207]

The one type of association which neither party can contract on his own with third parties is a *mufāwaḍa* partnership. The full and express agreement of all parties to a *mufāwaḍa* is required before any new partners can be added to the partnership.[208] The latter would, of course, have to meet the standards of equality with respect to personal status and property required for a valid *mufāwaḍa.*

If a partner should negotiate a *mufāwaḍa* without his colleague's permission, and the latter objected to it, the agreement is voided and is treated as an *'inān* partnership.

In addition to profits from outside investments, any wage earned by either of the partners (*iktisāb*) for rendering some service to a third party becomes part of their joint capital.[209]

Slaves in the *Mufāwaḍa*

Slaves fulfilled a variety of functions in medieval Islamic society; their services ranged from those of domestic servants to those of concubine, eunuch, business representative, or

[206] *Ibid.*, fol. 61b, l. 20.

[207] *Ibid.*, fol. 70b, ll. 14ff. For actual examples of partnerships within a partnership, often involving considerable sums of money, cf. Goitein, *Jewish Education in Muslim Countries*, pp. 124–125.

[208] Shaybānī, *Aṣl*, *Sharika*, fol. 70, l. 18.

[209] *Ibid.*, ll. 1ff.

mercenary.[210] In the context of this discussion of the conduct of the *mufāwaḍa* partnership, it would be convenient to adopt Shaybānī's functional classification of slaves—those that are intended for trade (*lil-tijāra*) and those that are intended for service (*lil-khidma*).[211]

Slaves acquired by the partnership for the purposes of trade are subject to the same general considerations as any other commodity of commerce. Each partner has the right to buy and sell this category of slaves and to trade with them in any manner that might bring advantage to the partnership. The freedom of action of the partners *vis-à-vis* jointly owned slaves of this type did not, therefore, necessitate any special definition or clarification.

The conduct of the partners in relation to service slaves or slaves that remained under their joint ownership for an extended period of time did require some definition.

Neither partner possessed the right of unilateral manumission of a jointly owned slave. While setting a slave free was a meritorious act, it constituted a *tabarru'*,[212] an act which is not effective with someone else's property. If a *mufāwaḍa* partner did manumit a partnership slave, the manumission is effective, but the freeing partner is obligated to reimburse his colleague from his private funds to the extent of one half the value of the slave. A partnership slave can, of course, be set free with the common approval of both partners.[213]

Either *mufāwaḍa* partner may unilaterally empower a slave for trade (*ma'dhūn lil-tijāra*)[214] or may grant him the status of *mukātab*, that is, the right for the slave to buy his freedom by

210 Cf. A. Mez, *The Renaissance of Islam*, trans. S. Khuda Bakhsh and D. S. Margoliouth, Patna, 1937, pp. 156–169.

211 Shaybānī, *Al-jāmi' aṣ-ṣaghīr*, p. 19, where this distinction has a practical significance in relation to the payment of the *zakāt* tax. In relation to partnership, this distinction is purely functional, one which makes possible a clearer presentation of each partner's rights *vis-à-vis* commonly owned slaves. There is nothing rigid about this classification, since the use to which a slave was put remained entirely at the discretion of the owners.

212 Cf. above, n. 167.

213 Shaybānī, *Aṣl*, *Sharika*, fol. 69, ll. 17–18; Sarakhsī, *Mabsūṭ*, 11:199.

214 This type of slave is also referred to as *'abd tājir*—"merchant slave"; cf. e.g., Shaybānī, *Aṣl*, *Sharika*, fol. 69, l. 21.

installments.[215] These actions are undoubtedly allowed because in neither case is there any loss to the partnership and because of the prevailing prejudices in Islamic law for the enfranchisement of slaves. The status accorded the slave by one partner is binding on his colleague.[216]

A partner may, without seeking the approval of his colleague, arrange for the marriage of a female slave belonging to both of them. He does not, however, have the right to dispose similarly of a male slave. Unilateral action with respect to female slaves was permitted because of the income to be derived by the partnership from the bride-price (*mahr*) paid by the prospective husband. In the case of a male slave, the opposite is true; the partnership would incur the expense of the bride-price in addition to the living expenses (*nafaqāt*) which the slave would be obligated to provide for his spouse.[217]

Limits of Mutual Surety

The mutual surety existing between the *mufāwaḍa* partners is operative in all activities connected with trade. By the application of juristic preference, the limits of their mutual surety are extended to include certain activities not directly related to their business affairs, such as their household and personal expenses. Where no explicit exceptions are made, the mutual surety of the partners is confined to their business-connected activities.

Any indemnity for which one of the partners may be liable as a result of some criminal action (*jināya*) is borne solely by him. His colleague is in no way obligated, not even to the extent of paying the fine and then collecting the sum from the offending partner. No consideration is given to the circumstances in which the crime occurred, whether it was intentional or unintentional, or whether or not it took place in the

215 Cf. Schacht, *Grundzüge*, p. 42, for the details of the *mukātaba* contract.

216 Shaybānī, *Aṣl*, *Sharika*, fol. 69, ll. 16–17; Sarakhsī, *Mabsūṭ*, 11:199; Re: predisposition of Islamic law toward the manumission of slaves, cf. Schacht, *Introduction*, pp. 129ff.

217 Shaybānī, *Aṣl*, *Sharika*, fol. 69. ll. 19–21: *Kāsānī*, 6:73. On the problem of disposition of jointly owned slaves, cf. also, Shaybānī, *Al-jāmi' aṣ-ṣaghīr*, p. 106; Shaybānī, *Amālī*, pp. 56–57; Abū Yūsuf, *Ikhtilāf*, pp. 93–97.

course of some commercial activity. The rule is quite absolute; a *mufāwaḍa* partner's surety for his colleague arises only from "causes of trade" and not from "causes of criminality."[218]

> If one of the *mufāwaḍa* partners commits a crime, in error or by premeditation, no liability attaches to his colleague. It makes no difference whether the crime is established by proof or by a confession. This applies to crimes committed against persons, as well as to less severe crimes, because this is not a part of trade. In the event that the criminal arranges for a monetary settlement corresponding to the penalty for this particular crime, the victim can bring no claim for the payment of this sum against the other partner. If a third party guarantees the payment of the penalty imposed, he cannot hold the other partner liable for the repayment of that sum. If one of the partners serves as a guarantor for the payment of a criminal fine imposed upon a third party, the guarantee is binding only on that partner, and not on his colleague, because this is not a part of trade.[219]

The commission of a crime by one of the partners and the imposition of a monetary fine upon him do not necessarily affect the continuity of the partnership. If it is possible for the criminal partner to pay the penalty from his own share of the proceeds, the validity of the partnership is not affected.[220]

All financial obligations connected with the marriage and family life of the partners, such as the payment of a bride-price or divorce settlement, or any other mandatory payments which a marriage contract might give rise to, are the exclusive responsibility of the partner involved. Neither the partner's wife nor any other member of his family can press a claim against his colleague for the fulfillment of any of these obligations. All these matters are not connected with trade and are legally considered in the same category as the liabilities resulting from a criminal act.[221]

Abū Ḥanīfa carries the separation of family and business

[218] *Kāsānī,* 6:73.
[219] Shaybānī, *Aṣl, Sharika,* fol. 70, ll. 13–17.
[220] *Ibid.*, fol. 71, l. 20–fol. 71b, l. 2.
[221] *Ibid.*, fol. 71b, ll. 4–6.

affairs to the point where he does not consider a business debt acknowledged by a partner to his wife as binding on the other partner. By analogy, he extends this rule to include all relatives whose relationship to the partner would invalidate their testimony in support of his claim. Abū Yūsuf holds, and his seems to have become the prevalent Ḥanafī opinion, that any business debt acknowledged by one partner is binding on his colleague, irrespective of the family relationship of the creditor.[222]

Dissolution of the Partnership

The circumstances affecting the termination of a contractual partnership are divided into two categories: (1) Those which lead to the dissolution of all contractual partnerships; and (2) Those which terminate only particular types of partnerships.

The death of one of the partners results in the immediate termination of a partnership regardless of whether or not the surviving partner is aware of this event. "For each of them is the agent of the other, and the death of the empowering agent has the effect of discharging the agent, whether the latter knew or did not know about it."[223] Any transactions conducted by the surviving partner after his colleague's demise, and in ignorance of that fact, are strictly on his own account. Heirs of the deceased partner have no claim to the profits, nor are they liable for any obligations which might arise from such transactions. Their rights and obligations are limited to the business transacted up to the time of their benefactor's death.

There are no provisions in Islamic law by means of which a partnership can remain intact after the death of one of its members. If the heirs wish to continue the association with the surviving partner, they must negotiate a completely new agreement.

If both partners were Muslims, the apostasy of one of them and his emigration to non-Muslim territory (*dār al-ḥarb*) results in the termination of the partnership. Apostasy has the same legal effects as the death of a partner. The same is true of the loss of mental competence by one of the partners, since

[222] *Ibid.*, ll. 11ff. [223] *Kāsānī*, 6:78.

this condition, like death and apostasy, severs the relationship of mutual agency existing between the partners.[224]

Any partnership can be terminated by the unilateral abrogation of one of its members. In this case, however, the dissolution of the partnership does not become effective until the other partner becomes aware of his colleague's action.[225]

The lapsing of equality in eligible capital is the one factor leading to dissolution of partnerships which is particular only to the *mufāwaḍa*. Equality in the ownership of eligible capital is not only a prerequisite for the formation of a valid *mufāwaḍa* partnership, but also for its continued operation. If one of the partners should inherit or receive a gift of property the form of which is eligible for partnership investment, this would lead to an inequality between the partners and to the termination of the partnership. The partnership would not come to an end at the time of inheritance, but only at the moment the partner took physical possession (*qabḍ*) of the property involved.[226]

224 *Ibid.*
225 *Ibid.*, pp. 77–78.
226 *Ibid.*, pp. 78–79.

IV

Ḥanafī Limited Investment Partnership (*'Inān*)

One can describe the *'inān* partnership as conceived in Ḥanafī law by stating that any contractual partnership (*sharikat al-'aqd*) which is not a *mufāwaḍa* partnership is an *'inān*. Any partnership which does not include all the commercial transactions of the parties concerned and which does not demand equality in investment, personal status, and the distribution of profits and liabilities is an *'inān* partnership. Unlike the *mufāwaḍa*, the *'inān* can take on a variety of forms *vis-à-vis* each partner's contribution to the common capital and the share of profit and liability allotted to each, as well as to the categories of trade and merchandise which it comprehends.

It is not only its structural features which distinguish the *'inān* from the *mufāwaḍa* partnership. Each *mufāwaḍa* partner is both the agent of (*wakīl*) and guarantor for (*kafīl*) his colleague. In the *'inān* partnership, the relations of the partners to third parties and those between themselves are based exclusively on the principle of agency. Each partner is only the agent and not the guarantor of his colleague; and this mutual agency is valid only in the area of commerce covered by their partnership or to the extent of their joint capital. As contrasted to the *mufāwaḍa*, this difference confines the partners' freedom of action in the conduct of business and severely curtails the rights and claims of third parties toward the partnership.[1]

Al-Qudūrī succinctly summarizes the main features and principles of the *'inān* partnership as follows:

> As for a limited investment partnership (*'inān*), it is contracted on the basis of mutual agency, but not mutual surety. It is valid in the case of a disparity between each partner's investment, and it is valid when they invest equally, but

[1] Cf. Sarakhsī, *Mabsūṭ*, 30 vols., Cairo, 1324/1906–1331/1912, 11:174: "As for an *'inān* partnership, it comprehends mutual agency, but not mutual surety; by virtue of mutual agency each partner is not liable for that which is upon (i.e., any obligation of) his colleague."

share the profits unequally. It is further permissible for either of the parties to invest only a part of their property, while the rest remains outside of the partnership. The form of the capital with which it is permissible to contract a limited investment partnership is the same as that which was indicated as permissible in a universal partnership (*mufāwaḍa*). It is permissible for one to invest dirhams and the other dinars. The price of whatever either of the partners buys for the partnership can be claimed from him alone. He may then demand remuneration from the other partner for the latter's share in it. If the entire partnership capital, or the capital of one of the partners is lost before anything is bought, the partnership is nullified. However, if one of them purchases something with his own share of the capital, and then the other partner's share is lost before anything is purchased with it, the purchased merchandise is common property in accordance with their partnership agreement, and the one who laid out the money may demand remuneration from his partner for the latter's share of its cost. The partnership is valid even if the two shares of capital have not been intermingled. The partnership is not valid, however, if it is stipulated that one of the partners receives a specified number of dirhams from the profit.[2]

Derivation of the Term *'Inān*

The derivation of the term *'inān* as a designation for the limited investment partnership was a subject of some dispute among Muslim legal writers. Aside from its inherent etymological interest, this discussion has some bearing on the historical derviation of the *'inān* partnership.

As for the term *'inān*, it is derived from the phrase "it presented itself to me," (*'anna lī*) that is, it appeared (*'araḍa*). Imru'-l-Qays said:

"A flock presented itself to us (*'anna lanā*), the cows among them like Duwar virgins mantled in their long-trailing draperies."[3]

[2] Al-Qudūrī, *Mukhtaṣar*, Istanbul, 1319/1901, p. 53.

[3] Imru'-l-Qays, died ca. A.D. 540; cf. Brockelmann, *Geschichte der*

Some of the Kufan scholars have claimed that this is a term which they themselves had innovated, and that the early Arabs had not used it in their speech. However, this is not so, for Nābigha al-Ja'dī had already said:[4]

"We made a partnership with Quraysh in their purity
And in their noble descent—an *'inān* partnership."

It is also said that the term is derived from the reins (*'inān*) of a pack animal, in the sense that the rider holds the reins with one hand and does something else with the other. Similarly, each of the partners transfers to his colleague the reins of disposition for only a portion of the joint capital. It could also be derived from the fact that a pack animal has two reins, one of them longer and the other one shorter; similarly, this partnership is permissible both with equal and unequal shares in the investment and profit on the part of the partners, and is therefore designated *'inān*.[5]

More detailed information concerning the Kufan attribution of the term *'inān* is provided by Ṭaḥāwī.

There are some legal scholars who consider the two terms *'inān* and *mufāwaḍa* as meaning the same thing. I have heard Bakkār b. Qutayba[6] report that Abū 'Āṣim an-Nabīl[7] was asked about the phrase *'inān* partnership as used by his colleagues, that is, Abū Ḥanīfa and his colleagues, and he (Abū 'Āṣim) said: "This term was employed by the scholars of Kufa, and in reality *'inān* and *mufāwaḍa* have one meaning with no difference between them." I mentioned this to Ibn Abī 'Imrān[8] and he refuted him saying: "Indeed, the term *'inān* in this connection has a meaning other than that

---

arabischen Litteratur (*GAL*), 1:24 (15), *Supp.*, 3 vols., Leiden, 1937–1943, 1:48–50. The lines quoted here are from his *mu'allaqa*; the translation is taken from A. J. Arberry, *The Seven Odes, The First Chapter in Arabic Literature*, New York, 1957, p. 65.

4 Died A.D. 684; cf. Brockelmann, *Supp.*, 1:92.

5 Sarakhsī, *Mabsūṭ*, 11:151–152.

6 Died 270/883; cf. Ibn Qutlūbughā, *Tāj at-tarājim*, Baghdad, 1962, pp. 19–20.

7 Mentioned *ibid.*, p. 7, as one of the teachers of al-Khaṣṣāf (d.261/874).

8 Unidentified.

of the term *mufāwaḍa*. An *'inān* partnership is one in which the communality is specified, whereas a *mufāwaḍa* is one in which the communality comprehends all things. The term *'inān* used in this sense is derived from the reins of a pack animal which serve to restrain the animal from some things."[9]

On the basis of the verse ascribed to Nābigha al-Ja'dī, W. Heffening has suggested that "historically it is probable that this *Sh. al-'Inān* is the older form; . . . on the other hand, the *Sh. al-Mufāwaḍa* (*societas questus*) seems to have been taken over from Roman-Byzantine law."[10] Without a thorough sifting of the evidence, which is in any case quite meager, the best one can do is speculate as to the origins of these two partnership forms among the early Muslims. Even if the verse ascribed to Nābigha is authentic, there is still the possibility, as suggested by Abū 'Āṣim, that in the early period *'inān* and *mufāwaḍa* were undifferentiated terms for partnership. Some support for this view is found in the fact that the Ḥanafī term *'inān* and the Mālikī term *mufāwaḍa* designate essentially the same type of partnership.[11]

On general evolutionary grounds one would suspect that the opposite of what Heffening suggests should hold true. Western legal historians have suggested that one of the oldest forms of partnership was that which originated in the family circle, and in which the duration and investment were unlimited and the scope all-embracing. Indeed, the medieval European term for partnership, *compagnia*, seems to have been derived from medieval Latin *cumpanis*—"one eating the same bread."[12] The *mufāwaḍa* partnership possessed features similar to those of the early medieval family *compagnia* and was eminently well suited to a society in which the extended

[9] Ṭaḥāwī, *Kitāb ash-shurūṭ aṣ-ṣaghīr*, ms. *Bayazit* 18905, fol. 95, ll. 13–18.

[10] *Encyclopaedia of Islam* (*EI*), 1st ed., Leiden, 1913–1934, 3:381.

[11] Cf. Saḥnūn, *Mudawwana*, 16 vols., Damascus, n.d., 12:68, and discussion of terminology at the beginning of Chapter 5.

[12] Cf. Robert S. Lopez and I. W. Raymond, *Medieval Trade in the Mediterranean World*, New York, 1955, pp. 185–186 and references there; also Max Weber, *Zur Geschichte der Handelsgesellschaften in Mittelalter*, Stuttgart, 1889.

family or tribe was the basic unit of social, political, and economic life. Such a situation, for example, existed in the Arabian trading cities in the decades preceding the rise of Islam, and it is conceivable that the commercial activities of the leading Meccan families were partially carried out in some form of proto-*mufāwaḍa* association.

Specified and General *'Inān* Partnerships

The *mufāwaḍa* partnership has essentially one form and is subdivided by Ḥanafī jurists only according to the nature of the capital invested by the partners, that is, either case, labor, or credit. In addition to its classification according to investment type, the *'inān* partnership is divided on the basis of its scope into two general categories: specified (*khāṣṣ* and general (*'āmm*).

> It is permissible in its general form, that is, when two people form a partnership for general trade; and it is permissible in its specified form, that is, when two people form a partnership for a specific category of merchandise, as, for example, cloth, or silk, or slaves, or garments, etcetera.[13]

The general *'inān* was formed for the purposes of general trade, with no restrictions with respect to the commodities that could be dealt with or the transactions that could be negotiated. Any legitimate trading activity designed to bring profit to the company came within its purview. In this respect it resembles the *mufāwaḍa* partnership and the companies of Western medieval trade. The only limitation to which the as-

[13] *Kāsānī*, 7 vols., Cairo, 1328/1910, 6:62. The terms *'inān khāṣṣ* and *'inān 'āmm* do not occur in Shaybānī's *Kitāb al-aṣl*. The specified *'inān* is designated by the following terms and phrases: *sharikat 'inān fī tijāra khaṣṣa* —"an *'inān* partnership in a specified trade," fol. 57b, l. 3; *wa-kānat tijāratuhumā ma'lūma khāṣṣa fī bāb dūna al-abwāb,*—"and their trade was known and specified and of a definite category," fol. 57b, l. 12; *sharikayn fī sil'a khāṣṣa*—"two partners in a specified commodity," fol. 69b, l. 17; the same phrase also in fol. 70, l. 15. A general *'inān* is termed: *sharikat 'inān fil-bay' wash-shirā',*—"an *'inān* partnership for the purpose of sale and purchase," e.g., fol. 69b, ll. 1 and 17. This latter phrase is usually found in juxtaposition to one of the designations for a specified *'inān* partnership.

sociates in a general *'inān* partnership were subject was the extent of their joint capital.

The specified *'inān* confined the partners to trade with a certain category of goods defined in the partnership agreement. This arrangement could be a continuing one, enduring over a considerable period of time and involving numerous transactions, or it could be limited to a single venture, the purchase of the desired merchandise and its subsequent division or resale. The mutual agency of the associates in a specified *'inān* extended only to those commodities or areas of trade agreed upon and no further.

> If, after having formed an *'inān* partnership in a specified trade with the condition that each partner may buy and sell for cash and credit, one of them buys something outside of this specified category, it belongs exclusively to him. By virtue of the partnership, each of them becomes the agent of his colleague; but agency is subject to specification. If they specify a certain type of goods, then each partner is as a stranger in relation to any goods purchased by his colleague other than those specified. These goods belong exclusively to the purchaser. As for the specified goods, their purchase or sale, for cash or credit, by one of the partners is binding on his colleague.[14]

The specified *'inān* bears a close resemblance to that form of commercial association in medieval English trade which M. M. Postan has described as an occasional partnership. Such a partnership "began with the purchase of a 'certain merchandise' and ended with its division or joint sale. . . . They regarded themselves as partners in a specified deal or, as they preferred to describe themselves, 'partners in certain merchandise.' "[15] On the basis of documentary evidence, Postan

[14] Sarakhsī, *Mabsūṭ*, 11:173–174.

[15] Postan, "Partnership in English Medieval Commerce," *Studi in Onore di A. Sapori*, 1:540. Even if purely coincidental, it is nevertheless interesting that the phrase used to characterize this early form of English partnership, "partners in a certain merchandise," is identical with one of the Arabic phrases used in the late eighth century to describe the same type of arrangement, *viz.*, "*sharīkayn fī sil'a khāṣṣa*," cf. Shaybānī, *Aṣl*, *Sharika*, fol. 69b, l. 17.

asserts that "the essential function of this partnership was financial. It had for its purpose to enable a large purchase to be made by persons who were unwilling to do it themselves or on their sole responsibility."[16]

In spite of the great difference, both geographical and historical, between the milieu of medieval Islamic and English trade, it would be reasonable to assume that the specific *'inān* partnership fulfilled a function in Islamic trade similar to that of the single-venture partnership in English trade. According to S. D. Goitein, most of the partnerships recorded in the Geniza documents were of short duration and limited to specific undertakings.[17] When these documents are published, a more definite evaluation of the role of specified short-term partnerships will be possible.

Formation of the *'Inān* Partnership

Personal Status

Participation in an *'inān* partnership is open to any person meeting the minimum standards of legal competence.[18] There are no restrictions with respect to personal status that are peculiar to this contract. Any person of either sex who is of age (*bāligh*) and in possession of his mental faculties (*'āqil*) may legitimately contract an *'inān* partnership.[19]

The several categories of persons excluded, because of some limitation in their personal status, from participation in a *mufāwaḍa* contract are eligible as participants in an *'inān* partnership. Similarly, a difference in personal status between prospective partners does not constitute a barrier to the formation of a valid *'inān* partnership. An *'inān* partnership negotiated between two *mukātab* or *mudabbar* slaves, or between two female *umm walad* slaves, or between two minors with

[16] Postan, *op.cit.*

[17] Cf. S. D. Goitein, *Mediterranean Society*, Berkeley and Los Angeles, 1967, pp. 169–170.

[18] For some of the factors affecting the formation of both the *mufāwaḍa* and *'inān* partnerships, cf. discussion in preceding chapter.

[19] These two characteristics are the minimum requirements for legal competence in all transactions; cf. J. Schacht, *Grundzüge*, Berlin, 1935, pp. 35ff.

the explicit approval of their guardians, is valid, as is a partnership between any of these and a free Muslim or *dhimmī*.[20]

Differences in religious affiliation between *ʿinān* partners, while not illegal, are frowned upon. "Abū Ḥanīfa said: 'A partnership between a Muslim and a *dhimmī*, while not recommendable (*makrūh*), is permissible for both of them.' This is also the opinion of Abū Yūsuf and Muḥammad. Ismāʿīl b. Muslim[21] has reported that al-Ḥusayn[22] said: 'There is nothing wrong with a partnership between a Muslim and a *dhimmī*, if it is the Muslim who oversees the selling and purchasing.' "[23] Exclusive supervision of the joint venture by a Muslim would remove any possible objection to a Muslim–non-Muslim partnership by preventing transaction and trade with commodities prohibited to a Muslim.

Male apostates from Islam are the only category of persons ineligible as associates in any type of contractual partnership with a Muslim.[24] Apostasy from Islam results in the suspension of all the apostate's legal rights; consequently, none of his transactions have any validity.[25] An *ʿinān* partnership between a Muslim and a female apostate is, for some reason, permissible, although it is not recommendable (*makrūh*).[26]

20 Shaybānī, *Aṣl*, *Sharika*, fol. 69, ll. 2–6; fol. 77, ll. 19–21: "Abū Yūsuf and Muhammad have asserted that anyone trading with only a portion of his property is to be considered in the category of a free man in relation to partnership." All these combinations are not permissible in a *mufāwaḍa* partnership.

21 Unidentified.

22 Al-Ḥusayn b. Jaʿfar al-Iṣfahānī, d. 212/827; cf. Ibn Qutlūbughā, *Taj at-tarājim*, p. 24.

23 Shaybānī, *Aṣl*, *Sharika*, fol. 77, ll. 17–19.

24 *Ibid.*, fol. 69, l. 8. A minority opinion is held by Abū Yūsuf, in whose opinion such a partnership is valid and is terminated only with the execution of the apostate or his escape to a non-Muslim jurisdiction; if the apostate repents and returns to Islam, the partnership is in no way affected. Cf. *ibid.*, ll. 10–12.

25 Cf. Schacht, *Grundzüge*, p. 53.

26 Shaybānī, *Aṣl*, *Sharika*, fol. 69, ll. 12–14. This distinction between male and a female apostate may be connected with the different penalties designated by Ḥanafī law for apostates of either sex. All are agreed that a male apostate is to be put to death, whereas a female apostate is imprisoned until she repents and again adopts Islam; cf. *EI*, 1st ed., *s.v. murtadd*, 3:737.

Form of Investment

"Partnership is not permissible with goods or with absent money. This is the position held by Abū Ḥanīfa, Abū Yūsuf, and Muḥammad."[27] The rule embodied in this legal tradition governs the form of investment permissible in the formation of all Ḥanafī contractual partnerships, no distinction being made in this respect between limited and unlimited investments.

In some circumstances, however, the more limited scope of the *'inān* contract does affect the formation of the joint capital. For example, mixed investments with different types of currency contributed by each partner are allowed for all partnerships. Any change in the value of either currency occurring before an initial joint purchase is made automatically invalidates the *mufāwaḍa* contract. This is not the case in an *'inān* partnership in which all considerations of equality are absent. Even a substantial change in the value of one of the invested currencies between the time the *'inān* contract was negotiated and the time of the initial joint purchase would not affect the partnership's validity.[28] Such a shift would leave the *'inān* partnership intact and affect only the amount of profit[29] or each partner's share of the losses.[30]

Circumvention of the prohibition against goods as an in-

[27] Shaybānī, *Aṣl, Sharika*, fol. 61, ll. 14–15. Problems connected with the investment types admissible in partnership are treated in detail in the preceding chapter in connection with the *mufāwaḍa*. The same general considerations are applicable to the *'inān*.

[28] Shaybānī, *Aṣl, Sharika*, fol. 61b, ll. 13–14.

[29] At the conclusion of the partnership, each partner withdraws the capital he invested, and the remaining sum of money is then divided according to their agreement. If the currency invested by one partner rose in value, the absolute amount of the profit would be reduced; the share of profit assigned to each partner, however, would not be affected.

[30] A partner's share in any losses follows strictly his share of the investment. A partnership becomes effective not at the time it is contracted, but only with the initial joint purchase. Indeed, the exact amount of each investment need not be known at the time of the contract, but must be precisely known at the time of purchase; cf. *Kāsānī*, 6:63. Therefore, the value of each partner's investment at the time of purchase determines his share in any losses.

vestment form in the *'inān* partnership can be accomplished by employing the legal fiction outlined for similar circumstances in a *mufāwaḍa* partnership. That is, each partner exchanges a portion of his goods for a portion of those of his colleague, establishing thereby a joint ownership over their respective properties.[31]

Both work and credit partnerships are permissible in an *'inān* form. Concerning the work partnership, Sarakhsī has the following to say:

> "This type of partnership can be either *'inān*, or *mufāwaḍa*, if all the latter's conditions are fulfilled. If it is a *mufāwaḍa*, then each of the partners can be held liable, on the basis of surety, for any obligations of his colleague. In the case of *'inān*, he can be held liable only for obligations undertaken by himself and not for those of his colleague, as is the case with the rules of agency."[32]

Concerning the *'inān* credit partnership, he states: "We have already explained that the credit partnership can at times be a *mufāwaḍa* and at others an *'inān*; in the latter case, it can be either general (*'āmm*) or specified, as is the case with cash *'inān* partnerships. This is so, because its permissibility is based on agency, and agency is valid for the purchase of a specified category of merchandise."[33]

Formation of the 'Inān *by Default*

There are several sets of circumstances which inadvertently give rise to an *'inān* partnership as a result of an invalidating element in an intended *mufāwaḍa* agreement. If the condition of equality required in a *mufāwaḍa* partnership is upset by one of the partner's extra-partnership income, the association is not cancelled, but is treated as an *'inān* partnership.[34] A *mufāwaḍa* partnership negotiated between two slaves, or between a free Muslim and a *dhimmī*, is similarly transformed

[31] Shaybānī, *Aṣl, Sharika*, fol. 62, ll. 10–11.
[32] Sarakhsī, *Mabsūṭ*, 11:155. [33] *Ibid.*, p. 168.
[34] Shaybānī, *Aṣl, Sharika*, fol. 61b, ll. 13–14.

into an *'inān* agreement.[35] A *mufāwaḍa* partner does not have the independent right to conclude another *mufāwaḍa* partnership with a third party; if he does so, the second partnership is treated as an *'inān*.[36]

Distribution of Profit and Loss in an *'Inān* Contract

> Abū Ḥanīfa said: "If the two partners in an *'inān* partnership agree that the profit and loss follow their respective investments, this is permissible. If one of them stipulates for himself a share in the profit proportionally larger than that of his colleague, this also is permissible. If, however, one of them assumes a share of the loss proportionally larger than that of the other, this is not permissible."[37]

Ḥanafī law permits some flexibility in the distribution of profits in an *'inān* partnership, but is absolutely rigid in regard to the contractual stipulations affecting the distribution of liability. In all partnerships forms, as well as in other forms of commercial association, such as the *commenda*, responsibility for losses is to be assigned strictly in accordance with the size of each party's investment. Any deviation from this rule invalidates the contract. This principle is based on numerous legal traditions[38] and is epitomized in one attributed to the fourth Caliph, 'Alī b. Abī Ṭālib: "The profit follows the conditions agreed upon, and the loss follows the capital."[39]

Contracts stipulating equal investment in the partnership and an unequal distribution of profit, or unequal investment and an equal distribution of profit, are both allowed in an *'inān* partnership. For example, a party contributing one third of the total capital of a partnership could reap one half or even two thirds of its profit. Some legal authorities considered this arrangement as a travesty of equity.[40] Answering their objections, Sarakhsī sought to provide the Ḥanafī recognition of this arrangement with both a theoretical and practical justification.

[35] *Ibid.*, fol. 68b, ll. 10–11.
[36] *Ibid.*, fol. 70, l. 21.
[37] *Ibid.*, fol. 61, ll. 16–18.
[38] *Ibid.*, ll. 15–19.
[39] *Ibid.*, ll. 18–19.
[40] Cf. Sarakhsī, *Mabsūṭ*, 11:156.

> We, however, assert that the claim to profit is based on the contractual stipulation. Each of the *'inān* partners is entitled to profit in accordance with what was stipulated for him. This is in keeping with the statement of the Prophet, God's blessing and mercy upon him: "Muslims must abide by their stipulations."[41] The permissibility of this contract is due to the people's need for it; and the need for this stipulation is a compelling one. For one of the partners may be more skillful than the other in some aspect of trade. In view of his skill, and the lack of it on the part of his colleague, the former would not agree to an equal claim to the profit. A claim to share in the profit can be based solely on work without the investment of any money, as is the case in the *commenda. A fortiori*, then, the claim to profit can be based on a combination of work and money.[42]

Capital and labor are the two considerations entitling one to profit, with a premium being attached to the quality of an individual's labor and skill. Following this concept to its ultimate conclusion, Ḥanafī law permits an *'inān* partnership in which all the parties invest capital, but in which the contract stipulates that all the work and trading be carried out by only one of them. An *'inān* partnership in which profit and loss follow the capital and in which only one partner works is permissible, as is one in which the same conditions pertain, except that the share of the profit assigned to the working partner is greater than his share of the investment. But an *'inān* partnership in which one party invests two thousand dirhams and the other one thousand, on the condition that profit be shared equally and the loss follow the capital and that all the work be done by the larger investor, is not permissible. This is so because the proportionally larger share of the profit assigned to the lesser investor cannot be justified either on the grounds of

[41] *al-muslimūn 'inda shurūṭihim*; concerning this maxim, cf. Schacht, *Origins of Muhammadan Jurisprudence*, Oxford, 1959, p. 174, where it is given as: *al-muslimūn 'alā shurūṭihim*, and p. 181. In an oral communication, Prof. Schacht assured me that the reading *'alā shurūṭihim* was to be preferred.

[42] Sarakhsī, *Mabsūṭ*, 11:157; cf. also, Shaybānī, *Aṣl, Sharika*, fol. 58, ll. 4ff.

capital or labor contributed. As Kāsānī phrases it, "the excess profit assigned to the lesser investor corresponds neither to labor or money contributed, nor to liability assumed."[43]

When all partners contribute both capital and labor, any distribution of profit mutually agreed upon is valid in an *'inān* partnership.

The Contract

A simple suggested formula for a written *'inān* partnership contract[44] is given at the very beginning of the chapter on partnership of the *Kitāb al-aṣl.*

"This is a document stating the agreement upon which *A* son of *B* and *X* son of *Y* have entered into a partnership. They entered the partnership in a God-fearing manner and with mutual fidelity. The capital of *A* is such and such, and the capital of *X* is such and such, and it is all in their possession. They may buy and sell with it either together or separately, and each one of them may trade according to his best judgment and may buy and sell for cash and credit. Whatever profit they may gain is to be divided between them according to their respective shares in the joint capital:[45] and whatever loss or setback they suffer is to be borne by them according to their respective shares in the joint capital. They have entered into a partnership on this basis in the month so and so of the year so and so."[46]

As in the case of the other partnership types, the formula for the *'inān* given in the *Kitāb al-aṣl* covers only the most essential elements of the contract, with no undue elaboration.

A more detailed version of an *'inān* contract is given by Ṭaḥāwī in his notarial handbook.

[43] *Kāsānī,* 6:63; cf. also Shaybānī, *Aṣl, Sharika,* fol. 58, ll. 20ff.; Sarakhsī, *Mabsūṭ,* 11:158–159.

[44] The problems connected with written contracts in Islamic law are discussed in Chapter 3 in the section dealing with "the *mufāwaḍa* contract."

[45] This particular division is exemplary and is only one of the several combinations of profit division in relation to investment permissible in the *'inān* partnership.

[46] Shaybānī, *Aṣl, Sharika,* fol. 57b, ll. 3–8. The basic technical terminology of this contract is the same as that of the *mufāwaḍa* partnership contract, and the comments made there apply here as well.

This is a document stating the agreement upon which *A* and *B* have entered into a partnership, an *'inān*[47] partnership and not a *mufāwaḍa*. They have entered into it in the fear of God and His complete obedience with mutual fidelity and good counsel both in private and public, and on the condition that:

a. Each party invests of his money one hundred uniform dinars of standard weight in gold, minted coin of good alloy which is to serve as the capital of this their partnership, and that they intermingle the money until it has become one and indistinguishable.

b. They may use this money, or any portion of it, as they see fit whenever they see fit, to buy the various types of goods.

c. They may pay the price of the goods that they buy to the person from whom they bought them from the money mentioned in this contract.

d. They may sell these goods, or any portion of them, as they see fit whenever they see fit, for cash and credit.

e. They may receive the price of the goods they sell and hand over what they sell to the person who has bought the goods from them.

f. They may hire, as they see fit, a person in connection with the goods.

g. They may appoint an agent for the goods, or for any portion of them, as they see fit whenever they see fit.

h. They may give the goods, or a portion of them, to be taken as a *biḍā'a* to any place that they see fit.

i. They may travel with the goods, or with a portion of them, anywhere they see fit, anytime they see fit.

j. They may trade with the goods according to their best judgment.

k. They may reinvest any revenues that come into their possession from the sale of the goods into any other category of goods they see fit, and the status of these latter goods is to be the same as that of the goods purchased with the

[47] The term *'inān* is not required for a partnership contract; cf. *Kāsānī*, 6:62. It is not mentioned in the contract formula suggested by Shaybānī and is included here primarily to distinguish it from a *mufāwaḍa* partnership.

original money mentioned in this contract and according to the conditions mentioned and described in this contract.

l. From whatever bounty God may grant them in this undertaking, and after the payment of any debts owed by them by virtue of the partnership mentioned in this contract, each partner is to withdraw his investment as mentioned in this contract, and whatever remains, after this, of the money mentioned in this contract is to be divided between them equally, neither of them receiving anything in excess of his colleague.

m. Whatever loss they incur is to be borne by them equally.

"They have formed and contracted between them the partnership mentioned in this contract according to the stipulations mentioned in this contract. It is a valid and permissible partnership.

"After negotiating the partnership mentioned in this contract, the parties separated physically, satisfied with it, and giving effect to it."[48]

The text of this contract derives from Ṭaḥāwī's shorter work on contract formulae and is intended to serve as a model contract for adherents of all Muslim legal rites. Ṭaḥāwī, although himself a Ḥanafī intentionally formulated the partnership contract in such a manner as to be acceptable to Ḥanafīs, Shāfi'īs, and Mālikīs alike. For example, the intermingling of the investments, or the insistence upon uniform currency on the part of each investor, is not required in Ḥanafī law, nor is the provision assigning the profit in accordance with the respective investments. These features are included by Ṭaḥāwī because they are required by Shāfi'ī law.[49] Differences between the schools are briefly noted by Ṭaḥāwī in his commentary on the contract, thus making it quite easy

[48] Ṭaḥāwī, *Kitāb ash-shurūṭ aṣ-ṣaghīr*, ms. Istanbul, *Bayazit*, 18905, fol. 94b, l. 17–fol. 95, l. 10. Several readings are based on the two other extant copies of the work, mss. Istanbul, *Murad Mollah* 997 and 998, which in certain instances have a better text.

[49] Cf. Chapter 2.

for any notary to change or exclude certain clauses in conformity with his client's wishes.

Whereas the contract in the *Kitāb al-aṣl* touches only cursorily upon the rights of the partners in the conduct of the partnership, that of Ṭaḥāwī spells them out in detail. This, indeed, is the most noteworthy difference between them. Partners are given the right to transact all partnership business "as they see fit whenever they see fit," thus obviating any incriminations and disputes in case of any unsuccessful venture. They may buy and sell in the name of the partnership, and they may reinvest in further ventures the proceeds of these sales. They may hand over their joint property as a *biḍā'a* to a third party, they may travel with it, and they may appoint agents to handle their goods and pay from the partnership funds all expenses connected with them. To cover transactions not specifically enumerated in the contract, such as the investment of partnership funds in a *commenda,* Ṭaḥāwī inserts the general provision, "and they may trade with the goods according to their best judgment."[50]

Conduct of the *'Inān*

The rights, duties, and obligations of *'inān* partners pertain only to that portion of their respective property invested in the joint undertaking. "In all matters that are not of their partnership, each of them is as a stranger in relation to his colleague."[51] In contrast to the *mufāwaḍa*, "in the *'inān* partnership the two have not become as one person."[52]

The principle of mutual agency upon which the *'inān* partnership is based determines the freedom of action of an *'inān* partner with respect to the joint capital, his relations with his associate, and with third parties.

> As for the *'inān* partnership, it comprehends mutual agency, but not mutual surety. By virtue of this mutual agency, each of them does not become liable for that which is owed by his colleague.[53]

[50] For the text of a contract formula for a *'inān* partnership between three parties, cf. Nasā'ī, *Sunan*, 8 vols., Cairo, 1930, 8:55–56. The general format of the contract resembles, but is not identical to, that of Ṭaḥāwī.

[51] Sarakhsī, *Mabsūṭ*, 11:175. [52] *Ibid.*, p. 174. [53] *Ibid.*

In an *'inān* partnership, liability of the partners toward third parties is several but not joint; within the partnership, liability for obligations arising from partnership affairs is joint. This principle covers all the transactions on behalf of the company in which its members are free to engage.

The rights and obligations of *'inān* partners have been appropriately compared with those of a *commenda* agent (*muqāriḍ, muḍārib*).

> Abū Ḥanīfa said: The *'inān* partner has the right to enter into a *biḍā'a* association and to entrust the capital as a *commenda*, even if his partner does not expressly permit him to do so. He is permitted to engage with their partnership capital in all those transactions in which a *commenda* agent may engage. This is also the opinion of Abū Yūsuf and Muḥammad.[54]

A *commenda* agent is free to trade with the capital entrusted to him in any manner intended to bring profit to the venture; all accounts, expenses, profits, and losses are settled between the agent and the investor. Obligations incurred by the agent toward third parties cannot be claimed directly from the investor; indeed, third parties need not even know of the latter's existence. The same is true of the *'inān* partnership. Third parties can gain satisfaction of their claims only from the partner with whom they had dealings; he alone is responsible for the entire sum involved. Only after payment of the debt or fulfillment of the obligation can the partner demand restitution from his associate for the latter's share. If an obligation is jointly undertaken by both partners, third parties can demand satisfaction from each of them proportional to the share of liability assigned to them in the partnership contract.

In Ḥanafī law, an agent does not normally have the right to transfer his mandate to another agent. This limitation, if applied to partnership, would seriously confine the area of independent action allowed to each partner. It would, for example, prevent a partner from investing the joint capital in a *commenda*, from giving it as a *biḍā'a* to another person, or

[54] Shaybānī, *Aṣl*, *Sharika*, fol. 61, ll. 11–12.

from appointing an agent to trade with it. Ḥanafī jurists get around this difficulty by exercising juristic preference based on the realities of commercial life.

> One of the *'inān* partners may empower a third party to act as an agent with the common property. This is based on juristic preference. By analogy, he would not have this right. Each of them is an agent of his colleague, and an agent cannot empower another agent. For the constituent,[55] while approving of his agent's judgment, may not approve of someone else's judgment.
>
> On the basis of juristic preference, however, empowering agents is part of the customary practice of merchants, and the partners cannot do without this right. For profit cannot be attained except by trade, both that close by and that far off.[56] Each partner is personally unable to engage in both kinds. Consequently, he has no alternative but that of empowering a third party as an agent for one of these kinds of trade, in order to accomplish their purpose which is profit.[57]

Purchase and Sale

Debts owed to and by each individual partner cannot be collected from, or claimed by, his associate. The same principle applies to the various problems connected with purchase and sale on behalf of the partnership. "If one *'inān* partner bought something for their trade and found a flaw (*'ayb*) in it, the other does not have the right to return it."[58] This is so, because the return of merchandise on these grounds is a right pertaining to the party directly involved in the transaction (*al-'āqid*); a constituent (*muwakkil*)[59] does not have the right to dispute with the seller for something purchased by his agent (*wakīl*).[60]

If one *'inān* partner grants a postponement in the payment

[55] Arabic: *muwakkil*, i.e., the one who empowers the agent. For the term constituent in this sense, cf. Henry C. Black, *Black's Law Dictionary*, 3rd ed., St. Paul, 1933, p. 78.

[56] Literally: "both that present and that absent."

[57] Sarakhsī, *Mabsūṭ*, 11:175; cf. also, *Kāsānī*, 6:69.

[58] Sarakhsī, *Mabsūṭ*, 11:175.

[59] Cf. above, n. 55.

[60] Cf. Shaybānī, *Aṣl*, *Sharika*, fol. 61, ll. 6ff.

of a debt owed to the partnership, the postponement is not binding on his colleague, and the latter can demand payment of his share either from the debtor or from his partner.[61]

Either partner may rescind a purchase or sale made by the other if he does so before the transaction is consummated.[62] *'Inān* partners also possessed the right of giving and taking pledges. However, only the partner conducting the sale, for example, could receive a pledge as a guarantee of payment. In case of non-payment, he would be obligated to compensate his colleague for the latter's share.[63]

Expenses

An *'inān* partnership, asserts Kāsānī, is contracted in accordance with the custom of the merchants and in recognition of the necessities of commerce.[64] Hiring services and equipment for the care and transportation of partnership property was considered to be such a necessity and was an independent right possessed by both *'inān* partners. In its importance, it is compared with each partner's right to purchase goods for the partnership. "Hire is in the same category as purchase; and since he possesses the right to buy, he also possesses the right to hire."[65] Like a *mufāwaḍa* partner, an *'inān* partner could, when necessary, use partnership funds to pay for the transportation of merchandise, with or without the express permission of his colleague. In case of any mishap, the loss was borne by the partnership as a whole.[66]

It is toward third parties that the chief difference between *mufāwaḍa* and *'inān* partners with respect to hiring expenses is discernible.

> In this respect (i.e., re: hiring expenses), the *'inān* partner is not comparable to the *mufāwaḍa* partner. An *'inān* partner is not bound to pay for any service hired by his colleague, if the hire is connected with the latter's private affairs. Simi-

[61] *Ibid.*, l. 5; Sarakhsī, *Mabsūṭ*, 11:174; *Kāsānī*, 6:68.
[62] Shaybānī, *Aṣl*, *Sharika*, fol. 74, ll. 4–5.
[63] *Ibid.*, fol. 70b (bottom); *Kāsānī*, 6:70.
[64] Cf. *Kāsānī*, 6:69.
[65] *Ibid.*, pp. 69–70.
[66] Shaybānī, *Aṣl*, *Sharika*, fol. 75b, ll. 20–21.

larly, if his colleague hires services in connection with their common trade, the hired person can only claim his fee from the party by whom he was hired and has no claim against his colleague. The partner who did the hiring can then demand half of this fee from his colleague. This applies, if the hire is connected with their common trade and if they are partners in selling and buying.[67] If, however, they are only partners in one specified commodity,[68] and one of the partners hires services in connection with this commodity, without being so instructed by his colleague, the former is liable for the entire fee and cannot legitimately demand any part of it from his partner.[69]

Travel Expenses

The consensus of Ḥanafi opinion grants each *'inān* partner the freedom to travel with partnership property for purposes of trade, even without the express permission of his colleague.[70] Echoes of a dispute concerning the propriety of this right in an *'inān* partnership are preserved in Kāsānī's legal treatise. Reluctance on the part of some early authorities to view unapproved independent travel of an individual partner as a right automatically pertaining to this form of commercial association was probably due to the fact that the *'inān* partnership was employed primarily for local and short distance trade. According to one tradition, Abū Ḥanīfa categorically denied this right to an *'inān* partner;[71] two opinions attributed to Abū Yūsuf limit the partner's travel "to a place which would not require him to spend the night away from home,"[72] or to a place which would not entail expenses of transportation and provisions.[73] Kāsānī explains away these hesitations by referring them only to dangerous travel conditions or to a situation in which the customary phrase *i'mal bi-ra'yiḳa,* "trade according to your judgment," was not enunciated by the partners in their mutual delegation of authority.[74] Under normal

[67] I.e., partners in a general *'inān*; cf. above, n. 13.
[68] I.e., partners in a specified *'inān*; cf. above, n. 13.
[69] Shaybānī, *Aṣl*, *Sharika*, fol. 69b, ll. 15–20.
[70] *Kāsānī*, 6:71.
[71] *Ibid.* [72] *Ibid.* [73] *Ibid.* [74] *Ibid.*

conditions, however, the right to independent, unrestricted travel in a general *'inān* partnership is granted to its members.

Having allowed him the right to travel, Ḥanafī law also allows the *'inān* partner to charge all his travel expenses to the joint fund.

> And he may expend funds from the entire capital[75] for anything he leases, for his expenses, his food, and his sustenance. This can all be charged to the partnership capital. This opinion was transmitted by al-Ḥasan[76] from Abū Ḥanīfa. Muḥammad said: This privilege is granted by juristic preference; according to analogy, he will not possess this privilege. For to expend funds from someone else's capital is not permissible except with that person's express permission. The basis of this exercise of juristic preference is common usage (*'urf*) and custom (*'āda*). For the custom of the merchants is that traveling expenses are charged to the partnership capital; and that which is a recognized practice has the force of a stipulation.[77]

Payment to third parties of debts incurred in the course of business travel follows the same procedures as those outlined above for all debts and expenses in the *'inān* partnership.

Transactions of the *'Inān* Partner

By juristic preference, *'inān* partners are endowed with the right to appoint third parties as agents in connection with partnership affairs.[78] As a consequence, the individual partners may freely invest partnership property in a *commenda*,[79] entrust it as a *biḍā'a*,[80] give it as a pledge,[81] or leave it as a deposit.[82] In all these transactions, profits and losses are charged to the account of the partnership.

[75] I.e., both from his own share of the capital and that of his partner.

[76] Probably al-Ḥasan b. Ziyād al-Lu'lu'ī, d. 204/819. Cf. Ibn Qutlūbughā, *Taj at-tarājim*, p. 22.

[77] *Kāsānī*, 6:71–72.

[78] Cf. Sarakhsī, *Mabsūṭ*, 11:175.

[79] Shaybānī, *Aṣl*, *Sharika*, fol. 61, l. 11; Sarakhsī, *Mabsūṭ*, 11:175; *Kāsānī*, 6:69.

[80] Sarakhsī, *Mabsūṭ*, 11:180.

[81] *Kāsānī*, 6:70–71.

[82] Sarakhsī, *Mabsūṭ*, 11:175.

An *'inān* partner may accept funds unconnected with the partnership as a *commenda*, and any resulting profit would accrue to him alone.[83] Generally, one *'inān* partner can have no claim on the extra-partnership earnings of his colleague. "Whatever a *mufāwaḍa* partner earns is shared between the partners; whatever an *'inān* partner earns belongs only to him, except if it is earned in connection with their partnership."[84]

An *'inān* partner may take a loan for use (*'āriyya*)[85] if the prosecution of partnership business requires it. For example, he may borrow a beast of burden to transport partnership goods from one place to another, and any liability arising from such a loan is borne by the partnership.[86] He may transfer debts owed the partnership by means of a *ḥawāla*, "because employment of the *ḥawāla* is a practice of trade and because the merchant has need of it."[87]

In all the transactions enumerated above, third parties can direct their claims only toward the partner who contracted (*al-'āqid*) the transaction giving rise to the claim.[88]

Neither partner may free, nor grant *mukātab* status, nor provide a wife for a commonly held slave without the express permission of his colleague, because none of these actions are directly connected with trade.[89] Permission of both partners is required before any other partnerships, either *'inān* or *mufāwaḍa*, are contracted with the common capital.[90] If the two *'inān* partners invest their capital in a *mufāwaḍa* partnership, the latter contract automatically cancels the first.[91] The *'inān* partner does, however, have the right to associate others in his own share of the partnership.[92]

Dissolution of the *'Inān*

The factors affecting the dissolution of contractual partnerships, including the *'inān*, have already been noted.[93] In ad-

[83] *Ibid.*; Shaybānī, *Aṣl, Sharika*, fol. 69, l. 9.
[84] Shaybānī, *Aṣl, Sharika*, fol. 70b, l. 3.
[85] Re: *'āriyya*, cf. Chapter 3, section on "Loans in the *Mufāwaḍa*."
[86] Shaybānī, *Aṣl, Sharika*, fol. 67, l. 21–fol. 70, l. 1.
[87] *Kāsānī*, 6:70; re: *ḥawāla*, cf. *Law in the Middle East*, 1:202.
[88] *Kāsānī*, 6:70–71.
[89] *Kāsānī*, 6:72.
[90] Sarakhsī, *Mabsūṭ*, 11:176.
[91] *Kāsānī*, 6:77.
[92] *Ibid.*, p. 69.
[93] Cf. Section on "Dissolution of Partnership" in Chapter 3.

dition to these, the specified *'inān* concludes with the accomplishment of the purpose for which it was contracted; that is, the purchase and subsequent division or resale of the commodities specified.

V

Mālikī Partnership

Sources

The two basic books of Mālikī law are the *Muwaṭṭa'*, composed in the latter half of the eighth century by the founder of the school, Mālik b. Anas,[1] and the *Mudawwana al-kubrā,* composed less than a century later by Saḥnūn b. Sa'īd at-Tanūkhī[2] on the basis of his discussions with 'Abd ar-Raḥmān b. al Qāsim,[3] who had reputedly studied with Mālik himself for twenty years. These two works provided the foundation for all subsequent Mālikī legal literature; together they constitute a reliable and comprehensive source for the early period of Mālikī doctrine.

Surprisingly enough, the institution of commercial partnership is not formally treated in the *Muwaṭṭa'*. The term partner (*sharīk*, pl. *shurakā'*) is mentioned in several instances, but usually only in reference to a jointly owned house, wall, or slave.[4] Commercial partnership is alluded to only in passing and not at all systematically, in the *Kitab al-buyū'* ("Book of

1 Born at Madina ca. 93/711 and died there 179/795; cf. C. Brockelmann, *Geschichte der arabischen Litteratur* (*GAL*), 2 vols., Leiden, 1937–1943, 1:184–185 (175). For the importance of the *Muwaṭṭa'* and an evaluation of Mālik's place in Muslim legal history, cf. Schacht's article in *Encyclopaedia of Islam* (*EI*), 1st ed., Leiden, 1913–1934, 3:205ff. References to the *Muwaṭṭa'* in this chapter are based on the Cairo edition of 1370/1951 edited by Muḥammad F'uād 'Abd al-Bāqī.

2 Born 160/776, died 240/854; cf. Brockelmann, *GAL*, *Supp.*, 1:99. As far as I know, there are only two printed editions of the *Mudawwana*—Cairo, 1324/5, in four volumes, and Cairo, 1323, in sixteen volumes. References in this chapter are based on the sixteen-volume edition. There is a French précis of the contents of the *Mudawwana* by G.-H. Bousquet, "La Moudawwana (Recension de Sah'noun)," *Annales de l'Institut d'Études Orientales d'Alger* 16 (1958):175–206; 17 (1959):169–211; 18–19 (1960–61): 73–165.

3 Born ca. 128/746, died 191/806; cf. Brockelmann, *GAL*, 1:186 (176).

4 E.g., Mālik, *Muwaṭṭa'*, Cairo, 1951, pp. 713–717, in connection with co-owners of a house; pp. 772–773, regarding the manumission of a jointly owned slave.

Sale") of the *Muwaṭṭa'*, where reference is made to partnerships in textiles and foodstuffs.[5]

This omission is puzzling since other forms of commercial association, such as the *qirāḍ (commenda)*[6] and the *musāqāt*[7] are systematically and thoroughly treated. The exclusion of so important an institution as partnership from its purview is perhaps to be explained by the fact that in the *Muwaṭṭa'*, Mālik, while aiming to give a survey of law and justice according to *ijmā'* (consensus) of Islam in Madina and to codify and systematize the customary law of Madina,[8] did not at the same time intend the *Muwaṭṭa'* to serve as a comprehensive and all-inclusive legal code. Whatever the reason for this omission, any inference that it signifies an ignorance on Mālik's part of commercial partnership would be absolutely unjustified. That Mālik was familiar with a developed form of commercial partnership is attested by his brief references to it in the *Muwaṭṭa'*,[9] by Shāfi'ī's citation of some of Mālik's views on partnership,[10] and, most importantly, by the lengthy treatment devoted to it in the *Mudawwana,* a treatment based largely on statements attributed directly to Mālik.[11]

Terminology and Classification

In respect to partnership, Mālikī law adopts a dual system of classification: (1) According to investment form, e.g., cash partnership, labor partnership, credit partnership, and cash and labor partnership;[12] (2) According to the force of the mandate mutually conferred: (a) general mandate partnership (*shari*ḳ*at al-mufāwaḍa*), and (b) restricted mandate part-

[5] *Ibid.*, pp. 676–677.

[6] *Ibid.*, pp. 687–702. For an English summary of the contents of the "Book of the *Qirāḍ*" in the *Muwaṭṭa'*, cf. *SPECULUM* 37:204–207.

[7] Mālik, *Muwaṭṭa'*, pp. 703–710. Ibn 'Arafa defines the *musāqāt* as: "The contract for the letting out of gardens is one in which one party agrees to undertake the cultivation of plants, etcetera, subject to his receiving a share in the fruits thereof"; quoted in F. H. Ruxton, *Mālikī Law*, London, 1916, p. 235.

[8] Cf. Schacht in *EI*, 1st ed., 3:205ff.

[9] Mālik, *Muwaṭṭa'*, pp. 676–677.

[10] Shāfi'ī, *Umm*, 7 vols., Cairo, 1321/1903–1325/1907, 3:206.

[11] Saḥnūn, *Mudawwana*, 16 vols., Damascus, n.d., 12:40–85.

[12] Cf. D. Santillana, *Istituzioni*, 2 vols., Rome, 1925–1938, 2:289.

nership (*sharikat al-ʿinān*).[13] Although identical in terminology, the forms of partnership association connoted by these two latter terms in Mālikī law diverge considerably from their counterparts in Ḥanafī law.

Mālikī Mufāwaḍa

By the term *mufāwaḍa*, Mālikī jurists understand a partnership in which each partner confers upon his colleague full authority to dispose of their joint capital in any acceptable manner intended to benefit their association. The emphasis is on the *tafwīḍ*,[14] i.e., on the delegation of discretionary authority to conduct trade with each other's capital. Each partner is his colleague's agent and can act in all commercial matters with respect to his own and his colleague's property without the latter's prior approval. The liability of the *mufāwaḍa* partners is both joint and several; any obligation incurred on behalf of the partnership toward third parties by one of the associates can be claimed in full from any of the other partners. "Each one of them is liable for any obligation undertaken by his colleague in connection with their work."[15]

In Mālikī usage, the implication of the term *mufāwaḍa* for partnership is confined to the nature of the relationship between the partners and does not extend, as it does in Ḥanafī law, to any other aspects of the association. There is no requirement for equality in the personal[16] and financial status of the prospective partners; nor does the Mālikī *mufāwaḍa* insist on the inclusion of all eligible capital within the partnership.

> Ibn Qāsim said: "Concerning the extent of the capital upon which people form a partnership: If it includes all things,

[13] In translating the latter two terms for Mālikī partnership, I have followed Santillana, *ibid.*, pp. 294–295; cf. also, D. Santillana and I. Guidi, *Il "Muḫtaṣar" O Sommario del Diritto Malechita di Ḫalīl Ibn Isḥāq*, 2 vols., Milan, 1919, pp. 364, 369.

[14] Indeed, this form of partnership is sometimes designated as *sharikat al-tafwīḍ*; cf. Santillana, *Istituzioni*, 2:294.

[15] Saḥnūn, *Mudawwana*, 12:47; cf. also, pp. 69–70; Santillana, *Istituzioni*, 2:299. This applies to all forms of partnership, i.e., cash, goods, and labor partnerships.

[16] Saḥnūn, *Mudawwana*, 12:70.

> then they have concluded a *mufāwaḍa* partnership; and if they have associated only in order to purchase one category of commercial commodities, such as slaves or pack-animals, then they have also formed a *mufāwaḍa* partnership."[17]

In addition to its flexible scope, the existence of extra-partnership wealth and revenues does not affect the validity of the Mālikī *mufāwaḍa.*

> I (Saḥnūn) said:[18] "Can two people be considered *mufāwaḍa* partners if one of them possesses capital in the form of goods or cash to the exclusion of his colleague?" He answered: "Yes." I said: "And will not the fact that one of them has dinars or dirhams or goods to the exclusion of his colleague invalidate the *mufāwaḍa* partnership between them?" He said: "Indeed it will not invalidate the *mufāwaḍa* partnership between them." I said: "Is this Mālik's statement?" He said: "This is my own view."[19]

It should be noted that the rules governing the investment in this form of partnership are in distinct contrast to those affecting the Ḥanafī *mufāwaḍa.*[20]

Mālikī 'Inān *Partnership*

Aside from the *mufāwaḍa*, Mālikī law recognizes one other partnership form. In the *Mudawwana* this form is not designated by any special term and can best be described simply as a non-*mufāwaḍa* partnership: "a partnership which is not a *mufāwaḍa* partnership, as when two people form a partnership in one commodity, or something similar."[21]

The term *'inān* for this partnership was unknown in the earliest period.

[17] *Ibid.*, p. 68.

[18] The *Mudawwana* is composed in the form of a dialogue, recording Saḥnūn's inquiries and Ibn Qāsim's replies on the various points of Mālikī Muslim law.

[19] Saḥnūn, *Mudawwana*, 12:69.

[20] Cf. Section on "Investment Form and Formation of Joint Capital" in Chapter 3.

[21] Saḥnūn, *Mudawwana*, p. 78.

> I said: "Does Mālik know of the *'inān* partnership?" He said: "I did not hear of it from Mālik, and I am not aware of any of the scholars of the Ḥijāz who knew of it."[22]

Mālik's ignorance of the term *'inān* led Shāfi'ī to conclude that he did not recognize the validity of this form of association.[23] A more accurate assessment, however, seems to be that of Averroes, who states that all Muslim jurists agreed on the validity of the *'inān* partnership "even if some of them did not know of this term and even if they differed concerning some of its rules."[24] It is possible that the term *'inān* to designate a partnership with restricted mandate was adopted into Mālikī usage from Ḥanafī law where it was employed for a corresponding form of association from the earliest period.[25]

The Mālikī *'inān* is characterized by the severe limitations it imposes on each partner's independent action with respect to their joint capital. "If it has been stipulated that one partner shall not be allowed to do anything without his co-partner, such a partnership is said to be one with limited powers (i.e., *'inān*)."[26] Each associate has the right to administer their joint affairs, but each act of management must have their joint consent. Only in cases of emergency is an individual *'inān* partner entitled to act without his colleague's expressed approval.[27] Only the *'inān* partner who personally conducted a given transaction is answerable to third parties for any obligation resulting from it.[28]

Although the scope of the Mālikī *'inān* is not clearly delineated in any of the sources, it appears to have been conceived as pertaining either to a single commodity[29] or to a single transaction.[30] In this respect, as well as in others, it is almost identical with the Ḥanafī specified *'inān* partnership (*'inān khāṣṣ*) discussed in the preceding chapter.

[22] *Ibid.*, p. 68; cf. also, Santillana, *Istituzioni*, 2:295, n. 30.

[23] Shāfi'ī, *Umm*, 3:206.

[24] Ibn Rushd (Averroes), *Bidāyat al-Mujtahid*, Cairo, 1952, 2:249.

[25] E.g., in the *Aṣl* of Shaybānī.

[26] F. H. Ruxton, *Mālikī Law*, London, 1916, p. 195; cf. also, I. Guidi and D. Santillana, *Il "Muḫtaṣar,"* 2 vols., Milan, 1919, 2:396.

[27] Santillana, *Istituzioni*, 2:295.

[28] *Ibid.*, p. 299.

[29] E.g., Saḥnūn, Mudawwana, 12:78.

[30] E.g., Guidi and Santillana, *Il "Muḫtaṣar,"* pp. 369–370; Ruxton, *Mālikī Law*, p. 195.

Proportional Principle (*Takāfu'*)

Before examining in detail the formation and operation of Mālikī partnership, a word should be said concerning the principle of proportionality, or balance (*takāfu'*), a factor pervading all aspects of the partnership relationship.

> I have heard from Mālik that partnership is not permissible unless there exists a balance (*takāfu'*) in the capitals.[31]

The ideal model of a Mālikī partnership is one in which there is a one-to-one ratio between the proportional share of the capital, labor, and equipment a partner contributes and his share of profits and losses; that is, if a partner's investment consists of one half or one third of the total joint capital, he should engage in a corresponding share of the work and, as a result, be entitled to the profits and liable for losses and other obligations in a like manner.

Mālikī law requires the maintenance of a strict equilibrium between all elements of input (i.e., capital, labor, and equipment) and all elements of output (i.e., division of profits and liabilities) in a partnership contract. Any stipulation or circumstance disturbing this equilibrium is declared invalid, and the consequent imbalance is restored by isolating the disproportional features from the partnership and treating them as elements of a hire (*ijāra*) contract.

> And this, in my opinion (Ibn Qāsim speaking) is comparable to what Mālik states concerning a partnership in which one of the partners invests one hundred dirhams and the other fifty dirhams on the condition that they share equally in the profit.[32] Mālik said: "This is not acceptable. They are to divide the profit in accordance with their respective investments, and the larger investor[33] is to compensate his colleague for the latter's work on twenty-five of the dirhams. They both work together on the fifty dirhams in excess of the lesser investor's investment; the greater investor works on twenty-five of them, and his colleague works on twenty-

[31] Saḥnūn, *Mudawwana*, 12:41.

[32] The assumption is that the work, too, is contributed in equal shares by each of the partners.

[33] Literally: "the owner of the fifty additional dirhams."

five of them. The latter is, therefore, entitled to an equitable compensation for his work.

"If they do not make any profit, but incur a loss, the loss is to be divided in accordance with their respective investment, and the fifty-dirham investor is still entitled to compensation for his work on the twenty-five dirhams of his colleague."[34]

The imbalance in the cash partnership discussed by Mālik was rectified by compensating the lesser investor for his share of the work in excess of his share of the total joint capital. A similar procedure is followed in partnerships of mixed investment, that is, a cash and work partnership, or a work partnership in which one or more of the associates provides some piece of equipment necessary for their work and in which the elements of the individual investments do not exactly correspond to the division of profits and liabilities. In these latter cases, however, there is the additional problem of determining which element of the investment is to serve as the basis for proportionality. The general rule in such instances is epitomized in the following statement: "Profit and increase, as well as loss, follow any component of the investment which cannot be hired; those components which can be hired are to be equitably compensated for."[35] In a cash and work partnership, it is each partner's cash contribution, since money is not hireable,[36] which determines his share of the profits and liabilities; any proportionally excessive work contributed by either partner is to be compensated for. In a work and equipment partnership, the extent of each partner's labor determines his portion of profit and loss, and the party contributing the equipment receives an equitable fee for the use of his property.

I said to Ibn Qāsim: "What is your opinion of a partnership between two fullers, one of whom provides the mallet and

[34] Saḥnūn, *Mudawwana*, 12:45; cf. also, p. 55 (bottom): "Mālik said: Loss is in accordance with their respective capitals, and the profit is in accordance with their respective capitals"; also pp. 59–60.

[35] *Ibid.*, p. 54.

[36] Cf. *ibid.*, p. 46. "Profit is to follow the capital since this is something which it is not permissible to hire, whereas men can be hired."

fulling tool and fulling material, while the other provides the stall, on the condition that their earnings be shared equally?" He said: "I do not approve of this. I did not hear anything concerning this case from Mālik; but I did hear from him that a partnership in which one party provides a pack animal and the other a millstone on the condition that they both share equally in the profit is not permissible. I consider the situation you describe to be comparable, and therefore not permissible, since the rent value of each party's contribution is different."

I said: "What is your opinion of a partnership between two fullers in which one provides the hammer and the fulling tool, and his colleague the other tools connected with this craft on the condition that they share equally in the profit? Is this permissible according to Mālik?" He said: "If the tools provided by the latter possess great value, it is not an acceptable arrangement; for Mālik has already registered his disapproval of an agricultural partnership in which one of the parties provides land which has a substantial rental value without fee on the condition that all the effort and work to be expended be divided equally between them." He (Mālik) said: "This is not acceptable, unless the landless partner pays half of the land-rent, and the work and effort be divided equally between them; similarly, a partnership in manual labor is not valid unless the tools are provided by both of them." I said: "What if one of the prospective partners provides the tools, and his colleague pays him half their rental value, and they then use them for a partnership on the condition that they share equally in the profits?" He said: "This is permissible."[37]

Underlying the principle of proportionality in partnership is the assumption that each of the partners will contribute, to some extent at least, to all the constituent elements of the investment. If the investment is so constituted that all the money is provided by one party and all the work by another, or all the equipment by one and all the labor by another, no part-

[37] *Ibid.*, pp. 43–44.

nership is said to exist; instead, the association is treated as a hire contract between the parties, each being entitled to some equitable form of compensation.

> I said: "What is your opinion of a partnership between three people in which one provides the millstone, the other the house, and the other the work-animal, on the condition that the owner of the animal do all the work?" He said: "The entire proceeds of the work are to go to the owner of the animal who executes the work, and he is obligated to pay the rental fee for the millstones and house." I said: "Is this also the case even if he does not earn anything?" He said: "Yes, even if he does not earn anything."[38]

Situations are conceivable in which certain disproportional features of a partnership contract cannot be integrated into the association by being separately treated as elements of a hire contract. Such would be the case if the partners contributed proportionally equal shares of capital and work, but stipulated that one of them be entitled to a greater share of the profits than his share in the investment. In this case, the offensive profit-sharing clause is voided, and the profit shared strictly according to the respective investments.[39]

Formation of the *Mufāwaḍa* Partnership

Personal Status

Any legally competent person[40] capable of disposition of property (*taṣarruf*) and of conferring a mandate can be a party of a *mufāwaḍa* partnership contract. This excludes minors, mentally incompetents, wastrels, and slaves acting without their masters' authorization. Slaves upon whom their masters have conferred the right to engage in trade (*ma'dhūn lahu*

[38] *Ibid.*, p. 45; cf. also, p. 60, where Ibn Qāsim rejects the validity of a cash partnership which stipulates that all the work be done by only one of the partners. He explains his rejection as follows: "The basis for this is that according to Mālik, a partnership is not permissible unless they combine in its work proportionally to their respective shares in the joint capital."

[39] *Ibid.*, p. 62.

[40] Regarding the standards of legal competence in Mālikī law, cf. Santillana, *Istituzioni*, 2:784, and references there.

fit-tijāra) are, however, fully eligible to enter into partnership agreements. Partnerships are valid when concluded between persons of the same status, e.g., two freemen or two authorized slaves, as well as when formed between persons of different status, e.g., a man and a woman or a slave and a freeman.[41]

Difference in religious persuasion constitutes for the Muslim a barrier to the formation of a partnership; it is, however, not an insurmountable difficulty.

> I said: "Is a partnership between a Muslim and a Christian or a Muslim and a Jew proper according to Mālik?" He said: "No, it is not, unless he (the Muslim) does not absent himself from the Christian or Jew when anything connected with purchase, sale, acquisition, or exchange is being transacted. And the latter is not to pay any debts, unless the Muslim be present together with him. If he acts in the manner I described to you, then the partnership is proper, and if he does not, then it is not proper."[42]

A valid partnership between a Muslim and a non-Muslim is possible only with the former's careful scrutiny and supervision of all the company's transactions. This requirement is, of course, intended to prevent any usurious transactions or any trading in commodities which are forbidden to a Muslim.[43] Any profits accruing to the Muslim partner from unsupervised transactions are suspect and are, therefore, not to be enjoyed by the partner, but are to be given as alms to the poor.[44]

In contrast to Ḥanafī law, Mālikī law does not demand equality in personal status as a prerequisite for a valid *mufāwaḍa* partnership. Partnerships are permissible between any legally competent Muslim, male or female, as well as slaves authorized to engage in trade and, under the proper conditions of supervision, between any of these and a non-Muslim.

Investment

Capital for partnership investment can take the form of cash (gold or silver coins), movable goods, or other property. It

41 Saḥnūn, *Mudawwana*, 12:70.
42 *Ibid.*, p. 70.
43 *Ibid.*, p. 70 (bottom).
44 Santillana, *Istituzioni*, 2:288.

cannot consist of commodities such as pork or wine, with which a Muslim is forbidden to deal, and the formation of the joint capital cannot involve a transaction such as the exchange of gold coins for those of silver, which is prohibited in Mālikī law of sale.[45]

Only the capital actually on hand at the partnership's inception can provide the basis for the distribution of profits and liabilities. Absent capital, or capital promised by one of the partners for future investment (*māl ghā'ib*), is not to be considered until it is actually delivered.[46]

The intermingling of the investments results in the formation of the social capital. This, however, is not a requirement for a valid partnership. The same result can be achieved by the use of one of the investments for a purchase on behalf of the partnership. Among the early major Mālikī authorities, Saḥnūn is alone in holding that "there can be no partnership except with the intermingling of the capital."[47]

Investment—Cash Partnership

The least problematical form of cash partnership is one in which the several parties contribute coins of the same metal, type, and value. In such a case, each partner's investment can be determined by the number or weight of the coins he contributed, and no element of exchange (*ṣarf*, *cambio*), a contract not permitted by Mālikī law, enters into the formation of the joint capital.[48]

The problem of *ṣarf* does, however, arise when each partner's investment consists of coins of the same metal, but of varying types, or of coins of different metals.

[45] *Ibid.*, p. 290. For Mālikī law of sale, cf. Frédéric Peltier's translation of the "Book of Sale" of the *Muwaṭṭa'*, *Le Livre des Ventes du Mouwatta de Mālik ben Anas*, Algiers, 1911.

[46] Saḥnūn, *Mudawwana*, 12:62.

[47] *Ibid.*, p. 67; cf. also, p. 66.

[48] Re: exchange (*ṣarf*), cf. Santillana, *Istituzioni*, 2:185–192; it applies only to the exchange of precious metals and certain types of foodstuffs. "Any profit or advantage gained or lost in the exchange of gold or silver, or in the exchange of foodstuffs is considered usury and, as such, prohibited. Foodstuffs, gold, and silver can only be exchanged for their exact equivalents." Ruxton, *Māliki Law*, p. 159. Cf. also, Guidi and Santillana, *Il "Muḫtaṣar,"* pp. 191–192; and translation, 2:186ff.

I said: "What is your opinion of a partnership in which I invest one hundred Hāshimī dinars and my colleague invests one hundred Damascene dinars, and the Hāshimī dinars have a different exchange rate than the Damascene dinars?" He said: "I cannot at this moment recall anything from Mālik concerning this problem, but I do not approve of this arrangement if the exchange rate of the Hāshimī dinars differs from that of the Damascene dinars, and if this difference is substantial. If, however, the excess in the exchange rate of the Hāshimī dinars is something trivial and not of any significant value, then I see nothing wrong with a partnership between them." I said: "What is the reason for your disapproval if the excess in the exchange rate of the Hāshimī dinars is great?" He said: "Because, if the excess in the exchange rate of the Hāshimī dinars is substantial and they form a partnership dividing the work and profit equally between them, this will mean that the capital of one of them will exceed that of his colleague. This excess will pertain to a *res certa*[49] in that his Hāshimī dinars will exceed in value the Damascene dinars of his colleague. And a partnership in which the capital of one partner is greater than that of his colleague is not permissible unless the profit and work are divided according to their respective shares in the joint capital.

"If they wish to form a partnership on the basis of the value of the Hāshimī and Damascene dinars on the condition that each one's share of the profit and loss follows the value of these dinars, this is also not permissible. This is so, because it is not permissible to form a partnership with dinars on the basis of their value; partnership is permissible only with gold in exchange for gold, and silver in exchange for silver, each investment being evaluated on the basis of weight. According to Mālik, it is not permitted on the basis of value."[50]

If at a particular moment the values of dinars or dirhams of different types are identical, or if the difference between them

[49] Arabic: *'ayn*, i.e., something which has individual, concrete existence; cf. Santillana, *Istituzioni*, 2:671.

[50] Saḥnūn, *Mudawwana*, 12:62–63.

is only nominal, these coins can serve as a valid partnership investment. Any change in the value of the coins subsequent to the contracting of the partnership is to be disregarded, that is, the division of profits and losses, as well as each partner's share of ownership in the joint property is determined by the value, at the time of investment, of the capitals of each.

> He (Ibn Qāsim) said: "No attention is paid to changes in the exchange value of the coins. If they wish to separate, they are to divide the joint property in their possession equally —be it in the form of commodities, foodstuffs, or cash. For, if they form the partnership with equal capital, then the joint property in their possession belongs to each of them accordingly."[51]

A partnership in which the investment of one party consists only of dinars and that of the other only of dirhams is not permitted.

> I said: "According to Mālik, a partnership with one of them investing dirhams and the other dinars is not valid, is it?" He said: "No, it is not permitted according to Mālik." I said: "And is the basis for Mālik's opinion the fact that a partnership is not valid unless their investments are of the same type of dinars and dirhams?" He said: "Yes."[52]

Attempts to circumvent this prohibition are checked by the fact that they must necessarily involve some form of *ṣarf*. For example, it would not be permissible for the dinar-investor to sell half of his dinars for half of his associate's dirhams, and then form a partnership with an equal number and corresponding types of dinars and dirhams being contributed by each.[53] The reason is, "because this would constitute a contract of exchange and a contract of partnership, and this is not per-

[51] *Ibid.*, p. 63.

[52] *Ibid.*, p. 64.

[53] This is reminiscent of the legal fiction (*ḥīla*) adopted by Hanafī and Shāfi'ī law to make possible a partnership in which one party's investment consists of cash and the other's of commodities; cf., e.g., Shaybānī, *Kitāb al-makhārij fil-ḥiyal*, ed. J. Schacht, Leipzig, 1930, p. 58.

missible."[54] If, at the outset of their negotiations, the two parties happened to have in their possession dinars and dirhams of corresponding type, a partnership in these would be possible between them since no element of *ṣarf* would be involved.[55]

The question of a partnership with copper coins (*fulūs*) as a component in the investment is not treated in the *Mudawwana*; for a *commenda*, however, investment in copper coins is absolutely disqualified.[56]

Investment—Partnership in Goods

The Mālikī school is alone among the major schools of Muslim law in recognizing the validity of a partnership investment in the form of goods. Except for a certain category of foodstuffs, all licit goods are eligible to become part of the joint capital of a partnership. In contrast to the uniformity of coin types required in a cash partnership, a partnership in goods can be formed with each party contributing commodities of any size, shape, or form.

At the time the partnership is contracted, the value of each partner's commodities is to be estimated in order to establish each one's share in the profits, losses, and work. Formation of the social capital is considered to occur by virtue of an implied mutual sale; i.e., whether or not the term sale was used or an exchange of property intended; the very contracting of a partnership in goods implies a sale of a portion of one party's goods in exchange for a portion of the other's.

> I said: "Is partnership in goods permissible? For example, if I possess garments and my colleague possesses wheat or livestock, and we form a partnership with these commodities, is the partnership between us permissible according to Mālik?" He said: "Mālik said that there is nothing wrong with this arrangement." Ibn Qāsim said: "In my view, the partnership is permissible if they form it on the basis of the

[54] Saḥnūn, *Mudawwana*, 12.65. Regarding the inadmissibility of mixed contracts, cf. Guidi and Santillana, *Il "Muḫtaṣar,"* 2:363 n. 1.

[55] Saḥnūn, *Mudawwana*, 12:65.

[56] Cf. *Ibid.*, p. 86, and Chapter 6, n. 25.

value of each one's merchandise; and on condition that each one will share in the work, profit, or loss in accordance with his respective capital."[57] I said: "What if each one's capital consists of a different type of merchandise? Is there no objection, according to Mālik, to their forming a partnership on the basis of the value of these commodities?" He said: "No." I said: "How are they to estimate the value of the goods in their possession, and how do they become partners? If the goods are of equal value, does each one sell half of his own goods in exchange for half of his colleague's, or do they just estimate the value without any mutual sale?" He said: "If they estimate their goods and find them to be of equal value, and if they testify to the effect that they formed an equal investment partnership, this constitutes a sale of half of one party's goods for half of those of his colleague. If they do this, a mutual sale is considered to have taken place, even if sale is not mentioned."[58]

The only commodities which Mālik does not countenance for the formation of a partnership are foodstuffs that can be measured and weighed. In his view, these goods are in the same category as silver and gold, thus making the conjunction of two or more investments in the form of foodstuffs a *ṣarf* contract, and thereby inadmissible.[59]

Indeed, Mālik disapproved of a partnership in which the investment of both parties consists of weighable or measurable foodstuffs. This applies if these investments are of different types, even if they are of equal value. For the status of these goods in sale approaches that of *ṣarf*; and just as he

[57] There is apparently an omission of several words in this sentence in the sixteen-volume edition of the *Mudawwana*; it mentions only that the loss follows each partner's share in the capital and says nothing of the division of work and profit. The missing phrases appear in the four-volume edition, Cairo, 1325, 4:30, and it is on this that I have based my translation.

[58] *Ibid.*, pp. 54–55.

[59] As far as I know, no historical explanation has been offered for Mālik's equating foodstuffs with gold and silver. One possibility that suggests itself is that it reflects an early Islamic or pre-Islamic barter practice in which foodstuffs served as a standard means of exchange. For example, cf. discussion of *darāhim tijāriyya* in Chapter 6.

disapproved of a partnership in which one party invested dinars and the other dirhams, even if the value of each is the same, so too did he indicate to me his disapproval of all measurable and weighable foodstuffs because of their affinity to *ṣarf*.[60]

It is the element of *ṣarf* which for Mālik distinguishes foodstuffs from all other commodities *vis-à-vis* partnership investment. "For according to Mālik, foods are in a category to which *ṣarf* is applicable; all other commodites involve only sale, against which there can be no objection."[61]

Mālik also refused to accept the validity of a partnership in which each partner's capital consisted of foodstuffs of the same type, quality, and quantity. By analogy to a cash partnership, this type of arrangement should be allowed, and no explanation is given for its rejection by Mālik. On this point, Ibn Qāsim dissents from his master's opinion: "I, however, consider this type of partnership permissible if it is formed on the basis of the weight of the foodstuffs, and not according to their value."[62] Ibn Qāsim's position on foodstuffs as a basis for partnership investment is summed up as follows: "I do not consider a partnership in foods permissible unless the investment is evaluated on the basis of weight. If the two investments correspond in weight and in quality, and the work is divided equally between the two partners, the partnership is permissible; if not, then the partnership is not proper."[63]

All Mālikī authorities admit the validity of a partnership in which the investment of only one of the parties consists of foodstuffs. For in such an arrangement, the formation of the common capital would result from a mutual sale and not from an illicit *ṣarf* contract.[64]

The following combinations of commodities are allowed as partnership investment according to Mālikī law: (1) Any licit goods, other than foodstuffs, invested by both parties; (2) Any goods, including foodstuffs, invested by one, and cash

[60] Saḥnūn, *Mudawwana*, p. 56.

[61] *Ibid.*, p. 59.

[62] *Ibid.*, p. 58.

[63] *Ibid.*, p. 58; cf. also, Santillana, *Istituzioni*, 2:291 (top).

[64] Cf. Saḥnūn, *Mudawwana*, 12:65–66.

invested by the other; (3) Goods invested by one and foodstuffs by the other; and (4) Foodstuffs of the same kind and quality invested by both (only according to Ibn Qāsim's dissent from Mālik).

Investment—Credit Partnership

"Partnership in obligations is not permissible; partnership is permissible only on the basis of property (*amwāl*) or manual labor."[65] This brief statement summarizes the Mālikī position *vis-à-vis* forms of investment admissible in a partnership. Partnership in obligations (*sharikat adh-dhimam*), that is, an association in which the communality consists of each partner's sharing in the obligations incurred by his colleague is explicitly rejected.

As a consequence, Mālikī law does not recognize the validity of a credit partnership.[66] A partnership in which the partners do not invest any capital, but instead authorize each other to buy on credit on the condition that each will be responsible for half the cost of the other's purchases and share in a like manner in the profit of their resale is not valid. The inadmissibility of credit purchases as a basis for partnership formation applies to arrangements in which the mutual delegation of authority (*tafwīḍ*) is general and unrestricted, as well as to those in which it is confined to a specific category of commodities; it applies to a partnership in which the partners are situated in the same locality, as well as to one in which they are active in different towns, each supplying the other with merchandise.[67]

A partnership on the basis of a credit purchase is possible only if all the prospective partners participate in the negotiation of the purchase transaction.

> I said: "What if two parties, without any capital, join together in a single transaction and buy a slave on credit?" He said: "This is permissible, and a partnership will exist

[65] *Ibid.*, p. 41.

[66] For a discussion of credit partnership, cf. *ibid.*, pp. 40–42. Santillana, *Istituzioni*, 2:290–291.

[67] Saḥnūn, *Mudawwana*, 12:40.

in regard to this slave. If the two of them purchase this slave jointly in a single transaction, it is their common property, and they are partners in this slave." I said: "Is this Mālik's opinion?" He said: "Yes, this is Mālik's opinion, because if any two people purchase a slave on credit, the purchase will be valid and the slave their joint property."[68]

Investment—Work Partnership

The equation of labor with cash as a valid form of partnership investment is also accepted in Mālikī law. Consequently, the basic structure of a Mālikī work partnership resembles its Ḥanafī counterpart fairly closely. There are, of course, differences in details, some of which may have had an influence on its manifestation in the economic life of the medieval Muslim world. In some respects the Mālikī work partnership is more restrictive, requiring, for example, that all its members follow the same trade or profession, thus excluding an association between a craftsman and an entrepreneur. In other respects it is more comprehensive, including as it does both skilled and unskilled work within its purview.

> If two people form a partnership on the basis of the work of their hands, their labor is to be considered in the same category as dirhams. Anything which is permissible in a partnership formed with dirhams is permissible in one based on the work of their hands.[69]

Both skilled and unskilled labor are, like money and goods, a valid form of partnership investment. Any two laborers, craftsmen, or professionals can share in the profits of their association with an investment of no capital other than their particular skills.

The division of profits and losses in a work partnership, as in other partnership forms, follows each partner's share in the total investment, which, in this case, would consist of the amount of labor each one contributes. No premium is placed on the quality of each partner's labor, and it is apparently

[68] *Ibid.*, p. 41. [69] *Ibid.*, p. 43.

only the quantity of work contributed by each that determines the division of profit.

> I said to Ibn Qāsim: "What is your opinion of two dyers or two tailors who form a partnership to work in the same stall, one of them being more skillful at his work than the other? Is this partnership between them permissible?" He said: "Mālik said that if the partnership is formed on the condition that they work in the same stall, then it is permissible." Ibn Qāsim said: "It is inevitable that some people will be more skillful than others in their work."[70]

Paralleling the uniformity of investment required in a cash partnership, a work partnership requires that all its members follow the same trade or profession and that they work in one place.

> I said: "In your opinion, is a partnership permissible between two blacksmiths, two fullers, two tailors, two cobblers, two saddlemakers, two bakers, or between any two people engaging in similar work?" He said: "Mālik said that if their trade is the same, be they two blacksmiths, or two bakers, or two tailors, or two fullers, and they form a partnership on the condition that they both work in the same stall, this is permissible. It is not permissible, however, that they form a partnership in which one works in this stall and the other in that stall, or this one in one village and his colleague in another village. Similarly, a partnership is not permissible between two people, one of whom is a blacksmith and the other a fuller: it is permissible only if both are blacksmiths, or both are fullers, and in the manner which I described to you."

> I said: "What is your opinion of a work partnership between two fullers who are not in need of any capital, with one third of the work assigned to one partner and two thirds to the other, on the condition that the former be entitled to one third of the income while providing one third of the dye, and the other be entitled to two thirds of the in-

[70] *Ibid.*, p. 42.

come while providing two thirds of the dye?" He said: "There is nothing wrong with this arrangement; it is like a partnership in dirhams. For if two people form a partnership on the basis of the work of their hands, their labor is to be considered in the same category as dirhams. Anything which is permissible in a partnership formed with dirhams is permissible in one based on the work of their hands." I said: "According to Mālik, is the same applicable to a partnership formed by a group of fullers or a group of blacksmiths working in the same stall?" He said: "Yes."[71]

A work partnership as conceived by the Mālikī assumes the participation of all its members in the actual work. An association in which all the work is assigned to one partner, while the other provides some necessary capital or equipment, but no work, is not a valid partnership. The non-working party is not entitled to any share of the income and can claim only the return of his investment and, if it happened to be in a form other than cash, some equitable rental fee for its use. In keeping with this view, a partnership between a worker and an entrepreneur on the basis of an equal division of the income is inadmissible because of the latter's non-participation in the actual work.

I said: "What is your opinion of an arrangement in which I place a person in a stall and say to him: 'I will accept the goods and you will do the work on the condition that whatever God grants us will be shared between us equally?'" He said: "According to Mālik, this is not permissible."[72]

Ibn Qāsim said: "Among the various types of work, there are some in the pursuit of which no capital is required; and there is nothing wrong with people entering into partnerships only on the basis of the work of their hands."[73] In addi-

[71] *Ibid.*, pp. 42–43. Later Mālikī authorities extend the validity of a work partnership to include different, but related, work; e.g., a dyer and a weaver. Cf. Santillana, *Istituzioni*, 2:301; Ruxton, *Māliḳī Law*, p. 196; Guidi and Santillana, *Il "Muḫtaṣar,"* 2:370–372.

[72] Saḥnūn, *Mudawwana*, 12:41. For an entirely different disposition of this case in Ḥanafī law, cf. discussion of "Labor Partnerships" in Chapter 3.

[73] *Ibid.*, p. 43.

tion to this category of work referred by Ibn Qāsim, there is also one in which the investment of money and/or equipment is essential. Formation of a partnership in any craft or profession of the latter category would thus involve a mixed investment of labor and capital. In such cases, the problem would be to determine which component of the investment is to serve as the basis for profit division, and then to establish an equilibrium between all the elements of each partner's investment and his share of the profit and liability. If it is the work which is the determining element of the investment, then any investment other than work must either be compensated for or canceled out by an investment of similar value by the other partner. The procedure for this has been discussed in a preceding section of this chapter.

All types of work, both physical and mental, are included within the purview of Mālikī work partnership. For example, two doctors or two teachers working out of the same place may associate in a partnership to share the income from the use of their services. In the case of doctors, however, any money spent on *materia medica* must be contributed equally by both partners.[74]

The Mālikī insistence on a single place of work as a prerequisite for a valid work partnership does not rule out associations between non-sedentary workers. Work which necessitates the mobility of the participants can serve as the basis for a partnership if the partners work together, helping and complementing each other's efforts. Although Mālik does not, for example, approve of treasure hunting in the graves and monuments of antiquity, there is no legal barrier to a partnership in the discovery of such treasures if the partners work together.[75]

Similarly, partnerships in the exploitation of resources found in the public domain, such as gathering brush-wood, hay, and wild fruits, or hunting and fishing, or mining and quarrying, are permissible if pursued together by all parties to

[74] Saḥnūn, *Mudawwana*, 12:48. One can assume that what holds true for partnerships between doctors and teachers would also apply to associations between all categories of "white collar" workers, such as scribes and others.

[75] *Ibid.*, p. 52.

the association.[76] Any equipment or materials necessary for these pursuits, such as boats, nets, traps, etcetera, must be jointly owned or their proprietors equitably compensated for their use.

Conduct of the Partnership

In the absence of any contrary stipulation, members of a Mālikī *mufāwaḍa* partnership are presumed to have discretionary powers in the administration of their joint capital. In all transactions which are recognized as a usual part of trade, each partner can act independently in the name of the partnership without exposing himself, in the case of loss, to any liability greater than that which would normally be his share.

> I said: "Is it, in your opinion, permissible for a *mufāwaḍa* partner to give part of the joint capital as a *biḍāʿa*, or invest it in a *commenda* without his colleague's express permission?" He said: "Yes, it is permissible if the two people involved established a *mufāwaḍa* partnership in the manner which I described to you, that is, if they delegate to each other the authority to transact business with the common capital, having said to each other, 'act according to your best judgment.'"[77]

Deposit

"Deposit is not a part of trade."[78] This, surprisingly, is Mālik's opinion of the status of deposits in commerce. As a consequence, members of a partnership do not possess the unqualified right to deposit any portion of the common property with a third party. If one of the partners should nevertheless do so, and the deposited property is adversely affected, the depositor is fully liable to his partner for the loss unless he can prove that there were compelling circumstances for his action.

> I said: "Is it permissible for him (the *mufāwaḍa* partner) to place the partnership goods in deposit?" He said: "Only

[76] *Ibid.*, pp. 49–52.

[77] *Ibid.*, p. 75.

[78] *Ibid.*, p. 77, *al-wadīʿa laysa min at-tijāra.* For the diametrically opposed Ḥanafī view, cf. section on "Deposits and Pledges in the *Mufāwaḍa*" in Chapter 3.

if there is a need for him to make the deposit is it permissible for him to do so." I said: "Is this Mālik's opinion?" He said: "It is my own view, but we did ask Mālik concerning the following: A man deposits money with another, and the latter in turn deposits it with a third party, after which the money is lost. Is the man with whom it was originally deposited liable? He said: "If this man intends to set out on a journey, or his house is unsafe, or if he has some similar excuse, then I do not consider him liable; if, however, he has no such excuse, I do consider him liable.'" He said: "We then said to Mālik: 'What about the case of a traveler who is given merchandise to take along with him, and he in turn gives it over to a third party?' Mālik said: 'He is liable; and one should not consider him in the same category as a sedentary depositary. For the traveler is aware of his itinerary and of the fact that he is in the course of his travels. Whereas the partner concerning whom you inquired, when he arrives in a town, he fears for the safety of the possessions he has with him, and he therefore deposits them with someone. Because the places where merchants alight when they are traveling are of the kind that you are well aware of; these are hostels, and similar places where they fear for the safety of their belongings. The partner, therefore, is not liable if he makes a deposit when in such circumstances. But if he makes a deposit when he does not find himself in any circumstances such as these, I consider him liable.'"[79]

Since "deposit is not a part of trade," any liability arising from a deposit left with one of the partners is borne by that partner alone, and none attaches to the partnership as a whole. A deposit of this kind is unrelated to their common trade and is considered strictly as a contract between an individual depositor and an individual depositary.[80]

Loans for Use (*'Āriyya*)

If a *mufāwaḍa* partner independently takes a loan for use in connection with the pursuit of the company's business, he

[79] *Ibid.*, pp. 75–76.

[80] *Ibid.*, p. 77.

alone is responsible for the full extent of any damage that might befall the borrowed object. This is so, because his colleague can justifiably reproach him for not having hired the services of the object in question instead of having borrowed it. In the case of hire, the liability would be restricted to the payment of a fee, and the responsibility for all damages would be that of the lessor. The partner, having exposed the partnership to unnecessary liability, is therefore solely responsible for all damages.[81]

> Ibn Qāsim said: "He alone is liable, because the man borrowed the pack animal or the ship, whose value is one hundred dinars, when he could have hired them at a fee of one dinar. This constitutes an injury to his colleague, and this is not permissible."[82]

Use of partnership funds or property to give loans for use is restricted to trivial things, or to matters which are intended to benefit the partnership. Neither partner has the independent right to grant loans for purposes other than these.

> I said: "Is a partner permitted to grant a loan for use from partnership material?" he said: "This is not permitted unless it involves only some trivial thing, as, for example, ordering a servant to water a man's animal. In this, I hope, there is no harm. A loan for use is a favor; and neither of them is permitted to grant favors out of the partnership property except with the permission of his colleague, or with the intention of thereby creating goodwill for the sake of their trade."[83]

This passage is possibly one of the earliest expressions of appreciation of the value of good public relations to the profitable prosecution of business. Partners are allowed to offer, independently, substantial discounts on their wares and even to bestow gifts from the partnership property for the purpose of attracting customers and maintaining good relations with them.[84]

[81] *Ibid.*, pp. 78–79.
[82] *Ibid.*, p. 79.
[83] *Ibid.*
[84] *Ibid.*, p. 80.

Commenda

For a *mufāwaḍa* partner to invest any of the joint capital in a *commenda* with a third party constitutes a legitimate exercise of the authority delegated to him by his colleague at the time their association was contracted.[85] Any resultant profits or losses are to be reckoned on the account of the partnership.

This is not the case, however, if one of the partners accepts a *commenda* investment from an outside party. In this case, all profits and liabilities are completely independent of the partnership, "because the acceptance of a *commenda* investment by one of the partners is not a part of their trade. He has the status of an employee who has hired himself out for the purposes of the *commenda*, and his partner has nothing to do with it."[86]

Partnership with Third Parties

A *mufāwaḍa* partner does not have the right, except with his colleague's express approval, to invest the company's capital in a *mufāwaḍa* partnership with a third party. He may, however, independently negotiate a partnership of short duration and limited scope.

> If, however, he negotiates a partnership which is not a *mufāwaḍa* partnership, for example, a partnership in one commodity, or something similar, this is permissible because it is a trade transaction like any other trade transaction.[87]

Expenses

All business expenses are covered by partnership funds. Money expended or debts incurred for such activities as travel, or for the acquisition, transportation, and maintenance of company property, can be recovered from the joint capital.

The disposition of personal and family expenses of the *mufāwaḍa* partners varies with their marital status. If both are single, or if both are married with families, all their regular personal expenses are on the partnership account. Neither partner need render any account of the funds expended on his

[85] *Ibid.*, p. 75. [86] *Ibid.*, p. 78. [87] *Ibid.*, p. 78.

household, since each partner's expenses are considered to cancel out those of his colleague. This holds true even if the partners are situated in two separate towns, each having a different price level. If one partner is single and the other is a family man, they are required to render an account of their personal expenses, and the difference between the single and married partner's expenditures are to be covered from the latter's personal funds.[88]

Personal expenses covered by the partnership include only the necessities of daily life; luxury items are expressly excluded.

> I said: "If one of the partners buys food or clothing for his own, or his family's use, may the seller of these items collect their price from either of the partners?" He said: "Yes, he may. Mālik told me that any food that they purchase, or any other expenditures for themselves and their families, are to be charged to the partnership capital; because if they both have families, their expenses cancel each other out. From Mālik's statement that their expenses cancel each other out, we may conclude that whatever household expenses they incur are to be charged to the partnership capital, and that the cost of clothing for themselves and their families is also charged to the partnership. . . . If the garments are of the kind that are not used in daily wear, such as fine linen, *shaṭawī*,[89] and silk brocade garments, etcetera, these are not to be charged to the partnership."[90]

A slave girl, purchased with partnership funds by one of the partners for his personal pleasure, is in the category of a luxury item; e.g., her cost is not to be borne by the partnership. The purchaser is required to reimburse the common fund to the extent of one half of her value.[91]

Purchase, Sale, and Debts

The liability for obligations arising from the commercial activity of the *mufāwaḍa* partners is joint and several. Third

88 *Ibid.*, p. 68; Santillana, *Istituzioni*, 2:298.

89 Cf. R. Dozy, *Supplément aux Dictionnaires Arabes*, 2nd ed., 2 vols., Leiden, 1927, 1:760: "étoffe précieuse."

90 Saḥnūn, *Mudawwana*, 12:69–70.

91 *Ibid.*, pp. 71–73.

parties, therefore, can treat with either partner, and vice versa, even if the particular transaction was conducted by one of them only. This applies to the rights and obligations pertaining to all purchases, sales, and debts, both those related to partnership business and those connected with the household affairs of the individual partners. The price of any partnership property sold by one partner can be collected by the other, and third parties can claim payment from one partner for goods sold to his colleague.[92] Similarly, any defective merchandise bought or sold by the partnership by one of its members can be returned to or by any of the other partners.[93]

A partner has the right to sell on credit, even if this right is not explicitly conferred in the partnership contract.[94] He can also make purchases on credit for the partnership; such transactions, however, are frowned upon by Ibn Qāsim if the amount involved in these purchases exceeds the total amount of the joint capital.

> I said: "What is your opinion of a *mufāwaḍa* partnership in which both partners invest equally on the condition that they make purchases with this capital and that they also buy and sell on credit, and that whatever profit God grants them be shared between them equally?" He said: "I do not approve of the formation of a *mufāwaḍa* partnership which involves purchases in excess of their capital; for partnership is not permissible except on the basis of actual capital. If they nevertheless make credit purchases, the purchased goods belong to them in equal shares."[95]

A *mufāwaḍa* partner's right independently to grant a postponement of the payment of a debt owed to the partnership, or to offer a discount on goods whose sale has already been negotiated, is governed by the same considerations as those affecting the loan for use (*'āriyya*). If an individual partner, motivated only by business considerations, granted a postponement or discount, e.g., in order to cultivate good will and attract customers, his colleague can raise no complaint against him. If,

[92] *Ibid.*, p. 69.
[93] *Ibid.*, p. 81.
[94] *Ibid.*, p. 71.
[95] *Ibid.*, p. 71.

however, this was done purely as a personal favor, his colleague can demand the immediate payment of his share of the debt or the discount.[96]

A partner is entitled to no special consideration in the price of any joint property he wishes to purchase exclusively for himself.[97]

Slaves

Neither partner has the independent right to set free a jointly owned slave or to grant him any change in status. If he does so, he is liable to reimburse his colleague for the latter's share in the slave.[98]

Exclusions from Mutual Liability

A *mufāwaḍa* partner is in no way liable for any obligations of his colleague arising from the following categories of activities: (1) Criminal acts; (2) Wrongful appropriation or use of someone else's property (*ghaṣb*); (3) Marriage and divorce; (4) Surety provided by a partner for the commercial activities of third parties.[99]

End of the Partnership

The termination of the Mālikī *mufāwaḍa* partnership is affected by the same factors affecting that of the Ḥanafī *mufāwaḍa*.[100] The partnership is terminated by the mutual consent of the partners, by the accomplishment of its aim, by the expiration of the term stipulated in the contract, or upon the death of one of the partners.[101]

[96] Saḥnūn, *Mudawwana*, 12:73–74.
[97] *Ibid.*, p. 75. [98] *Ibid.*, p. 81. [99] *Ibid.*, p. 81.
[100] Cf. section on "Dissolution of Partnership" in Chapter 3.
[101] Cf. Saḥnūn, *Mudawwana*, 12:84; Santillana, *Istituzioni*, 2:300.

VI

The *Commenda* (*Muḍāraba, Qirāḍ, Muqāraḍa*)

Origins and Early History

In the medieval period, the partnership and *commenda* contracts were the two basic legal instruments for combining financial and human resources for the purposes of trade. This holds true for the medieval West as it does for the medieval Muslim world.[1] In Islamic law and in Western commercial practice these two institutions were the chief methods for pooling capital and bringing together investors and managers. Having discussed partnership in preceding chapters, we will now focus our attention on the *commenda*.

The *commenda* is an arrangement in which an investor or group of investors entrusts capital or merchandise to an agent-manager, who is to trade with it and then return to the investor(s) the principal and a previously agreed-upon share of the profits. As a reward for his labor, the agent receives the remaining share of the profits. Any loss resulting from the exigencies of travel or from an unsuccessful business venture is borne exclusively by the investor(s); the agent is in no way liable for a loss of this nature, losing only his expended time and effort.[2]

[1] For the West, cf. Robert S. Lopez and J. W. Raymond, *Medieval Trade in the Mediterranean World*, New York, 1955, pp. 174ff.; also R. de Roover, "The Organization of Trade" in *Cambridge Economic History of Europe* (*CEH*), 3:46-55. For medieval Near Eastern trade, cf. S. D. Goitein *A Mediterranean Society*, Berkeley and Los Angeles, 1967, pp. 169–179; also "Commercial and Family Partnerships in the Countries of Medieval Islam," *Islamic Studies* 3 (1964):315–337.

[2] This paragraph describes a unilateral *commenda*, the simplest, paradigmatic form of the contract, i.e., a *commenda* in which the entire capital comes from the investor's side, and none from the agent. It is possible for the investing function to overlap and embrace the agent as well. In a bilateral *commenda*, part of the capital is furnished by the agent. (Re: these two types, cf. Lopez and Raymond, *Medieval Trade in the Mediterranean World*, p. 175.) The agent's contribution is, in a sense, not really part of the *commenda*, and is not governed by its rules, since the agent enjoys the total profit from his share. Its chief importance within the *commenda* is that

The *commenda* combined the advantages of a loan with those of a partnership; and while containing elements characteristic of both, it cannot be strictly classified in either category. In all Islamic legal writings, it is treated as a distinct and independent contract with a separate section or book (*kitāb*) devoted to it. As in partnership, profits and risks are shared by both parties, the investor risking capital, the agent his time and effort. However, in the *commenda* no social capital is formed, and the investor does not become directly or jointly liable with the agent in transactions with third parties; indeed, third parties need not ever be aware of the investor's existence.[3] As in a loan, the *commenda* generally entailed no liability for the investor beyond the sum of money or quantity of commodities handed over to the agent; and in the event of its successful completion, the agent returned the capital plus a share of the profits (the latter, corresponding to the interest in an interest-bearing loan).

The agent's complete freedom under normal trading circumstances from any liability for the capital in the event of partial or total loss and the disjunction between the owners of the capital and third parties are novel and distinctive features of the *commenda* which made it a particularly suitable instrument for long-distance trade. Its introduction, probably from the Islamic world,[4] in the Italian seaports of the late tenth and

---

the willingness of the investor to conclude the contract may be contingent on the agent's providing some capital as well. In view of the fact that the investor receives no direct financial benefit from imposing such a condition, the rationale behind it was probably less direct; e.g., the investor might calculate that a larger total sum in the venture would increase the opportunities of profitable trading activities, or he might feel that the agent's direct financial stake in the transactions would make him at once more cautious and more enterprising. Cf. below for a discussion of the problems involved in a bilateral *commenda*.

3 For the exceptional circumstances in which this principle is qualified, cf. below, "Distribution of Liability."

4 Cf. A. L. Udovitch, "At the Origins of the Western *Commenda*: Islam, Israel, Byzantium?", *SPECULUM* 36 (1962):198–207. Since very little is known of early medieval Western and Byzantine commercial law, we cannot exclude the possibility of an indigenous European or late-Roman antecedent to the Italian *commenda*. In the present state of our knowledge, however, the Islamic-Near Eastern origin of this commercial institution seems most likely.

early eleventh centuries, was germinal to the expansion of medieval European trade.[5] Although commercial arrangements resembling the *commenda* were known in the Near Eastern and Mediterranean world from the earliest times,[6] it is the Islamic form of the contract (*qirāḍ, muqāraḍa, muḍāraba*) which is the earliest example of a commercial arrangement identical with that economic and legal institution which became known in Europe as the *commenda*.

It appears very likely that the *commenda* was an institution indigenous to the Arabian peninsula which developed in the context of the pre-Islamic Arabian caravan trade. With the Arab conquests, it spread to the Near East, North Africa, and ultimately to Southern Europe. The *commenda* was the subject of lengthy and detailed discussion in the earliest Islamic legal compendia (late eighth century). Its legal treatment in these early treatises bears the hallmark of long experience with the *commenda* as an established commercial institution.

Although not mentioned in the Qur'ān, numerous traditions attribute its practice to the Prophet and his leading companions. According to one tradition, Muḥammad, in the early part of his career, acted as an agent in a *commenda* contract with an investment provided by Khadīja, his wife-to-be.[7] Another tradition attributed to Muḥammad an unequivocal endorsement and approval of those engaging in trade by means of a *commenda*. "The Messenger of God, may God bless him and keep him, was sent at a time when people were using the *commenda* in their dealings and he confirmed them in this practice. He also urged them towards it in his statement, may God keep him and bless him, 'He who has a family with three daughters and is a captive, then help ye him O servants of God, engage in a *commenda* in his behalf and go into debt on his

[5] Cf. Lopez and Raymond, *Medieval Trade in the Mediterranean World*, and further literature cited there.

[6] E.g., the Babylonian *tapputum* for which cf. G. Astuti, *Origini e svolgimento storico della commenda fino al secolo XIII*, Turin, 1932, pp. 104–108 and references there; also the Byzantine *chreokoinonia* and the Jewish *'isqā*, for which cf. my article referred to in note 4.

[7] Cf. Shirbīnī, *Mughnī al-muḥtāj*, 2:309 (bottom) in Nawawī's *Minhāj aṭ-ṭālibīn*, 4 vols., Cairo, 1374/1955.

behalf.' "[8] 'Umar and 'Uthmān, the second and third of the rightly guided Caliphs were parties to *commenda* contracts. The former invested the money of orphans of which he was guardian with merchants who traded between Madinah and Iraq.[9] 'Āisha and 'Abdullah b. 'Umar used to invest orphans' money and other money left in their safekeeping in *commendas*.[10] Ibn Mas'ūd, a prominent companion of the Prophet, and 'Abbās b. 'Abd al-Muṭṭalib, the uncle of the Prophet, engaged in *commenda* trading, the latter having obtained Muḥammad's approval for the conditions he imposed upon agents to whom he entrusted his money.[11] The two sons of 'Umar used the provincial tax money which they were transporting to the capital of the early Caliphate at Madinah as a *commenda*, buying Iraqi merchandise which they then sold at a profit in Madinah, and keeping half the profit for themselves and returning the original sum with the remainder of the profit to the treasury.[12]

From the sparse indications available, it appears that this form of commercial association continued through the early centuries of the Islamic era as a mainstay of caravan and long-distance trade.[13] In one of the very few medieval Arabic

[8] Sarakhsī, *Mabsūṭ*, 30 vols., Cairo, 1324/1906–1331/1912, 22:19. For the use of the *commenda* in pre-Islamic Arabian trade between the Quraysh and other tribes, cf. M. J. Kister, "Mecca and Tamīm," *Journal of the Economic and Social History of the Orient* (*JESHO*) 8 (1965):117ff.: although no Arabic term denoting *commenda* is used, the arrangement which is described is in effect that of a *commenda*.

[9] Shaybānī, *Aṣl, Muḍāraba*, fols. 42a, 42b; Sarakhsī, *Mabsūṭ*, 22:18, l. 21ff.; Ibn Sa'd, *Kitāb aṭ-ṭabaqāt al-kabīr*, ed. E. Sachau, Leiden, 1904, vol. 3, part 1:41; Balādhurī, *Ansāb al-ashrāf*, ed. S. D. Goitein, Jerusalem, 1936, vol. 5, part 2.

[10] Shaybānī, *Aṣl, Muḍāraba*, fol. 42b, ll. 12–14, Sarakhsī, *Mabsūṭ*, 22:18, cf. also Santillana, *Istituzioni*, 2 vols., Rome, 1925–1938, 2:324 where the author points out that the same practice was recommended for orphan's money in the statutes of Italian towns.

[11] Shaybānī, *Aṣl, Muḍāraba*, fol. 42a; Sarakhsī, *Mabsūṭ*, 22:18, ll. 8–12.

[12] Sarakhsī, *Mabsūṭ*, 22:18; for variant versions of this tradition, cf. *Sharḥ az-Zurqānī 'alā muwaṭṭa' al-imām Mālik*, Cairo, n.d. 3:345.

[13] Cf. Sāliḥ al-'Alī, *At-tanẓīmāt al-ijtimā'iyya wal-iqtiṣadiyya fil-baṣra fil-qarn al-awwal al-hijrī*, Baghdad, 1953, pp. 242–243; indeed, it is likely that it was via the *commenda* that Medinese notables like az-Zubayr amassed their large fortunes from the *amṣār* and other newly conquered territories. Cf. also, A. A. Dūrī, *Ta'rīkh al-'Irāq al-iqtiṣādi fil-qarn ar-rābi' al-hijrī*, Baghdad, 1948, pp. 121ff.

treatises of commerce, ad-Dimashqī's *The Beauties of Commerce* (probably eleventh century), the *commenda* is cited as one of the three methods by which trade is carried out;[14] Ghazzālī lists it among the six commercial contracts "the knowledge of which is indispensable to anyone seeking gain in trade."[15] The Geniza documents are replete with numerous examples of *commenda* agreements which account for a considerable share of the commercial activity reflected in these documents.[16] Thus we can confidently conclude that not only in law, but in practice as well, the *commenda* constituted one of the most widespread tools of commercial activity.

Three Arabic terms are used to designate the *commenda*: *qirāḍ, muqāraḍa*, and *muḍāraba*; the terms are interchangeable with no essential difference in meaning or connotation among them. The divergence in terminology was probably originally due to geographical factors. The terms *qirāḍ* and *muqāraḍa* apparently originated in the Arabian peninsula, and the term *muḍāraba* was of Iraqi provenance. Subsequently, the difference was perpetuated by the legal schools, the Mālikīs and Shāfi'īs adopting the term *qirāḍ* and to a lesser degree, *muqāraḍa*, and the Ḥanafī's the term *muḍāraba*.

> The term *muḍāraba* is derived from the expression 'making a journey' (*aḍ-ḍarb fil-arḍ*), and it is called this because the agent (*al-muḍārib*) is entitled to the profit by virtue of his effort and work. And he is the investor's partner in the profit and in the capital used on the journey and in its dispositions.
>
> The people of Madina call this contract *muqāraḍa*, and that is based on a tradition concerning 'Uthman, may God look favorably upon him, who entrusted funds to a man in the form of a *muqāraḍa*. This is derived from *al-qarḍ* which

[14] H. Ritter, "Ein arabisches Handbuch der Handelswissenchaft," *Der Islam* 7 (1917):58; quoted in English translation in Lopez and Raymond, *Medieval Trade in the Mediterranean World*, p. 24. Re: the dating of this treatise cf. Cl. Cahen, "A propos et autour d'Ein arabisches Handbuch der Handelswissenschaft," *Oriens* 15 (1962):160–162.

[15] Ghazzālī, *Iḥyā' 'ulūm ad-dīn*, 4 vols., Cairo, 1957, 2:66.

[16] Cf. S. D. Goitein, "Commercial and Family Partnerships," *Islamic Studies* 3 (1964):315, n. 1, and *idem, A Mediterranean Society*, pp. 169ff.

signifies cutting; for in this contract the investor cuts off the disposition of this sum of money from himself and transfers its disposition to the agent. It is therefore designated by that name (*muqāraḍa*). We, however, have preferred the first term (*muḍāraba*) because it corresponds to that which is found in the book of God, may He be exalted. God, may He be exalted, said: "While others travel in the land (*yaḍribūna fil-arḍ*) in search of Allah's bounty,"[17] that is to say, travel for the purposes of trade.[18]

As in the case of partnership, the law justifies the licitness of the *commenda* contract on the religious grounds of traditional practice (*sunna*), the consensus of the community (*ijmā'*)[19] and, more interestingly, on the practical grounds of its economic function in society. After quoting a series of traditions describing the *commenda*'s use in trade by the Prophet and his companions, Sarakhsī adds that it is also allowed:

> Because people have a need for this contract. For the owner of capital may not find his way to profitable trading activity, and the person who can find his way to such activity, may not have the capital. And profit cannot be attained except by means of both of these, that is, capital and trading activity. By permitting this contract, the goal of both parties is attained.[20]

Sarakhsī's summary of the *commenda*'s economic function is as accurate and to the point as that made by any contemporary student of medieval economic institutions. It includes the most important functions of the *commenda* in trade which have been described as "the hiring of capital" and the "hiring

[17] *Qur'ān*, 73:20.

[18] Sarakhsī, *Mabsūṭ*, 22:18. Cf. also Shirbīnī, *Mughnī al-muḥtāj*, 2:309, who states that the *qirāḍ* "was the usage of the people of the Ḥijāz"; Zurqānī, *Sharḥ 'ala muwaṭṭa' al-imām Mālik*, 4 vols., Cairo, 3:345, and Santillana, *Istituzioni*, 2:323, n. 125.

[19] Sarakhsī, *Mabsūṭ*, 22:18; the Shāfi'īs add a third traditional ground for the *commenda's* permissibility, that of its analogy (*qiyās*) to the agricultural lease contract (*musāqāt*); cf. Shirbīnī, *Mughnī al-muḥtāj*, 2:309.

[20] Sarakhsī, *Mabsūṭ*, 22:19, cf. also *Kāsānī*, 7 vols., Cairo, 1328/1910, 6:79.

of trading skill."[21] By pointing to its economic function, Sarakhsī also provides an explanation for its widespread use in medieval trade. To paraphrase him, profit can be realized only by the combination of capital and trading activity, and in certain commercial contexts such as long-distance trade, the *commenda* becomes the ideal instrument to attain this profitable goal.

Uniformity of Legal Treatment

In contrast to partnership, the legal treatment of the *commenda* in the three major schools of early Muslim law is sufficiently uniform to permit its discussion within the compass of a single chapter. There are, to be sure, differences between the schools on individual legal points; but the basic structural features of the *commenda*, as well as the character of the relationships between its principal parties, are similar in all the schools. This greater uniformity, as compared with partnership, may be explained by its probable development from a single indigenous institution of the Arabian caravan trade. Its elaboration in Islamic law was thus influenced and guided by its unitary origin. The Ḥanafī *commenda* emerges as at once the most comprehensive, practical and flexible form of this contract. Using these criteria it is followed in descending order by the Mālikī and Shāfi'ī versions. For this reason, I have made the Ḥanafī *muḍāraba* the basis of the following remarks, pointing wherever necessary to parallels or deviations in the other two law schools.

Investment Form

The criteria for the eligibility of various types of property for investment in a *commenda* are the same as those for partnership.[22] These are summarized by Abū Ḥanīfa in the following statement:

Abū Ḥanīfa said: "One cannot have a *commenda* except

[21] Cf. M. M. Postan, "Credit in Medieval Trade," *Economic History Review* 1 (1927): 234–261; and *idem*, "Partnership in English Medieval Commerce," *Studi in Onore di A. Sapori*, 1, Milan, 1927, pp. 521–549.

[22] Cf. above, Chapter 3, "Investment Form and Formation of Joint Capital."

with dinars and dirhams. It cannot be formed with anything except these, nor with any other objects that are measured or weighed, nor with any type of goods. It can only be formed with dinars and dirhams. Abū Yūsuf expressed the same opinion. Muḥammad (i.e., Shaybānī), however, on the basis of *istiḥsān*, said that a *commenda* can be formed with *fulūs* (copper coins) just as with dinars or dirhams since the former are currency comparable to dinars and dirhams; but it cannot be created with anything except these."[23]

Coins of Various Types

Any gold, silver, or copper coins[24] which were in circulation and were accepted as legal tender were eligible for investment in a *commenda*. Gold and silver coins possessed intrinsic value, and as such were recognizable as legal tender in the Middle Ages, at all times and in all places. It is, therefore, self-evident that they should be eligible for investment in any and all commercial contracts. Copper coins on the other hand, were a fiduciary currency with little or no intrinsic value. The temporal and geographical extent of their circulation was considerably more limited than that of silver and gold coins. It is therefore worthy of note that in spite of the difference of opinions among the early legal scholars, subsequent Ḥanafī law included copper coins within the category of currency permissible for *commenda* investments. However, non-circulating copper coins were excluded; they were held to be commodities and not currency, and hence ineligible for *commenda* investment.[25] Essentially the same principle applied to unminted

[23] Shaybānī, *Aṣl, Muḍāraba*, fol. 43a, ll. 9–13. Part of the last sentence required a slight correction in the text of the *Aṣl*; it reads: *liannahā thaman min ad-danānīr wad-darāhim*. The correct reading is found in Sarakhsī's *Mabsūṭ*, 22:21—*liannahā thaman mithl ad-danānīr wad-darāhim*. In this passage, I have translated *thaman* as currency because of the requirements of the context. Literally it means price. Cf. J. Schacht, *An Introduction to Islamic Law*, Oxford, 1959, 1964, p. 152.

[24] For the equal status of gold, silver, and copper coins (*dinar, dirham, fals*) for investment and subsequent *commenda* transactions, cf. *Shaybānī, Aṣl, Muḍāraba*, fol. 164b, ll. 4–7.

[25] Shaybānī, *Aṣl, Muḍāraba*, fols. 52b, 53a, especially fol. 53a, ll. 9ff., Sarakhsī, *Mabsūṭ*, 22:21; Mālikī and Shāfi'ī law absolutely disqualify copper coins (*fulūs*) for *commenda* investments, cf. Saḥnūn, *Mudawwana*, 16 vols.,

silver and gold. Except in areas where the precious metals in unminted form were used in exchange as currency, they were considered as ordinary commercial commodities and thus invalid for *commenda* investment.[26] The requirement that the *commenda* investment consist of legal tender was also applied to various marginal types of dirhams. Thus, for example, *zuyūf* and *bahraj* dirhams were valid for investment in a *commenda* whereas the *sattūq* and lead dirhams were invalid for this purpose.[27] The distinction would appear to be based on the fact that *bahraj* and *zuyūf* dirhams, while debased coins of low silver content, were nevertheless an accepted medium of exchange; on the other hand, *sattūq* dirhams were apparently counterfeit, spurious coins, unacceptable for any transaction.

Another type, the "commercial dirhams" (*darāhim tijāriyya*),[28] at first rejected for the purposes of *commenda* investment, was later allowed in response to economic realities.

Damascus, n.d., 12:86. Shirbīnī, *Mughnī al-muḥtāj*, 2:310, al-Ghazzālī, *Al-wajīz fī fiqh al-imām ash-Shāfi'ī*, Cairo, 1317/1900, 2:221.

26 Shaybānī, *Aṣl*, *Muḍāraba*, fol. 52b, Sarakhsī, *Mabsūṭ*, 22:21. Cf. also Saḥnūn, *Mudawwana*, 12:87.

27 Shaybānī, *Aṣl*, *Muḍāraba*, fol. 52b; *Kāsānī*, 6:82. Cf. also, R. Brunschvig, "Conceptions monétaires chez les juristes musulmans (VIIIe–XIIIe siècles)," *ARABICA* 14 (1967):134–137, where these terms are briefly discussed. Consultation of lexicographical works yields very little clarification regarding the precise meaning of these terms. Whatever technical meaning they conveyed in the early Islamic centuries had apparently already become blurred and indistinct by the time the great lexicographers compiled their works. For example, the *Lisān al-'arab* (s.v. *bahraj*, *zuyūf* and *sattūq*) describes all three as bad and sub-standard dirhams. However, from the stories, traditions and lines of poetry cited, it appears that the *bahraj* and *zuyūf* dirhams, while bad, were nevertheless accepted for most transactions; the *bahraj* is explicitly described as dirham of low and poor silver content (*fiḍḍatuhu radī'a*, *Lisān al-'arab*, Beirut ed., 2:217, col. 1). The *sattūq* dirham, on the other hand, is described as a coin without any redeeming quality (*lā khayr fīhi*, *Lisān al-'arab*, 10:152, col. 2). This corresponds to *Kāsānī*, 6:82: "The *sattūq* and lead dirhams are not to be compared with the *bahraja* and *zuyūf* dirhams since the *sattūq* and lead dirhams do not contain any silver and are just like any other commodities, and are in the same category as raw lead or raw brass."

28 These are not to be confused with the commercial dirhams in William Popper, *Egypt and Syria under the Circassian Sultans, University of California Publications in Semitic Philology* 16 (1957):53, and 60–67. Popper used this term to describe the Mamluk *darāhim fulūs* (copper dirhams), and it does not, as in this case, correspond to any term in the Arabic sources.

He (Abū Yūsuf) was asked concerning a *commenda* with commercial dirhams and he said, "Were I to permit that, then a *commenda* in foodstuffs in Mecca would be permissible." That is to say that the people of Mecca used foodstuffs as a medium of exchange just as the inhabitants of Bukhara use wheat. The shaykh, the noble *imām* (Sarakhsī) may God have mercy upon him said, "Our shaykh, the *imām*, may God have mercy upon him, used to say: 'In my view, the correct opinion is that a *commenda* with commercial dirhams is permissible, because they are among the most widely used currency among us, comparable to dinars in other countries.' "[29]

As far as I have been able to ascertain, nothing is known about the exact nature and use of these "commercial dirhams." From the present context it would appear that they refer to some sort of token coinage based on an important local commodity whose circulation was restricted to one town or to a town and its immediate environs. If this supposition is correct, what we have here is a primitive, purely local currency, just one stage beyond the level of barter, existing side by side with a more universally accepted system of currency. The simultaneous production and employment of purely local currency co-existing with more widely accepted and higher quality coins is attested in other areas of the medieval world.[30] The "commercial dirhams," like coinage of a similar type in other areas, were used exclusively for local, internal trade, and probably primarily for small transactions. These may have been used to substitute for the absence, or to supplement the shortage of other petty coins such as *fulūs* and the fractional dirhams (*qiṭ'a*, pl. *qaṭā'i'*).

Another interesting aspect of this passage is the change of doctrine on this point which occurred between the time of Abū Yūsuf (d. 182/798), one of the epigones of the Ḥanafī school, and that of Sarakhsī's teacher (ca. mid-eleventh century). In the some two hundred years that separate them, the

[29] Sarakhsī, *Mabsūṭ*, 22:21.

[30] E.g., in Byzantium, cf. Robert S. Lopez, "The Dollar of the Middle Ages," *Journal of Economic History* 11 (1951):209–234.

"commercial dirhams" that were originally ruled out as a valid form of *commenda* investment were allowed by Ḥanafī doctrine because of the prevalence of their use. This is more than an example of the responsiveness of Ḥanafī law to economic needs and realities; from an economic point of view it indicated that commerce had at its disposal the entire reservoir of monetary resources of the medieval Islamic world. This not only facilitated the financing of trade, but could also stimulate its velocity by making available all types of currency in an age when the supply of standard, good-quality coins was not always adequate.

Inadmissibility of Goods as Investment

There are two general considerations underlying the rejection of goods and commodities for investment in a *commenda*.[31] The first is the opposition to risk and unjustified enrichment which permeates the entire Islamic law of obligations;[32] and the second, its corollary, is the strict requirement in Islamic law that the object of any contract be determined (*ma'lūm*) i.e., clearly known and defined.[33] In explaining the ineligibility of commodities for the formation of a *commenda,* Kāsānī says:

> "The *commenda* in goods leads to uncertainty concerning the amount of the profit at the time of division. This is so because the value of the goods is known only by estimation, chance, and conjecture, and will differ with the difference of those who do the estimating. And uncertainty in turn leads to dispute, and dispute leads to discord."[34]

Uncertainty regarding the value of the goods leads to the undesirable possibility of dispute and discord. But the possible fluctuation in their value may lead to the even more undesirable result of inequitable advantage and enrichment for

[31] For the inadmissibility of goods for *commenda* investment cf. Shaybānī, *Aṣl, Muḍāraba,* fols. 52b, 53a; Sarakhsī, *Mabsūṭ,* 22:33; for the Mālikīs, *Muwaṭṭa',* 3:348; Saḥnūn, *Mudawwana,* 12:87; for the Shāfi'īs, Shirbīnī, *Mughnī,* 2:310; E. Sachau, ed., *Muh. Recht,* Berlin, 1897, p. 520.

[32] Schacht, *Introduction,* p. 144.

[33] *Ibid.,* p. 147.

[34] *Kāsānī,* 6:82.

one of the parties and the converse disadvantage to the other. This last consideration seems to be paramount in the Mālikī rejection of goods for *commenda* investment. Concerning a *commenda* in commodities that can be weighed or measured, Saḥnūn asks 'Abd ar-Raḥmān b. al Qāsim:[35]

> "Why have you disapproved of this?" He said: "Because of the danger of his (the agent's) taking the wheat or barley and its value on that day will be one hundred dirhams, and after trading with it, its value on the day he returns will be one thousand dirhams. His entire profit is thereby swallowed up. Or, its value on the day he returns it may be fifty dirhams and he will have profited from it."[36]

Since the profit in a *commenda* emerges only after the investment has been returned intact to the investor, any marked rise in the market value of goods serving as the basis for the *commenda* would cancel out any profit for the agent. Any drop in market value would put the investor at a disadvantage and provide the agent with unjustified, and, in a sense, unearned profit.[37]

The only legal school which purportedly permitted goods as a *commenda* investment was that of Ibn Abī Laylā.[38] Rather surprisingly, a similar position is attributed by Sarakhsī to Mālik:

> Mālik, may God have mercy upon him, said: "A *commenda* in goods is valid, because a commodity is an estimable property which is usually relied upon in trade. As far as the purpose of the *commenda* is concerned, it is equivalent to currency. For just as it is permissible at the *commenda*'s completion for the capital to be in the form of goods, so is it permissible for it to be in this form at its beginning.[39]

[35] For the dates of these two early Mālikī jurists, and for the question and answer format of the Saḥnūn, *Mudawwana*, cf. above, Chapter 5, notes 2, 3, and 18.

[36] Saḥnūn, *Mudawwana*, 12:87.

[37] For a more elaborate Ḥanafī explanation of this point of view cf. Sarakhsī, *Mabsūṭ*, 22:33.

[38] Cf. *Ibid.*, p. 38.

[39] *Ibid.*, p. 33. Cf. also *Kāsānī*, 6:82.

No source is given for this statement. In the *Muwaṭṭa'* and in all subsequent major Mālikī works, exactly the opposite position is taken.

> Mālik said: "The *commenda* is valid only if the investment is in the form of cash of either gold or silver. It may not consist of any goods or merchandise."[40]

This apparent misinterpretation of Mālikī doctrine may be the result of a variant tradition for which the source is now lost, or more likely, the result of a misunderstanding of Mālikī doctrine on this point. For, according to Mālikī law, as well as in Ḥanafī law, it is possible to circumvent this prohibition, and to form a *commenda* with merchandise by means of a simple legal device.[41] The statement attributed to Mālik by Sarakhsī might have been a generalization based on the *commenda* in goods through the use of the proper legal device.

The exclusion of goods and merchandise as valid types of investment would, in the context of medieval trade, have proved an even greater handicap in a *commenda* arrangement than would the similar prohibition in a partnership contract. The *commenda* was one of the chief instruments by which long-distance trade was carried out. Any skillful merchant following the injunction of the trade manuals of his day to buy goods in a market that is low, and to sell in one that is high, would naturally be interested in having his merchandise transported to a market where there was an adequate demand for them and in which they would fetch an attractive price.[42] It was not always possible for a merchant personally to meet the requirements of such a situation;[43] thus, a *commenda* arrangement with an itinerant merchant would provide a convenient and profitable solution. This, however, would require

40 Mālik, *Muwaṭṭa'*, 3:348.

41 Cf. above, Chapter 5, "Partnership in Goods."

42 E.g., cf. al-Jāḥiẓ (pseudo-Jāḥiẓ?), *Kitāb at-tabaṣṣur bit-tijāra*, ed. H. H. 'Abd al-Wahhāb, Cairo, 1935, pp. 9–10; French translation, by Ch. Pellat in *ARABICA* 1 (1954):154–155. Also, Ibn Khaldūn, *The Muqaddima*, trans., Franz Rosenthal, 2:338ff. and Maxime Rodinson, *Islam et le Capitalisme*, Paris, 1966, pp. 47ff.

43 Cf. Sarakhsī, *Mabsūṭ*, 22:38 for the division of trade into two types, local and long-distance, and for the impossibility of the man to take care of both at once.

a *commenda* investment in the form of merchandise, which is ruled out by all major Islamic legal schools. The requirements of the law were undoubtedly not strong enough to withstand the pressures of the market place. We can be reasonably certain that *commenda* arrangements were frequently formed with investments in the form of goods and merchandise.[44] It was probably in response to this reality that both Ḥanafī and Mālikī law developed a simple legal device to accommodate it. An investor may entrust goods to an agent and instruct him to sell them, and to use the cash realized from the sale as the investment in a *commenda* at a mutually agreed upon division of the profits.[45] Or, as al-Khaṣṣāf suggests, the investor can sell his goods for cash to a party whom he trusts, then hand over the proceeds to the agent who can immediately repurchase them for the *commenda*.[46] These possibilities all but nullify the force of the prohibition against goods as an investment in a *commenda*. The only exception would be a case in which the invested goods were not to be sold, and proceeds of their sale employed in further trade, but were instead themselves to be used in some manufacture or service capacity.

Non-Commercial and Industrial *Commenda*

Islamic law viewed the *commenda* primarily as a commercial contract, that is, one in which the investment would be used in trade, in a series of purchases and sales with hope of ultimately realizing a profit. Its use for non-commercial purposes seems to have been considered unusual, and was in certain cases completely disqualified. Merchandise was, *a priori*, ineligible for *commenda* investment, but could be made eligi-

[44] In the West, investments in the form of goods and merchandise frequently served as the basis for *commenda* agreements; cf. Lopez and Raymond, *Medieval Trade in the Mediterranean World*, p. 179 (investment of silk and paper), p. 181 (investment in cloth).

[45] Shaybānī, *Aṣl*, *Muḍāraba*, fols. 55b, l. 14–56a, l. 6; Sarakhsī, *Mabsūṭ*, 22:36–37; Mālik, *Muwaṭṭa'* 3:353; Saḥnūn, *Mudawwana*, 12:87. According to the Mālikīs, however, the agent is entitled to an equitable fee (*ajr mithluhu*) for accomplishing the sale of the goods the proceeds of which are to constitute the *commenda* capital.

[46] Al-Khaṣṣāf, *Kitāb al-ḥiyal wal-makhārij*, ed. J. Schacht, Hanover, 1923, p. 27. A similar resolution for this problem is found within the context of the partnership contract.

ble by the employment of a simple legal device involving the sale of the goods in question. However, if the object of the investment itself was necessary in all the subsequent *commenda* transactions, a circumventory sale of this kind would not be possible. For example, if one party provides a net or a pack animal for another to use for fishing or transporting goods on the condition that the proceeds from their activities are to be shared, this is an invalid *commenda*. It is treated as a hire (*ijāra*) contract with the agent keeping the entire proceeds, and the owner of the object entitled to an equitable rental fee for the use of his property.[47] The fact that these arrangements were considered invalid by Ḥanafī law does not necessarily mean that they were not practiced. On the contrary one might speculate that the enumeration of the various types of arrangements of this kind and the careful attention devoted to determining which party is entitled to the profit, and which to an equitable remuneration, indicate that such letting-out arrangements, even though disapproved of, were indeed practiced.[48]

It would be appropriate at this point to make some general comments concerning the relationship of the *commenda* contract and, to a lesser extent, also that of partnership, to a simple hire contract. S. D. Goitein has already pointed out that in medieval Near Eastern society the *commenda* and partnership contracts fulfilled essentially the same function and to a large extent displaced employment and loan contracts. Labor partnerships and industrial *commendas* were quite frequently nothing but veiled forms of employment.[49] From the Geniza documents it is apparent that employment as a form of economic collaboration was eschewed, since dependence upon others for a livelihood was considered degrading and

[47] Shaybānī, *Aṣl, Muḍāraba*, fols. 53b and 54b; in certain circumstances, the proceeds go to the owner, and the agent is entitled to an equitable wage.

[48] Schacht, *Introduction*, p. 85, n. 1: "Hostile references to practice in works of Islamic law are an important source of information on it for the Middle Ages."

[49] Cf. Goitein, *Mediterranean Society*, p. 170.

humiliating.[50] Consequently, many enterprises, no matter on how modest a scale, requiring the combined efforts of more than one person would be organized in the form of partnerships and *commendas*. It is largely for this reason, no doubt, that the legal description of these institutions contained provisions for their use in both long-distance and large-scale commercial ventures (for which they were ideally suited) as well as for local and small-scale trade and manufacturing.

There are, of course, substantial similarities between labor partnerships and industrial *commendas* on the one hand and the hire contract on the other. In all three arrangements, one party provides the capital, be it in the form of cash goods or equipment, while the other supplies the time and labor. This connection is perhaps most clearly manifested in the event of an invalid *commenda* or partnership. In almost all such cases, the nature of the relationship is altered; the invalid arrangement is transformed into a regular hire contract in which the investor becomes the employer and the agent the employee.[51]

While the degree of specialization and the division of economic functions in medieval Islamic society were fairly advanced, they were not complete; considerable overlappings existed between the commercial and other economic sectors. Therefore, the basically commercial view[52] of the *commenda* held by Ḥanafī lawyers did not preclude their approval of a *commenda* in which the employment of capital was associated with crafts or manufacturing activities. A person could entrust his capital to an agent on the condition that the latter buy raw materials and turn them into finished consumer products and

[50] *Ibid.*, pp. 92ff., where a Tunisian merchant who had fallen on hard times and was forced to enter the service of others complains: "I eat bread in the service of others; every minute of the day I gulp the cup of death because of my degradation and that of my children."

[51] Numerous examples of this can be found throughout the present discussion. Aspects of this relationship are explored in Alberto Gaiani, "The Juridical Nature of the Moslem *Qirāḍ*," *East and West* 4, no. 2 (July, 1953): 81–86.

[52] The Muslim lawyers of all schools understood trade and commerce to consist primarily of buying and selling. Perhaps the most concise definition is that offered by al-Ghazzālī: "Trade is the pursuit of profit by means of selling and buying and not by means of craft or manufacture." Al-Ghazzālī, *Wajīz*, 2:220.

then sell them on the basis of shared profit.[53] Even though this is not a purely commercial arrangement, i.e., one which involves only buying and selling, it was allowed because it was an accepted practice of merchants in pursuit of their primary goal, *viz.*, the attainment of profit.

> For the work which is stipulated for the agent is the kind that the merchants practice in the pursuit of the attainment of profit. It is comparable to buying and selling. Similarly, if the investor instructs the agent to use the capital to purchase leather and hide and then to cut it into boots, buckets and leather bags, this is all part of the practice of the merchants in the pursuit of the attainment of profit, and its stipulation is permissible in a *commenda*.[54]

An arrangement of this kind is what one might term an industrial or labor *commenda*, in which elements of manufacture and production are tied to the more usual commercial functions of the *commenda*. At present we have no way of knowing how extensive such arrangements were, and what importance, if any, they had in the financing and organization of industrial production in the Islamic cities of the early Middle Ages. However, the legal instruments for the association of capital and industry were available at least from the eighth century onward, and the Geniza documents contain several examples of exactly this type of commercial-industrial arrangement, arrangements involving minting, weaving, and textile-dyeing.[55]

The Mālikīs and the Shāfiʿīs were more consistent in their insistence on the *commenda* as a pure, undiluted commercial instrument. They reject a *commenda* which requires any manufacturing activity on the part of the agent, considering such an arrangement a hire contract in which all profits and losses accrue to the investor, with the agent-worker being entitled to an equitable remuneration for his work.[56]

53 Shaybānī, *Aṣl, Muḍāraba*, fols. 70a–70b; Sarakhsī, *Mabsūṭ*, 22:54.

54 Sarakhsī, *Mabsūṭ*, 22:54.

55 Cf. Goitein, *Mediterranean Society*, pp. 88–89, and Appendix C, no. 2 (p. 362), no. 5 (p. 363), and no. 20 (p. 366).

56 Saḥnūn, *Mudawwana*, 12:89.

Ready Cash, Debts, and Deposits

All forms of Islamic partnership, with the sole exception of the credit partnership, require that the investment be on hand (*māl ḥāḍir*) in order for the contract to be valid and effective. For the *commenda*, the situation is somewhat more flexible. Even if the investor's capital is not on hand, but is on deposit with someone, or owed to him by another party, it is nevertheless possible according to Ḥanafī law to enter into a *commenda* agreement. In the case of a deposit the investor may instruct the agent to collect his money from the depositor and use it as capital for a *commenda*, or he may directly arrange with the depositee to change the status of his capital from that of a deposit to that of a *commenda* investment.[57] Similarly, in the case of a debt, the investor may empower the agent to collect it from the debtor and to use the money collected as a *commenda* investment.[58] Actually this arrangement combines a transfer of debt contract (*ḥawāla*) with that of a *commenda*. The advantages of such a combination would have been especially important in long-distance trade, facilitating the flow of capital and investment. For example, if merchant *A* is leaving with goods or capital for some distant point at which merchant *B* has an unpaid debt from *C*, *A* can be empowered to collect from *C* and invest in goods on a *commenda* basis for the return trip.

For a creditor to ask the debtor to use the amount of money owed as a *commenda* investment is not permissible because "a *commenda* cannot be formed with liable money (i.e., money for which the agent has some liability). A *commenda* can be formed only on the basis of capital whose origin is absolutely free of liability."[59] Undoubtedly another reason for excluding this type of arrangement, although not stated in the sources, is the easy abuse to which it could be put in concealing a usurious loan. Indeed, it is fear of such abuse that the Mālikīs explicitly offer as their reason for rejecting the conversion of

[57] Shaybānī, *Aṣl, Muḍāraba*, fols. 47b–48a; Sarakhsī, *Mabsūṭ*, 22:29.

[58] Shaybānī, *Aṣl, Muḍāraba*, fols. 74a, 98a; Sarakhsī, *Mabsūṭ*, 22:29, pp. 58–59.

[59] Shaybānī, *Aṣl, Muḍāraba*, fol. 48a.

a debt into a *commenda* investment in the hands of the debtor. For, under the cover of a false *commenda* agreement, the creditor could assure himself not only the recovery of his debt but also an illegal return on his loan in the guise of his share of the *commenda*'s profits.[60] Mālikī law consistently disqualifies any extraneous operations and procedures in the formation of a *commenda* agreement. Thus it also rules out the conversion of a deposit into a *commenda* investment, or the collection of a debt owed to the investor in order to use the collected funds as the basis for a *commenda*. In all such cases, the agent would be entitled to some fixed remuneration for the services rendered to the investor, and only after the collection of the debt or deposit could the *commenda* take effect.

There may have been a practical consideration that underlay the Mālikī insistence on insulating the initiation of the *commenda* from other commercial arrangements such as loans and deposits. From the Geniza and from Jewish *responsa* literature we learn that a frequent point of contention between collaborating merchants concerned the nature of their relationship; e.g., one party might claim it to be a *commenda* or partnership, while the other might contend that it was a loan or deposit or *ibḍāʿ*. The likelihood of such disagreements was enhanced by the fact that collaboration often extended over long periods, several or more years not being uncommon, thus tending to blur the precise nature of the original contract.[61] Perhaps the Mālikī position is to be viewed as a partial attempt to avoid muddying the commercial waters by reducing the likelihood of confusions and disagreements as to the exact nature of the relationship between the parties.

Nevertheless, the Ḥanafīs do permit what might be described as a "mixed investment," i.e., an arrangement whereby the investor entrusts a given sum of money to an agent, half or any other fraction of which is a *commenda* investment, and

[60] Saḥnūn, *Mudawwana*, 12:88. Cf. also Santillana, *Istituzioni*, 2:326, where this possibility is discussed in some detail.

[61] Cf. Goitein, *Mediterranean Society*, pp. 176–177.

the remainder either a loan, deposit, or *ibḍāʿ*.[62] It would seem that the purpose of such arrangements was to extend the possible variations in the distribution of profits and risks. By conferring the status of a loan on part of the sum, the investor enjoys greater security with respect to his capital. The agent is liable under all circumstances for the return of that portion. But by the same token, the investor, is reducing his prospects for profit by a similar fraction. By designating some of the money as a *biḍāʿa*, the investor achieves less protection for his capital, but at the same time creates a compensating broader base for his profit. Employment of these hybrid arrangements were probably a function of market conditions.

Alienation of Money on Part of Investor

The transfer of control over the investment from the investor to the agent is an absolute requirement for a valid *commenda.* The money must either be physically handed over (*dafʿ al-māl*) to the agent and remain in his possession while he is conducting *commenda* affairs; or, in cases in which the money is not on hand, authority over its disposition must be transferred to the agent. A clear separation must occur between the investor and the capital invested.

> If a man takes out 1000 dirhams of his money and says to another man: "Work with this on a *commenda* basis; use it to buy and sell on the condition that whatever God, may He be exalted, grants in connection with it be shared between us equally." But the investor does not actually hand over the money to the agent, and the latter nevertheless bought and sold. In this case, regardless of whether the agent profited or lost, the profit goes to the investor and the loss is also borne by him. The agent is entitled to an equitable remuneration for his work.
>
> This is an invalid *commenda.* A *commenda* can only be valid if the investor hands the money over to the agent, and if it is the agent who trades with the money without the investor stipulating that he work with him.[63]

[62] Shaybānī, *Aṣl, Muḍāraba*, fols. 132a–133b; Sarakhsī, *Mabsūṭ*, 22:130ff.
[63] Shaybānī, *Aṣl, Muḍāraba*, fol. 96a, l. 15–fol. 96b, l. 4. Cf. also

Requiring the agent to have clear possession of the investment and primary responsibility and authority over its disposition emphasizes one of the *commenda*'s innovative features —a feature which contributed to its importance in long-distance trade, namely, the independence of the agent and the possible anonymity of the investor *vis à vis* third parties. This, however, in no way implies a transfer of ownership of the investment capital from the investor to the agent. While the agent's control over the disposition of the investment is almost absolute, its ownership unequivocally remains with the investor.[64]

The transfer of the capital to the agent's possession does not in itself make the *commenda* effective in the sense that it creates any legal obligations between the parties. As in the case of partnership, it is the initial act of trading that puts the contract into force.[65]

Provisions for Profit-Sharing

Any proportional division of profit agreed upon between an investor and an agent is acceptable in a *commenda* contract. The only requirement, and one which is a *sine qua non* of a valid *commenda* contract, is that division of profit between the parties be strictly proportional.[66] Solely on the basis of the legal sources, it is not possible to know what the accepted standard division was, if indeed any standard practice at all existed on this point.[67] Most of the cases discussed in the

---

Sarakhsī, *Mabsūṭ*, 22:84. For the Mālikīs, cf. Saḥnūn, *Mudawwana*, 12:112–113. The Mālikīs go a step further by not allowing the investor to send along a personal representative, or family-member to safeguard the investment and oversee the agent's activities, cf. *Mudawwana*, 12:113.

[64] On the problem of ownership of *commenda* property and its changing aspects as the agent's trading activities progress, cf. below, "Investor and Agent During Operation of the *Commenda*."

[65] Shaybānī, *Aṣl, Muḍāraba*, 107b, and Santillana, *Istituzioni*, 2:327.

[66] Shaybānī, *Aṣl, Muḍāraba*, fol. 43b, ll. 1–6; Sarakhsī, *Mabsūṭ*, 22:22ff.; Saḥnūn, *Mudawwana*, 12:89; Shirbīnī, *Mughnī al-muḥtāj*, 2:312-313; al-Ghazzālī, *Al-wajīz*, 2:222.

[67] In Italy the usual division was ¾ profit to the investor and ¼ to the agent; cf. Lopez and Raymond, *Medieval Trade*, p. 175; the Geniza documents reveal no standard practice in this regard, but a wide variation in the distribution of profit shares, conditioned by an equally wide variety of

legal texts are introduced by the formulaic phrase: "If a man handed over to another money in the form of a *commenda* on the basis of half the profit." However, this is not necessarily an indication of any prevalent practice since the cases discussed are of a theoretical nature for which any randomly chosen fraction would have sufficed; the one-half may just be a convenient, obvious fraction used to illustrate the points in question. There are instances of other fractions used to illustrate different points e.g., 1/3–2/3 division, and 1/4–3/4, 2/5–3/5, and 19/20–1/20. Any such division is valid and is left to the discretion of the parties concerned at the time the *commenda* is being negotiated.

Any violation of the proportional division rule renders the *commenda* invalid, and it is treated as a regular hire (*ijāra*) contract, with the agent entitled to an equitable remuneration (*ajr mithluhu*) for his work, but thereby disqualified from any share in the profit. On the other hand, in case of loss, the agent is free of responsibility "because in this matter he is a trusted person."[68] One violation frequently discussed in the sources is when one of the parties stipulates a specific sum of money from the profit instead of, or in addition to, his proportional share of the profits. Such an arrangement could conceivably lead to an inequitable situation in which one party would get all the profit and the other none, and is therefore invalid.[69] In certain circumstances it could also come perilously close to a usurious transaction.

---

commercial and extra-commercial considerations. Cf. Goitein, *Mediterranean Society*, pp. 174ff.

[68] Shaybānī, *Aṣl, Muḍāraba*, fol. 43b, ll. 13–14.

[69] *Ibid.*, ll. 6–14; Sarakhsī, *Mabsūṭ*, 22:22. While the Mālikīs also forbid the stipulation of a fixed sum in addition to share of profit for either party (cf. Saḥnūn, *Mudawwana*, 12:109), by analogy to the *musāqāt* (agricultural lease) contract, they do admit a *commenda* in which all the profit is assigned to the agent (cf. *Mudawwana*, pp. 89–90). For obvious reasons, this is not the case when all the profit is assigned to the investor. The Ḥanafīs do, however, outline the following method for circumventing the proportional-profit-provision: The investor hires an agent to carry on trade in return for a fixed wage and entrusts to him the necessary capital to do so. The agent then gives the funds to the investor on a *commenda* basis; the investor then returns them to the agent as a *biḍā'a*. The agent, thus, continues to receive his fixed wage plus a share of the *commenda* profit. Cf. Shaybānī, *Aṣl, Muḍāraba*, fol. 142a.

Just as the object of the *commenda* contract must be clearly determined and known (*ma'lūm*), so too should the provisions of the contract regarding the division of profit be clearly spelled out. Ideally, the exact disposition of the entire profit should be mentioned in the agreement; that is, each party's share should be stated, and the designated shares should add up to the total profit. Strict application of legal reasoning would require that a *commenda* contract in which this condition is not met be declared invalid; however, Ḥanafī authorities exhibited a degree of flexibility in this regard, and validated some such arrangements on the basis of *istiḥsān*. For example, if a *commenda* contract mentions only the investor's share of the profit, but not that of the agent, it is acceptable on the basis of *istiḥsān* and the remainder of the profit is assigned to the agent.[70] If no definite division of the profit is mentioned, but the investor merely says to the agent: "on the condition that whatever God, may He be exalted, grants us will be between us," or if he said: "on the condition that we be partners in the profit," then the *commenda* is valid and the profit is shared equally between both partners.[71] If the profit division is not explicitly stated, but is referred to indirectly, e.g., if the investor says that the profit will be divided in a way "similar to that which *A* stipulated to *B*," the *commenda* is valid only if both parties are aware of the stipulations referred to. If either party is ignorant of them, the contract is invalid.[72]

Any unassigned portion of the profit automatically reverts to the investor "since it is profit on his capital." So, for example, if one-half is assigned to the investor and one-third to the agent, and no mention is made of the disposition of the remaining one-sixth of the profit, it is given to the investor.[73]

The status of a stipulation which assigns any part of the

[70] *Ibid.*, fol. 45a (bottom).

[71] *Ibid.*, fol. 70, Sarakhsī, *Mabsūṭ*, 22:54–55. This is the opinion of Abū Yūsuf; Shaybānī disagrees, considering such an arrangement invalid and treating it as a hire contract. The disposition of this case might be construed as evidence that normally profits were divided on a ½–½ basis; however, this is not necessarily so since the phrase used here by the investor regarding the profit division implies an equality between the two parties.

[72] Shaybānī, *Aṣl, Muḍāraba*, fol. 47a–b; Sarakhsī, *Mabsūṭ*, 22:27.

[73] Shaybānī, *Aṣl, Muḍāraba*, fol. 46a.

commenda profit to an outside third party, that is, someone other than the investor or the agent, varies in accordance with the agent's economic relationship to the third party. The principle which emerges from the various cases discussed is that such stipulations are to be honored only when the agent has a vested economic interest in relation to the third party concerned. In all cases where this does not apply, the share assigned to the third party reverts to the investor. Thus, a *commenda* which provides for one-third to the agent's slave is valid, even if the slave was not active in the *commenda*, because the property of the slave belongs to his master, thus establishing the agent's vested interest in the provision. The agent is therefore entitled to two-thirds of the profit. Similarly, the assignment of one-third of the profit to a party to whom the agent is indebted is a valid provision and would result in one-third of the profit going to the investor and two-thirds to the agent. However, if a portion of the profit was assigned to charity or to the wife of some other relative of the agent, the stipulation is considered null and void and that share reverts to the investor.

> His wife is not comparable in this respect to the slave of the agent, because he does not possess the property of his wife. For the agent has no right in anything of this kind that belongs to her. As for the slave, however, any property that belongs to him belongs to the agent, and stipulating profit for his slave is the same as stipulating profit for himself. However, stipulating profit to his wife, or his sons, or his father, or his brother, or his sister, or his *mukātab* slave[74] are all alike. And anything that he stipulates to any of these reverts to the investor.[75]

Thus, in the absence of a clear-cut and direct vested interest in the third party's share, the profit stipulated for the agent's relatives or other persons reverts to the investor.

In a *commenda*, the right to any portion of the profit is

[74] Re: the special status of a *mukātab* slave, cf. *EI*, 2nd ed., 1:30 and Schacht, *Introduction*, pp. 129–130.

[75] Shaybānī, *Aṣl, Muḍāraba*, fol. 48b, ll. 12–17.

earned either by virtue of the money invested, or by virtue of the work invested. Since neither of these grounds can be claimed by any of the third parties involved, the profit reverts to the investor, excluding even provisions assigning part of the profit to charitable causes such as pilgrims, the poor, and the indigent.[76] Mālikī law differs on this point, accepting the assignment of part of the profit to an outside third party, e.g., the poor, and insisting that a provision of this kind be fulfilled.[77]

A more general, unarticulated consideration may be involved in the treatment of this problem, namely, that of unjustified enrichment. Any opening to profit and enrichment without risking labor or capital would provide possibilities for various types of usurious transactions. For example, *A* might lend money to *B* on the understanding that *B* will stipulate a share of the profits for him in his *commenda* with *C*, thus assuring for himself the return of his money plus the possibility of an additional amount which would be equivalent to interest.

A multiplicity of agents or investors in one *commenda* contract does not affect the principles of profit sharing. As long as the shares are proportionally assigned, the same degree of flexibility with respect to the size of the shares exists as in a simple *commenda*, i.e., with one investor and one agent.[78] On the assumption that each of the agents in the same *commenda* will invest an approximately equal amount of work, Mālikī law applies some limitations in regard to the assignment of profit-shares. To avoid having one agent unjustly profit from the work of his colleague, it insists on an equal share for each of the agents.[79] However, in the case of a bilateral *commenda*, one in which both the agent and the investor contribute to the trading capital, the flexibility in assigning profit shares is somewhat restricted. The investor's share must be limited only to his contribution to the total capital, since there is no basis on which he can claim profit

[76] *Ibid.*, fols. 48a–50a; Sarakhsī, *Mabsūṭ*, 22:28.
[77] Saḥnūn, *Mudawwana*, 12:91.
[78] Shaybānī, *Aṣl, Muḍāraba*, fols. 49b–50b.
[79] Saḥnūn, *Mudawwana*, 12:90.

on capital he did not contribute and with which he didn't work. The agent is entitled to the entire profit on his own share of the capital in addition to a share of the profit from the investor's contribution.[80]

A *commenda* is invalid in which the profit stipulation is equivocal, e.g., if the investor gave the capital on condition that either one-half *or* one-third of the profit was to be the agent's. This is invalid because the condition is not determined or known.[81] Similarly, an arrangement in which the shares of profit are not stated, but left to the discretion of one of the parties at the time of the profit division, is invalid, and the agreement is treated as a hire contract.[82] The same is true of an arrangement which, even though designated as a *commenda*, makes no provisions whatsoever for profit-sharing.[83] For the Mālikīs, such an omission, important as it is, does not prevent the contract from being considered a *commenda*. They resolve the difficulty by transforming the defective contract into a *qirāḍ mithluhu*, i.e., a similar, or average *commenda*, with the assignment of profit to follow the provisions prevalent in the marketplace for *commendas* negotiated under similar circumstances.[84] The designation of a contract as a *commenda* is totally disregarded in cases in which either all the profit is assigned to the agent or to the investor; such arrangements are treated for what they really are, namely, a loan and a *biḍāʿa* respectively.[85]

In spite of the insistence on having the shares of profit clearly fixed in the contract, Ḥanafī law does permit some variables in this regard. A *commenda* agreement with a flexible profit

[80] Shaybānī, *Aṣl, Muḍāraba*, fol. 51a. For a similar principle in Western bilateral *commendas*, cf. Lopez and Raymond, *Medieval Trade*, p. 175.

[81] Shaybānī, *Aṣl, Muḍāraba*, fol. 46a.

[82] *Ibid.*, fols. 46b–47a.

[83] *Ibid.*, fol. 45b.

[84] Saḥnūn, *Mudawwana*, 12:90. The Mālikīs apply the concept of *qirāḍ mithluhu*—average or usual *commenda*—to solve a variety of problems that can arise in connection with this contract; e.g., a disagreement between the agent and investor regarding each one's share of the profit is resolved by referring to an average or usual *commenda* contracted in similar circumstances; cf. Saḥnūn, *Mudawwana*, 12:90–92.

[85] Shaybānī, *Aṣl, Muḍāraba*, fols. 45a–b.

provision, dependent on what goods the agent trades with is permissible.[86] Such arrangements are probably allowed in recognition of the varying degrees of risk involved in obtaining, transporting, and profitably trading with different categories of merchandise.[87]

In the legal sources, the *commenda* is frequently and aptly referred to as a "partnership of profit," and the parties to it as "partners in the profit." The two fundamental components of this "partnership of profit" are the work and capital invested, and it is basically only on the grounds of these two that either party can lay claim to a share in the profit. Within this framework, however, a wide, almost limitless, range of profit-sharing possibilities is allowed.

Contract

The same general considerations, *vis-à-vis* written contracts that were discussed above in relation to partnership apply to the *commenda* as well.[88] That written contracts, although not required, were frequently used is shown both directly and indirectly in the legal discussions of the *commenda*. In a case brought before the early legal scholar 'Āmir ash-Sha'abī,[89] it is recorded that a man came with a written document (*sakk*) which contained proof that a certain deceased person had one thousand *mithqāl* of his money as a *commenda* investment.[90] This is noteworthy not only because of the written document involved, but also because it is described as containing evidence (*bihā al-bayyina*) of the investment. Suggested formulae for *commenda* contracts are given by Shaybānī in the *Aṣl*, and one is also found in Ṭaḥāwī's *Kitāb*

86 Shaybānī, *Aṣl, Muḍāraba*, fol. 95a; Sarakhsī, *Mabsūṭ*, 22:82. For alterations in the proportional profit assignments in Mālikī law cf. Saḥnūn, *Mudawwana*, 12:90 and 108–109.

87 For profit rates on different commodities in medieval Near Eastern commerce, cf. Goitein, *Mediterranean Society*, pp. 202–203 and passim.

88 Cf. above, Chapter 3, "The Contract."

89 'Āmir b. Shurāḥīl ash-Sha'bī, a traditionist from Kūfa, d. 109/727–728. Cf. Ibn Ḥajar, *Tahdhīb at-tahdhīb*, 5:65–69.

90 Shaybānī, *Aṣl, Muḍāraba*, fol. 43a; cf. also fol. 53a, line 13, where it is assumed that the agreement will be in a written form: *fa-inna al-muḍāraba jā'iza 'alā ḥālihā alladhī kātaba 'alayhi*.

ash-shurūṭ aṣ-ṣaghīr. A translation of Shaybānī's formulae follows:

If a man entrusts another with capital in the form of a *commenda* on the basis of half profit, and the agent wishes to draw up a document as proof against the investor containing the conditions of the *commenda,* and setting forth his portion of the profit, he (the notary) writes: This is a document in favor of *A* son of *B* drawn up on the part of *X* son of Y which says: "I have handed over to you such and such a number of dirhams of good weight in the form of a *commenda* on the condition that you use them to buy and sell for cash and credit in all categories of trade and in other related matters, and that you act in these matters according to your judgment. And whatsoever God, may He be exalted, grants, half of it is mine, and half of it is yours for your work. I have handed this money over to you and you have taken possession of it from me, and it amounts to such and such, in the month——of the year——; it is in your possession according to what we have stated in this our document concerning this *commenda.*" Witnessed——.

And if the investor wishes to have a document drawn up as proof against the agent concerning the *commenda,* he (the notary) writes: This is a document in favor of *X* son of *Y* drawn up by *A* son of *B,* that says: "You have handed over to me such and such a number of dirhams of good weight as a *commenda* on the condition that I use them to buy and sell on cash and credit in all aspects of trade, and in other related matters, and that I act in all these matters according to my judgment. And whatsoever God, may He be exalted, grants, half is yours and half is mine for my work in it. You have handed over this money to me, and I have taken possession of it from you, and it amounts to such and such, in the month——of the year——; and it is in my possession according to what we have stated in this our contract of this *commenda.*" Witnessed——.[91]

[91] Shaybānī, *Aṣl, Muḍāraba,* fol. 140b.

What we have here is not one contract, but essentially an exchange of documents between the two parties. The documents are not identical, and are written in the subjective style[92] in which the parties address each other directly using the first and second person. Although similar in content, the purposes of each document are apparently different. The agent is interested in obtaining a statement from the investor primarily in order to clearly spell out his share of the profit; we can assume that the investor's interest in a similar statement from the agent is primarily for the purpose of confirming the amount of the investment and the fact that the agent acknowledges having taken possession of the capital. Both documents contain essentially the same four elements: (1) The nature of the contract, i.e., a *commenda,* (2) The object, i.e., the amount of the investment, (3) The provisions regarding profit division, and (4) The agent's authorization to use it in trade as he sees fit.[93]

Shaybānī's suggested contract formula undoubtedly represents an early format of the recording of contractual relationships—a format in which the parties addressed each other directly, and consequently one in which the wording of each party's declaration was different. In Ṭaḥāwī's manual, some two hundred years later, the *commenda* contract given is formulated in the objective style, and instead of separate declarations, Ṭaḥāwī prescribes that two copies of the identical contract be drawn up, presumably one for each party.

The translation of Ṭaḥāwī's contract follows:

> If a man gives to another money as a *commenda* on condition that the agent works with it in any field of trade that he (the agent) sees fit, and in any city that he wishes to, and on condition that whatever profit God grants them in this matter be shared between them equally, and both wish

[92] Cf. above, Chapter 3, n.139. For a recent thorough and illuminating discussion of the style of Arabic written documents including those which are cast, as this one is, in the form of a dialogue, cf. J. A. Wakin, *Islamic Law in Practice: Two Chapters from Ṭaḥāwī's Kitāb Al-Shurūṭ Al-Kabīr,* pp. 73ff.

[93] For the general similarity of the points included here to those enumerated in Geniza letters and contracts, cf. Goitein, *Mediterranean Society,* pp. 171–172.

to draw up a document between them in this matter, then he (the notary) writes: "This is a document stating that to which the witnesses named in this document testify. They all testify that *Fulān* and *Fulān,* whose identity they have ascertained and whom they know in a manner that is legally sound. . . ." Then the scribe should arrange the contract by inserting the various formulae until he finishes writing the first date.[94] Then he should write:

"*Fulān,* the person named in this document, handed over to *Fulān,* also named in this document, one hundred uniform dinars of standard weight, in gold, minted coin of good alloy on the basis of a valid and sound *commenda* on condition that:

a. "This *Fulān* (the agent) may use it to buy any and all categories of trading goods as he sees fit, from whom he sees fit, anytime he sees fit, in any and all places he sees fit.
b. "He may pay the price of anything he buys in this regard from the money mentioned in this document.
c. "He may sell these goods or any part of them that he sees fit, for whatever he sees fit, either for cash or credit in any and all places that he sees fit.
d. "He may take possession of the price of what he sells in this regard, and may deliver what he sells to the one to whom he sold it.
e. "He may hire in this regard whomsoever he sees fit, to go wherever he sees fit on land and on sea, and he may pay, as he sees fit, the wage of whomsoever he hires in this regard from the money mentioned in this document and from that which he might profit by virtue of the *commenda* mentioned in this document.
f. "He may administer the capital in this fashion, and dispose of the funds that may come into his possession and the funds accruing from that which he sells just as he could freely dispose of them previously (i.e., prior to the

[94] For an explanation of the order of clauses and formulae and the dating formulae in Arabic documents, cf. Wakin, *Islamic Law in Practice*, pp. 69–72 and 81–119.

purchase and resale of *commenda* goods), by virtue of the *commenda* agreement mentioned in this document.[95]

g. "From whatever profit God grants from this money by virtue of *Fulān*'s (the agent's) activities with it within the *commenda* agreement mentioned in this document, the agent will hand over to *Fulān* the investor his investment, mentioned in this document, after payment of any debts that he, the agent named in this document, may have incurred on account of the *commenda* agreement mentioned in this document.

"Then, whatever profit which God may have granted on the money mentioned in this document is to be shared between the two of them in so many and so many shares. To *Fulān* (the investor) from this sum, by virtue of his capital mentioned in this document, *X* number of shares from the total number of shares; and to *Fulān* (the agent) from this sum by virtue of his time and effort expended on it, *Y* number of shares from the total number of shares mentioned in this document.

"And *Fulān* (the investor) handed over to *Fulān* (the agent) the entire amount of *X* dinars mentioned in this document, and *Fulān* (the agent) took possession of them from him. They were transferred into his possession during the session in which the two of them concluded the *commenda* agreement mentioned in this document and before the two parties separated from one another physically.[96] This was done on the condition that *Fulān* (the agent) will conduct himself in a God-fearing manner with respect to that which was entrusted to him in the *commenda* mentioned in this document, and that he will act in a trustworthy manner with it, and that he will be zealous with it, and that he will generally conduct himself in accordance

[95] This clause emphasizes the agent's continuing control over the *commenda* property; i.e., his right to dispose of it extends not only to the actual capital entrusted to him, but also to all the money and goods that he subsequently acquires on behalf of the *commenda.*

[96] This refers to the *majlis*, the session or meeting at which agreements and contracts were normally concluded; cf. Schacht, *Introduction*, p. 145.

with what the precepts of God demand. For God, may He be exalted and magnified, will not diminish the reward of one who does good works."

Then he (the scribe) writes:

"This document was written in two copies."

And after that he mentions the testimony for the investor and for the agent, in a manner similar to that which we described earlier in a previous passage of this book, until he finishes writing the date with which the document concludes.[97]

In keeping with its disregard for formalism, Islamic law does not insist on the use of any particular term or formula for the creation of a *commenda*, "for in contracts, consideration is given to the meaning and not to the phrasing."[98] Any agreement negotiated without the explicit use of the term, but in which one party entrusts another with some capital to work with in return for share of the profit, is treated as a *commenda* regardless of the particular phrases used to arrive at this agreement. Any of the following phrases used by the investor in addressing the agent result in the creation of a *commenda.*

(1) This thousand is with you on the basis of one-half profit. (*hādhā al-alf ma'aka bin-niṣf*)[99]
(2) Whatsoever God grants you in this is to be shared between us half and half. (*mā razaqaka allah min shay' fī dhālika fahuha baynanā niṣfayn*)[100]
(3) Whatever profit there will be in this is to be shared between us. (*mā kāna fī hādhā al-māl min ribḥ fahuwa baynanā niṣfayn*)[101]
(4) Whatever you profit with this capital will be shared

[97] This translation is based on the three Istanbul mss. of Ṭaḥāwī's *Kitāb ash-shurūṭ aṣ-ṣaghīr: Murad Mollah* 998, fols. 114b–115; *Murad Mollah* 997, fols. 107–108; *Bayazit* 18905, fols. 92b–93.
[98] Sarakhsī, *Mabsūṭ*, 22:23 (bottom).
[99] Shaybānī, *Aṣl*, *Muḍāraba*, fol. 44a.
[100] Shaybānī, *Aṣl*, *Muḍāraba*, fol. 43b, l. 15, also 111a.
[101] Shaybānī, *Aṣl, Muḍāraba*, fol. 43b, l. 16, also 111a.

between us half and half. (*mā ḳāna laḳa fī hādhā al-māl min faḍl fahuwa baynanā niṣfayn*)[102]

(5) On the condition that whatever gain you earn with this money will be between us half and half. (*'alā an mā ḳasabta fī hādhā al-māl min ḳasab fahuwa baynanā niṣfayn*)[103]

The only objection to these phrases and others conveying the same meaning is that they do not fully enough spell out the conditions of the agreement. This shortcoming, however, is overlooked because, as Shaybānī says, "it is the practice of the people and their usage."[104] Therefore, if the investor uttered any of the above phrases without further elaboration, and without mentioning the term *commenda (muḍāraba, muqāraḍa, qirāḍ)*, the arrangement is held to be a valid *commenda*, "because the essential character of the obligation (*ḥuḳm*) is based on that which is intended, and no attention is paid to differences of expression if they convey the same intention; and the intention of these phrases is the stipulation of the sharing of the profit."[105]

A special problem is posed by the use of single terms, other than the *commenda*, terms which have ambiguous connotations, but are used with the intention of creating a *commenda*. The terms in question are *mu'āmala, mu'āwaḍa*, and *mufāwaḍa*. All three terms connote some mutual commercial arrangement, and one, *mufāwaḍa*, has a technical meaning in Ḥanafī and Mālikī partnership law.[106] If any of these three terms are used by the investor in conjunction with a profit sharing provision they are considered to constitute a *commenda*, e.g., if he said "take this money as a *mufāwaḍa* or as a *mu'āmala* or as a *mu'āwaḍa* on the basis of half profit, this

[102] Shaybānī, *Aṣl, Muḍāraba*, fol. 43b, ll. 16–17.

[103] Shaybānī, *Aṣl, Muḍāraba*, fol. 11a. For other phrases which vary but slightly from those given above, and which are considered to create a *commenda*, cf. Shaybānī, *Aṣl, Muḍāraba*, fols. 44b–45a; *ibid.*, fol. 111a; Sarakhsī, *Mabsūṭ*, 22:23–24.

[104] Shaybānī, *Aṣl, Muḍāraba*, fol. 45a, l. 3.

[105] Sarakhsī, *Mabsūṭ*, 22:21–22. Re: *ḥuḳm*, in this sense, cf. Schacht, *Introduction*, p. 214.

[106] Cf. above, Chapters 3 and 5.

is a *commenda*. His saying *mufāwaḍa* or *muʿāmala* or *muḍāraba* (*commenda*) is equivalent and it is a *commenda* in all respects."[107]

Conduct of the *Commenda*

To judge from the considerable attention they receive in the legal sources, the most problematic aspects of the operation of the *commenda* are those concerned with the agent's conduct of *commenda* trade. By far the largest portion of the legal discussions is devoted to elaborating and defining the extent of the agent's freedom of action and to clarifying his relationship to the investor and to third parties. These discussions take place within the same framework as those concerning the rights and duties of a partner in his conduct of partnership business. Like partnership, the *commenda* is classified as a contract of fidelity (*ʿaqd al-amāna*); like a partner, the agent is considered a trustworthy and faithful party (*amīn*) with respect to the capital entrusted to him, and therefore not liable for any loss occurring in the normal course of business activities; and, like a partner, the agent becomes liable for the

[107] Shaybānī, *Aṣl*, *Muḍāraba*, fol. 44b, ll. 6ff. Re: *muʿāwaḍa* cf. Sarakhsī, *Mabsūṭ*, 22:23. Re: *muʿāmala*, Shaybānī, *Aṣl*, *Muḍāraba*, fols. 44b, ll. 8–10, and 45, l. 6. Sarakhsī, *Mabsūṭ*, 22:23; the term *muʿāmala* occurs a number of times in the Geniza documents where it is understood as a form of general commercial co-operation as opposed to a formal contract, cf. Goitein, *Mediterranean Society*, p. 169. It is possible that in light of its use in legal sources, this interpretation might have to be reconsidered. Re: *mufāwaḍa* in the sense of *commenda*, cf. Shaybānī, *Aṣl*, *Muḍāraba*, fol. 42b, ll. 5–7; *ibid.*, fols. 44b, ll. 7–8, 45b, ll. 5–7; 49a, l. 4; Sarakhsī, *Mabsūṭ*, 22:23. Cf. also Ṭaḥāwī (*Kitāb ash-shurūṭ aṣ-ṣaghīr*, ms. Bayazit, 18905, fol. 95, ll. 13–18), who quotes an old tradition to the effect that originally the terms *ʿinān* and *mufāwaḍa* had the same meaning in the context of partnership law. The fact that the term *mufāwaḍa* was in an early period used also to designate a *commenda* (cf. Shaybānī, *Aṣl*, *Muḍāraba*, fol. 42b, ll. 5–7 where in a tradition concerning ʿUthmān's commercial activity it is stated, "and *mufāwaḍa* is a *commenda*") would seem to indicate that this term was originally an undifferentiated term for commercial associations in which the specific conditions and rules were determined by the agreement of the parties in that particular case. Thus, the term *mufāwaḍa* could have designated different types of partnership as well as a *commenda*. It probably took on a specific meaning sometime in the late eighth century, and even then it was used differently by the different law schools.

property in his care as a result of any violation of this fidelity (*amāna*).

There are a number of considerations which determine the boundaries of the agent's freedom of action. Generally, his actions must be consonant with the over-all purpose of the contract, namely, that of achieving a profit, and they must fall within the bounds of recognized and customary commercial practice. More specifically, his freedom of action depends on the type of mandate he receives from the investor, and on whether or not any specific conditions or limitations are imposed at the time the contract is negotiated.

Commenda with Limited and Unlimited Mandate

With respect to the agent's activities while trading with the investment entrusted to him, Ḥanafī law distinguishes two types of contracts: a limited mandate, and an unlimited mandate *commenda*. A *commenda* with an unlimited mandate is one in which the investor authorizes the agent to act completely at the latter's discretion in all business matters. Such authorization is conveyed by the investor's statement to the agent: "act with it (the investment) as you see fit." (*i'mal fīhi bira'ika*). In this case the agent may:

(1) Buy and sell all types of merchandise as he sees fit.
(2) Buy and sell for cash and credit.
(3) Give goods as *biḍā'a,* leave them as a deposit or pledge.
(4) Hire helpers as needed.
(5) Rent or buy animals and equipment.
(6) Travel with the capital.
(7) Mingle it with his own resources.
(8) Give it as a *commenda* to a third party.
(9) Invest it in a partnership with a third party.

Sarakhsī summarizes this as follows:

> If the investor says to the agent, "act with it as you see fit," then he may practice all of these things except the loan.[108]

[108] A loan is excluded from the practice of merchants, because it is viewed as a favor on the part of the lender, and not as a commercial transaction from which some advantage can be expected.

> For the investor has consigned the control of this capital to the agent's discretion in a comprehensive way; and we know that his intention is the inclusion of all that is the customary practice of the merchants. The agent, thereby, has the right to engage in *commenda*, a partnership, and to mingle the capital with his own capital because this is of the practice of the merchants.[109]

This comprehensive and unrestricted mandate permits the agent the widest latitude *vis à vis* the techniques of commerce he may employ in the pursuit of profitable trade. He is free to transmit this unrestricted mandate to a second agent, "and the second agent is equivalent in this respect to the original agent."[110] Indeed, the original agent is to share in the profits even if he himself did no trading whatsoever with the capital, but simply reinvested it in a *commenda* with a second agent.[111] This opens the way for the use of the *commenda* as an instrument of financial entrepreneurship. Capital could be entrusted to a well-known and experienced trader who could then skillfully reinvest it with others, sharing in the profit but not risking any losses.

In the absence of any blanket authorization, the agent's freedom of action is somewhat restricted, especially with regard to transactions with third parties. If the investor does not use the phrase "act according to your judgment," or a substitute phrase conveying the same intention, in his instructions to the agent, the agent may not engage in any of the last three practices enumerated above; i.e., he may not mingle the investment with his own capital, nor may he invest it in a *commenda* or partnership with third parties. However, he may engage in the other enumerated commercial activities.

> If a person entrusts to another capital in a *commenda* and he does not say "act with it according to your judgment," then the agent may use it to purchase anything he sees fit to from the categories of trade and he may sell, because he

109 Sarakhsī, *Mabsūṭ*, 22:39–40. Cf. also p. 48; Shaybānī, *Aṣl*, *Muḍāraba*, fols. 57a, 64a–b, and 109b; *Kāsānī*, 6:7–8.

110 Shaybānī, *Aṣl*, *Muḍāraba*, fol. 109b, l. 8.

111 *Ibid.*, fol. 110a.

stands in the investor's stead with regard to trade. For the investor's aim in handing over the capital to him is the achievement of profit, and this comes about by means of trade. Similarly, by the very nature of the contract, the agent possesses the right to do anything that is part of the practice of the merchants. He may, in our opinion, sell for cash and credit. . . . And he may give it as a *biḍā'a*, because giving it as a *biḍā'a* is part of the custom of the merchants and the agent will have need for it in order to achieve profit. For trade is of two kinds: local, in one's own town, and long-distance, in another town. And the agent cannot personally supervise both of these types by himself. And if he is not permitted to give the capital as a *biḍā'a*, and to have the power of appointing agents, and the right to leave it as a deposit, then he will have to miss out on one of the two types of trade because of his preoccupation with the other type. He may engage hired help with him to buy and sell; he may hire horses and pack animals for the merchandise which he buys, for these are part of the practice of the merchants and the agent cannot dispense with them in the attainment of profit. . . . And he may travel with it . . . because his goal is the achievement of profit, and this is usually only achieved by travelling with the capital, and the agent possesses this right by the very nature of the *commenda* contract.[112]

Thus, even in a limited mandate *commenda* contract, the agent's freedom of action extends almost unto the commercial horizons in which he functioned. The only criterion for the legitimacy of the agent's actions is the customary practice of the merchants. This standard is applied with remarkable consistency to all the agent's activities, even to the point of bending and adapting rules of law to the requirements of the marketplace. For example, merchants trading in foodstuffs usually rent and do not buy pack animals to transport their merchandise. Consequently, an agent engaged in this trade would not be permitted to use *commenda* funds to purchase

[112] Sarakhsī, *Mabsūṭ*, 22:38–39.

a pack animal.[113] However, if the agent is trading in a place in which it is the custom of the food merchants to buy pack animals, then on the basis of *istiḥsān*, such a purchase on the part of the agent is to be considered a legitimate *commenda* expense. If not specifically interdicted from doing so, the agent is permitted even to purchase a ship, if that is the practice of the merchants in the area in which he is operating.[114] "Because the agent possesses the full rights of trade with that which was entrusted to him here, and everything he purchases is of the contracts of trade."[115]

That the customary practice of the merchants almost exclusively determines the legitimacy of the agent's conduct of *commenda* trade is exemplified in connection with the problems of accepting a transfer of debt (*ḥawāla*)[116] in payment for *commenda* merchandise he sells. An agent may accept a *ḥawāla* from a purchaser "because this is part of trade, and of that which the merchants practice amongst themselves."[117] Further, he may accept the *ḥawāla* even if the debt is being transferred to someone less prosperous (*aʿsar*) than the purchaser, thereby entailing a greater risk of nonpayment. Sarakhsī points out that in this case, the considerations governing the *commenda* agents' actions differ from those applying to others who are entrusted with the safekeeping and welfare of property other than their own. For example, a guardian of the property of minors is restricted in the disposition of their property only to transactions which are unequivocally in the minors' better interests. In disposing of any of their property, the guardian or father is not permitted to take the risk of accepting a *ḥawāla* to a person who is less prosperous than the purchaser "because their transactions (i.e., of the father or guardian) are restricted by the condition of that which is best and most ad-

113 If the agent does so, the animal becomes his own property, and he is obliged to pay back the investor the price of the beast. If the animal was used to transport *commenda* merchandise, the investor would be obligated to pay the agent an equitable fee (*ajr mithluhu*) for the services rendered.

114 Shaybānī, *Aṣl*, *Muḍāraba*, fol. 61b.

115 Sarakhsī, *Mabsūṭ*, 22:45.

116 Re: *ḥawāla*, cf. Schacht, *Introduction to Islamic Law*, pp. 148–149.

117 Shaybānī, *Aṣl*, *Muḍāraba*, fol. 63b. l. 16.

vantageous."[118] By contrast, "the *commenda* agent is not restricted by any similar condition, but only by that which is the customary practice of the merchants."[119] This unequivocal right to engage in all normal commercial operations is repeated and emphasized in connection with several other types of transactions. So, for example, with regard to the agent's pledging (*rahn*) *commenda* property as security for a debt, Sarakhsī says:

> Just as the agent possesses the right to pay off a *commenda* debt with the *commenda* capital, so too does he possess the right to give it as a pledge. For this is part of the practice of the merchants; and in all matters that are part of the practice of the merchants, the agent is in the same category as the owner of the capital.[120]

It is in their conception of the scope of the agent's freedom of independent action with the *commenda* capital that the most substantial divergence between the Ḥanafī and the other early schools of Islamic law is to be found. For the Mālikīs and Shāfiʿīs, the agent's task was the achievement of profit primarily by means of buying and selling for cash. In their view, the right to engage in any other transactions did not inhere in the mandate the agent received from the investor. Without the express permission of the investor, the agent was not permitted to sell *commenda* goods on credit, to accept a *ḥawāla* in payment for them, to entrust them as a *biḍāʿa* to outside parties, to invest them in a *commenda* or partnership with third parties, nor even to leave them as a deposit, except in extreme and extenuating circumstances. Engaging in any of these activities without authorization subjects the agent to liability for the investment in case of loss.[121]

Compared with the nearly unrestricted flexibility with which Ḥanafī law endows the *commenda* agent, his freedom to dis-

118 Sarakhsī, *Mabsūṭ*, 22:47.

119 *Ibid.*, p. 47.

120 Sarakhsī, *Mabsūṭ*, 22:123; cf. also, Shaybānī, *Aṣl*, *Muḍāraba*, fols. 123b–124a.

121 Saḥnūn, *Mudawwana*, 12:103–123; Shirbīnī, *Mughnī*, 2:315; al-Ghazzālī, *al-Wajīz*, 2:223.

pose of *commenda* property in Mālikī law is severely limited, confined almost entirely to the rudimentary transactions of buying and selling on a cash basis. These radically divergent conceptions of the agent's role and activities might be explained by the difference in the economic ambience of these two schools. Presumably, the Mālikī *qirāḍ* reflected the commercial practices and needs of Medinese long distance trade, and was the contractual mainstay of this trade which in the first centuries of the *hijra* traveled from Mecca and Madina to the trading centers of Iraq and Syria in the northeast and northwest, and probably to a lesser extent, in the post-conquest period, to Yemen in the south. No large inhabited urban areas intervened between Mecca-Madina and the trading entrepôts of Iraq, Syria, and Yemen. It is very likely that the transactions requisite to carry out this trade were fairly simple and straightforward. Money or goods invested with an agent in Madina would be carried to Syria or Iraq, reinvested in merchandise there and in turn transported back to Madina where it would hopefully be resold at a profit. Thus, the need for credit transactions, *ibḍāʿa*, deposit, and the like were probably infrequently felt; simple buying and selling sufficed to assure a profit for most ventures.

However, in Iraq, whose commercial practice is reflected in the opinions of the Ḥanafī school, quite a different situation prevailed. The traveling trade initiated in, or transiting through, Iraq emanated over numerous routes traversing a series of urban trade centers in the direction of Syria, Byzantium, Central Asia and the Far East. To exploit fully the profitable commercial opportunities along these routes, the *commenda* agent would require the flexibility of freely employing a variety of commercial techniques. This reality undoubtedly contributed to the formation of the Ḥanafī conception of the agent's function in conducting *commenda* trade and thus endowed him with a much greater freedom to do so.

As for the Shāfiʿī conception of the *commenda,* it apparently developed entirely in disregard of economic considerations, with attention only to the requirements of its legal theory. The end result, of course, is an institution more confined and restricted than that found in either the Ḥanafī or Mālikī schools, a commercial instrument less responsive to the opportunities of trades and less efficient for their profitable exploitation.

Specific Restrictions

In his brief comments about business methods in the treatise *The Beauties of Commerce*, ad-Dimashqī says concerning the *commenda*: "The agent is not bound to indemnify the investor for accidental loss of the investment so long as he does not go beyond the localities agreed upon."[122] This did not apply to all *commendas*; it was true only for cases in which a geographical limitation on the agent's activities was specifically included in the agreement. This was but one of a variety of specific restrictions that the investor could impose on the agent. These specific restrictions could appear in a limited as well as in an unlimited mandate *commenda*, and could relate to the place, object, or methods of trade. The only requirement was that the restriction be what Sarakhsī terms a "beneficial stipulation," that is, a useful and beneficial condition from the investor's point of view.

Imposition of a geographical restriction, for example, fulfilled the above requirement, since the investor might have considered it desirable to have quick and direct access to his capital.[123] In such a case, the agent may not move the capital out of the restricted area or transfer it to anyone else who would do so. If he does so, he becomes liable for any loss.[124] The effects of geographical restrictions are interpreted rather leniently in the legal sources. Unless explicitly made a condition of the contract or formulated as a command to the agent, the geographical restriction is viewed as casual advice on trading policy and is not binding on the agent.[125] Even a valid restriction to one city, is interpreted, on the basis of

[122] Ad-Dimashqī, *Maḥāsin at-tijāra*, p. 40, trans. Ritter in *Der Islam* 7 (1917):58; also in Lopez and Raymond, *Medieval Trade*, p. 25.
[123] Sarakhsī, *Mabsūṭ*, 22:40.
[124] Shaybānī, *Aṣl, Muḍāraba*, fols. 57a–57b.
[125] Shaybānī, *Aṣl, Muḍāraba*, fol. 58a; Sarakhsī, *Mabsūṭ*, 22:40.

istiḥsān, as including the adjacent areas outside the city.[126] An explicit restriction to work only in a specific market, or a specific place in the market, is construed in an economic and not strictly geographic sense, i.e., as an injunction to trade only at the general price level of that market.

> If the investor entrusts him with a *commenda* on the condition that he works with it in the market of Kūfa, and the agent works with it in Kūfa but not in that place, then according to analogy he is a violator and liable because he violated a stipulation imposed upon him by the investor. But by *istiḥsān*, his transactions are effective in the *commenda* and he is not liable. Because a stipulation which is not beneficial is not taken into consideration, and there is no benefit in confining his transactions to the market. For the investor's intention applies to the price level of Kūfa, not the market itself; in any place in Kūfa in which he transacts business, his transactions conform to that which the investor stipulated. Do you think that if the investor instructs him to work with the investment in the changer's market and he works in a different market, or if he instructs him to work in the house of so and so, and he works in some other place that he will be liable? He will not be liable for anything in this connection by reason of the unity of the city.[127]

Inclusion of a geographical restriction in a *commenda* contract transforms its function from that of an instrument primarily facilitating long-distance trade into a means of investment for local trade. The legal treatment of this type of *commenda* also provides us with a clue to its economic motivation. It permitted the investor quick access to his capital, i.e., instead of waiting for the agent to return from a journey of undetermined duration, the investor could at any time instruct the agent to convert the investment into cash, retrieve his capital and hopefully some profit, and then invest it elsewhere or use it for some other purpose. Such an arrangement would also involve less risk and uncertainty since trade would be car-

[126] Shaybānī, *Aṣl, Muḍāraba*, fol. 57b.
[127] Sarakhsī, *Mabsūṭ*, 22:48.

ried on in economic circumstances and within a price structure with which the investor was familiar. Conversely, the rate of profit would undoubtedly be lower; nevertheless, the *commenda* with a geographical restriction could transform the *commenda* into a satisfactory means for short term investment.

The investor's right to impose restrictions on the agent's trading activity also includes the object of trade; he may limit the agent to buying and selling only a specific commodity such as wheat, barley, slaves, or to a category of merchandise such as textiles, foodstuffs, etc.[128] A restriction on merchandise does not preclude the use by the agent of investment funds for necessary incidental expenses such as transportation, storage, and hired help. If necessary, even paying for the services of a broker is an admissible expense.[129] The general rule in a restricted *commenda* of this kind is that the agent may do "anything that merchants engaged in that branch of trade do."[130] This rule is of economic importance, and probably reflects the experience of merchants trading in different markets with commercial customs varying from place to place. It gave an agent, even in a restricted *commenda*, the freedom to adapt his manner of doing business to local conditions, thus permitting him to compete on an equal footing with his colleagues in different locations where commercial practices may have varied in some details from those of his own home base. Failure to endow the *commenda* agent with such freedom could have put him at a severe disadvantage when trading in foreign parts. Since the *commenda* was presumably used primarily for long-distance trade, this type of flexibility for the agent was almost a *sine qua non* for a profitable venture.

Restricting trade to one commodity or class of commodities meets the standards of a "beneficial stipulation" (*sharṭ mufīd*) because the investor might consider the agent skillful and knowledgeable only in certain types of merchandise to the exclusion of others, and thus wish to confine the agent's activity to his specialty.[131] A *commenda* of this kind is a legal

[128] Shaybānī, *Aṣl, Muḍāraba,* fol. 58b.
[129] Shaybānī, *Aṣl, Muḍāraba,* fol. 58b, Sarakhsī, *Mabsūṭ,* 22:42.
[130] Shaybānī, *Aṣl, Muḍāraba,* fol. 61a, l. 16.
[131] Sarakhsī, *Mabsūṭ,* 22:41.

expression of an economic and social reality, *viz.*, the occasional specialization of the merchant class in the medieval Islamic world. The advanced degree of specialization in trade in the eleventh and twelfth centuries has been documented by S. D. Goitein on the basis of the Geniza records, where two hundred and sixty-five different occupations in trade and industry are mentioned.[132] Surnames such as *bazzāz, ṭa‘‘ām,* etc., referred not to the production of silk or of foodstuffs, but rather to the specialization of the person in trading with these commodities. It is not surprising then that as universal an instrument of trade as the *commenda* should lend itself to adaptation to this reality.

The investor may also impose binding restrictions on the agent's trade policy. He may designate the parties from whom the agent is to buy goods and to whom he is to sell them. This is a "beneficial stipulation" because people differ from one another regarding their trustworthiness and reliability in fulfilling obligations, and the investor has the right to protect his investment by confining the agent's transactions only to people in whom he has confidence.[133] The investor may forbid the agent to give the goods as an *ibḍā‘*[134] and may limit the agent's operations only to cash transactions excluding any credit purchases or sales, so as to be able to retrieve his capital quickly whenever he so desires.[135] On the other hand, a restriction on the agent to sell only for credit and not for cash is not binding; if the agent then sells for cash he does not become liable for the capital in his trust, "because he has done better than that which he was commanded."[136] Sarakhsī does not consider the agent's disregard of his instructions in this case to be a violation of his trust and fidelity since selling for cash is a more efficacious means of attaining the primary purpose of the *commenda.*

132 Cf. S. D. Goitein, "The Main Industries of the Mediterranean Area as Reflected in the Records of the Cairo Geniza," *JESHO* 4 (1961):171, and *idem, Mediterranean Society*, pp. 99ff. and pp. 155–156.

133 Shaybānī, *Aṣl, Muḍāraba*, fol. 59a; Sarakhsī, *Mabsūṭ*, 22:42.

134 Shaybānī, *Aṣl, Muḍāraba*, fol. 62b; Sarakhsī, *Mabsūṭ*, 22:46.

135 Shaybānī, *Aṣl, Muḍāraba*, fol. 61a; Sarakhsī, *Mabsūṭ*, 22:44.

136 Shaybānī, *Aṣl, Muḍāraba*, fol. 61a.

> Because this is better for the investor; any violation for the better with respect to his instructions is not a violation in the *commenda*. It is as if the investor instructs him to sell the goods for a thousand dirhams and not to sell them for any more than a thousand. If he then sells them for two thousand, he does not become a violator, since he accomplished that by which the aim of the instructor is achieved and with additional benefit.[137]

Thus, the investor's right to impose restrictions on the agent, and to guide his trading policy applies only in so far as it is beneficial and coincides with the primary purpose of the *commenda*, that of achieving a profit. When his instructions conflict with this goal, they are overridden and the rules of the marketplace prevail.

Under certain circumstances, the agent's disregard of the investor's stricture to sell only on credit and not for cash is regarded as a violation of his fidelity. The agent is free to disobey his instructions only "if he sold the goods for cash in accordance with a price designated for him. If, however, he sold them for less than that, the agent is a violator, since his actions are not conducive to attaining the aim of the investor with respect to value. For an object is sold on credit for more than it is sold for in cash."[138] Again, it is the economic advantage to the *commenda* which determines the status of the agent's actions; it is not the action itself which determines whether he is adjudged a violator, but rather the economic context in which it takes place.[139]

Restrictions imposed by the investor after the *commenda* is already functioning apply only to that portion of the capital which is not yet committed to other merchandise and which is still in cash form;[140] if it has already all been committed, the restriction becomes effective only after the agent has com-

[137] Sarakhsī, *Mabsūṭ*, 22:44.

[138] Sarakhsī, *Mabsūṭ*, 22:44–45.

[139] Cf. Goitein, *Mediterranean Society*, p. 199, for an actual incident of this kind, in which the investor insisted on the agent selling his goods on credit, and not accepting a cash payment.

[140] Shaybānī, *Aṣl*, *Muḍāraba*, fol. 60a; Sarakhsī, *Mabsūṭ*, 22:43.

pleted the series of transactions he is engaged in, and the capital of the investment is converted into cash form.[141]

In cases of disagreement between the investor and the agent as to whether or not a restriction was stipulated, unless proven otherwise, the presumption is that the *commenda* is unrestricted and covers all forms of trading activity and all types of merchandise. The *commenda,* by its very nature, implies the freedom to engage in a wide range of trading activities, since this is necessary to achieve its goal of the attainment of profit. In case of a dispute, therefore, and in the absence of contrary evidence, the word of the party claiming the more comprehensive character of the contract is accepted.[142]

Even in the absence of any restrictions, there are certain commodities in which the agent is prohibited from investing the *commenda* capital. These include wine and pork, which no Muslim may possess, trade in or profit from, certain types of slaves such as a *mudabbar*, *mukātab*, and *umm walad*, the purchase of which would not be to the economic advantage of the *commenda*.[143] The principle in this regard is that "the agent may not use the *commenda* capital to purchase anything the sale of which will be impossible for him."[144] If the agent invests in any of these, the purchase is considered a private one, and not on the account of the *commenda.*

Purchase and Sale

The agent's freedom to invest and otherwise dispose of the *commenda* capital is predicated on the assumption that this will be done responsibly and reasonably. An agent cannot be held liable for any loss resulting from a reasonable use of the

141 Shaybānī, *Aṣl*, *Muḍāraba*, fols. 68b–69a; Sarakhsī, *Mabsūṭ*, 22:53.

142 Shaybānī, *Aṣl, Muḍāraba*, fols. 59a, 62a; Sarakhsī, *Mabsūṭ*, 22:43. For the Mālikī discussion of restrictions in a *commenda* cf. Saḥnūn, *Mudawwana*, 12:111–120; the investor may impose restrictions in the agent's activities similar to those discussed in Ḥanafī law, but they must be of a reasonable nature, and not inimical to the purpose of the contract.

143 Shaybānī, *Aṣl*, *Muḍāraba*, fols. 69a–69b; Sarakhsī, *Mabsūṭ*, 22:54. Re: wine and pork, cf. Juynboll, *Handbuch des Islamischen Gesetzes*, pp. 175–180; Schacht, *An Introduction to Islamic Law*, pp. 120, 131, 135. Re: *mudabbar*, *mukātab*, and *umm walad*, cf., *EI*, 2nd ed., *s.v.*, *'abd.*

144 Sarakhsī, *Mabsūṭ*, 22:58; cf. also Saḥnūn, *Mudawwana*, 12:124–125.

commenda funds. If, however, the loss resulted from some unreasonable transaction on the part of the agent, he is held liable. In regard to buying and selling *commenda* property, the criterion of reasonableness is "that by which people will be fooled." For example, if the agent used a thousand dirhams to purchase a commodity worth only five hundred, he is liable because the difference between the purchase price and the worth of the goods is more than that by which people would normally be deceived. But if he used the same sum (1000 dirhams) to buy goods worth nine hundred and fifty dirhams, he is not held liable for the difference because this is a *ghabn yasīr*, "a slight deception," and is a misjudgment that is easy to make.[145] The same standard applies to the sale of *commenda* goods by the agent; that is, the negative difference between their value, or their original purchase price, must not be greater than the amount that people would normally be fooled by, otherwise the agent is liable for the difference.[146]

The Mālikīs do not apply the standard of *ghabn yasīr* to the agent's buying and selling activity. It is expected that he will exercise all the skill and care necessary to protect the capital entrusted to him. If he is clearly negligent in this respect, he would become liable for any loss that might occur, as exemplified in the following:

> I said: "What is your opinion of the following case? I give a man capital as a *commenda* with which he buys some merchandise and pays the seller for it. When he wishes to take possession of these goods, the seller denies that he received their price from him. Is the agent liable for anything or not?" He said: "I do not recall any statement from Mālik on this matter, but I consider him liable, because he caused the loss of the investor's capital by failing to have the sale witnessed when he paid the price."[147]

[145] Shaybānī, *Aṣl*, *Muḍāraba*, fols. 60b–70a; Sarakhsī, *Mabsūṭ*, 22:54.

[146] Shaybānī, *Aṣl*, *Muḍāraba*, fol. 70a. This is the opinion of Abū Yūsuf and Shaybānī; Abū Ḥanīfa, however, holds that any sale on the part of the agent is valid and binding on the *commenda*.

[147] Saḥnūn, *Mudawwana*, 12:123.

Presumably, other clear-cut cases of negligent and careless business practices would also make the agent liable in the Mālikī view.

As the investor's "representative in trade," the agent possesses the full range of options that any buyer or seller trading with his own money or goods would have the right to exercise. If he sold some goods in which the purchaser found a fault, he has the right (a) to take back the goods and refund the purchase-price; (b) to deny that the fault exists; (c) to contest it, claiming that fault came about after the goods were sold; or, and most significantly, (d) to appease the buyer either by reducing the price, or by offering him additional goods.[148] The agent cannot be reproached or held liable for exercising this last option if the additional goods he offered reasonably corresponded in value to the fault in the goods sold, and "if he discounted in accordance with what people discount for that fault."[149] In the absence of any fault or claim of a fault from the buyer, the agent may not offer a reduction from the regular price "because this is not part of trade; it is rather in the category of a gift."[150] If he does so, he can be held accountable by the investor, and the amount of the reduction is "a debt of the agent to the investor."[151]

An interesting insight into the commercial ethos and the social organization of trade in the medieval Islamic period is provided by the discussion of the agent's right to transact *commenda* business with members of his family. The legitimacy of *commenda* purchases and sales from and to members of his family by the agent are subject to the same scrutiny as are any of his other purchases and sales; that is, they must not exceed the bounds of "that by which people are fooled." Since there is room for suspecting that the agent may tend to be less vigilant when dealing with his family than he would be with strangers, Abū Ḥanīfa holds that a stricter standard should be imposed. In his view, even that slight difference between the value of goods and the price received or paid, which in other

[148] Shaybānī, *Aṣl, Muḍāraba*, fols. 72b–73a, Sarakhsī, *Mabsūṭ*, 22:57.
[149] Shaybānī, *Aṣl, Muḍāraba*, fol. 64a, ll. 2–3.
[150] Shaybānī, *Aṣl, Muḍāraba*, fol. 64b, l. 6.
[151] Sarakhsī, *Mabsūṭ*, 22:47.

circumstances is overlooked as a *ghabn yasīr* (slight deception), is not to be tolerated when the agent is trading with members of his family, and when the latter are the beneficiaries of the agent's miscalculation. The prevalent Ḥanafī position rejects Abū Ḥanīfa's view, and holds that economic self-interest will prove stronger than attachment to kith and kin.

> For the agent is a partner in the profit and this will prevent him from neglecting to scrutinize and look into the value and quality of the goods—even when trading with his father and son. For he will prefer himself to the both of them. For this reason, it is permitted for him to trade with them in accordance with the value of the goods.[152]

The very fact that this problem is raised would seem to indicate that the *commenda* was not primarily confined to the members of the same family, but involved outsiders. To a lesser extent, the same is probably true of partnerships. Although extended family ties undoubtedly played an important role in the commerce of the medieval Islamic world, its major institutions had already moved beyond the family framework and its ethos was already liberated from a narrow family outlook placing primary emphasis on economic self-interest.[153]

Murābaḥa

In its relationship to other commercial transactions, the *commenda* might be designated as a *horizontal* contract. Since its purpose was the attainment of profit, both for the investor and the agent-manager, by means of trade, it transversed all known commercial practices and techniques. In the pursuit of profit the agent would doubtlessly have to avail himself of a variety of transaction. Any thoroughgoing treatment of the agent's activities with the investment entrusted to him would, therefore, necessarily become a focal point for the discussion of all other trade practices as they related to the conduct of the *commenda*. The aim of these discussions is always to define

[152] Sarakhsī, *Mabsūṭ*, 22:58, and also p. 57; Shaybānī, *Aṣl, Muḍāraba*, fols. 73a–73b.

[153] Cf. also Saḥnūn, *Mudawwana*, 12:122.

the limits of the agent's freedom of action in such transactions as purchase, sale, deposit, credit, etc., with particular reference to the fact that the money he is trading with is not his own, and that he bears no liability for its partial or total loss under normal trading circumstances. As indicated above the agent's rights coincide almost completely with the customary practice of the merchants; the only inhibitions placed upon the agent's disposition of the investment relate to such "favors" as loans, gifts, and the like. Consequently the legal discussions of the various trade practices which the agent, in company with all other merchants, may engage in contain no new elaborations of these transactions. They are essentially summaries, in the context of a *commenda* contract, of the major commercial operations that the agent is likely to make use of, and except for a different emphasis, do not deviate in any significant way from the more detailed independent treatment that these institutions receive elsewhere in the legal compendia. Their significance in the context of the treatment of the *commenda*, especially in the extensive and full discussions that we find in Shaybānī, and the *Mudawwana* of Saḥnūn lies in the fact that they were singled out by these legal scholars as the transactions most likely to be needed by the agent, and thus probably reflect their relative importance and frequency of use in actual trade. It is in this connection that one should take note of a particular form of sale which is the subject of a detailed discussion in the "Books of *Commenda*" —that of the *murābaḥa*—or fixed-profit sale.

According to the lawyers, and in conformity with what one would expect to be the case, the most common form of sale was the *musāwama*, i.e., the sale of goods at any price mutually agreed upon by the buyer and the seller.[154] In addition, Islamic law also discusses in great detail three forms of sale which have as their starting point the cost of the sale's object to the seller. These are: the *tawliya*, resale at the stated original cost with no profit or loss to the seller; the *waḍīʿa*, resale at a discount from the original cost; and the *murābaḥa*, the resale at fixed surcharge or rate of profit on the stated original

[154] Cf. Samarqandī, *Tuḥfat al-fuqahā'*, Damascus, 1964, 2:132.

cost.[155] As Schacht has already pointed out, the exact economic function these institutions fulfilled in trade, especially the *murābaḥa*, is far from clear.[156] Al-Marghīnānī suggests that their purpose, particularly of the *tawliya* and *murābaḥa* sales, was the protection of the innocent general consumer lacking expertise in the various items of trade from the wiles and stratagems of sharp traders.[157] By basing the sale's price on the original cost of the item to the seller, the customer was provided with a modicum of protection against unfair exploitation by an unscrupulous merchant.

This view of the economic function of these three forms of sale, while not explicitly articulated, is nevertheless largely confirmed by the treatment of them in earlier Ḥanafī literature. The chief concern is to avoid any fraud on the part of the seller by setting out detailed guidelines regarding the considerations that are to enter into determining the cost of any item. Foremost among these, of course, is the price paid by the seller for the goods in question. In addition, a variety of expenses connected with the maintenance, improvement and transport of the goods may be included in the cost which forms the basis of the *murābaḥa* sale. The custom of the merchants served as the criterion for determining exactly which expenses were to be included. The general rule emerging from the numerous cases discussed is that money expended directly on the goods or on services indispensable to their sale (e.g., brokerage fees) may be included, whereas the personal expenses of the merchant and other expenses not directly involved with the goods are not to be figured into the stated original cost on which the *murābaḥa* transaction is based. As an additional protection to the customer, the lawyers insist that the seller avoid any misleading statements. He must be scrupulous in how he designates the sum serving as the basis of the *murābaḥa*. If he includes various expenses in this sum, he may not, directly or indirectly, lead the buyer to believe that

155 Cf. Schacht, *Introduction to Islamic Law*, pp. 153–154; Schacht, *Grundzüge*, Berlin, 1935, pp. 71–72.

156 *Ibid.*

157 Al-Marghinānī, *Al-hidāya*, Cairo, n.d., 3:56.

the *murābaḥa* is based on the purchase price, but must use some expression indicating that this is what it cost him, and not that this is what he paid for it. All these safeguards, however, are undermined by the legitimacy of transacting a *murābaḥa* sale on the basis of any sum that is not misleading or fraudulent. That is, even if the commodities in question were purchased by the seller for a hundred dirhams, or cost him that much after he included various and sundry expenses associated with the goods, he may nevertheless transact a *murābaḥa* sale on the basis of any higher figure he chooses as long as he does not claim that the sum bears any relationship to his cost. Thus for example, he may say to the customer, "I will sell you these commodities as a *murābaḥa* on the basis of three hundred dirhams and fifty dirhams profit," even though the base sum, in this case the three hundred dirhams, is far higher than his original cost.[158] This possibility serves further to complicate any attempt on our part to reconstruct the precise economic function of the *murābaḥa* sale in medieval Islamic commerce. Lacking, as we do, any detailed information concerning the practices of the medieval Islamic marketplace, we can only broadly speculate that the *murābaḥa* was one of a variety of forms of sale utilized in commerce and that its use was restricted to circumstances which made its particular provisions expeditious. A buyer, for example, may have been willing to pay a retailer who was at hand a fixed surcharge on the cost of certain commodities in order to save himself the trouble of obtaining them from a wholesaler who may have resided at some distance.

One can envisage other hypothetical conditions under which the use of the *murābaḥa* could have been particularly effective. One is the tantalizing possibility that it served as a form of commission sale. This possibility is supported by the fact that one is allowed to acquire goods on credit and then resell

[158] For sources on the preceding discussion of the *murābaḥa* cf. Shaybānī, *Al-aṣl, Kitāb al-buyū' was-salam*, ed. Sh. Shiḥāta, Cairo, 1953, pp. 155–175; Sarakhsī, *Mabsūṭ*, 13:78–91; and 22:73–89; Shaybānī, *Aṣl, Muḍāraba*, fols. 84bff. In the nineteenth century, and perhaps earlier, the term *murābaḥa* was used in some parts of the Islamic world as an euphemism for usury; cf. M. Rodinson, *Islam et capitalisme*, Paris, 1966, p. 59.

them on a *murābaḥa* basis, with the surcharge of either a fixed sum or a fixed rate of profit based on the purchase price. The only limitation placed on the seller is that he informs the buyer that the goods in question were acquired on credit. Honesty and probity require that this information be given, according to Sarakhsī, since customarily goods sold on credit fetch a higher price than those sold for cash.[159] Whether the possibilities of commission sales inherent in the *murābaḥa* were realized in medieval Islamic commercial life is a problem concerning which we can at this point, make no definitive judgment. Whatever its possibilities, and whatever economic functions it fulfilled, the *commenda* agent possessed the right to engage in this transaction under the same conditions as applied to any other trader.

Investor and Agent During Operation of the *Commenda*

One of the conditions of a valid *commenda* is the alienation of the investor from his capital; i.e., there can be no effective *commenda* while the capital is still in the investor's possession and not in that of the agent. By extension, this same notion prevents the investor from insisting on his own full participation in the commercial conduct of *commenda* business. If the investor made his own participation in its conduct a condition of the *commenda* the contract is invalid because of the absence of any separation between the investor and his capital. If the parties proceed on the basis of the condition, the contract is considered a hire agreement with all profit and loss accruing to the investor, and the agent being entitled to an equitable wage.[160] This does not rule out "informal" help from the investor to the agent, but excludes any compulsory participation in *commenda* affairs as a result of a clause or stipulation in the contract.

It is the agent who possesses supreme authority in the conduct of *commenda* business. After the capital is in his posses-

159 Sarakhsī, *Mabsūṭ*, 22:78. For a brief discussion of the significance of this fact, cf. A. L. Udovitch, "Credit as a Means of Investment in Medieval Islamic Trade," *Journal of the American Oriental Society* (*JAOS*) 87 (1967): 262.

160 Shaybānī, *Aṣl, Muḍāraba*, fol. 96a; Sarakhsī, *Mabsūṭ*, 22:83–84.

sion, the agent may, if he wishes, delegate the investor to trade with it. This arrangement would be considered as a *biḍā'a,* and the original *commenda* would remain intact. If the investor takes it upon himself to act without the agents' permission, the status of the *commenda* and the allocation of the profits depends on whether the investment is in the form of cash or of goods. If, for example, the investor, without the agent's permission, took the capital, still in cash form, from the agent's house and traded with it, the *commenda* would cease with the investor's retrieval of his money, and all subsequent profit would go only to the investor. However, if the investor takes goods which the agent bought with the capital and sells them without the latter's permission, any resulting profit is to be divided according to the *commenda* agreement. The agent shares in the profits of the investor's unauthorized activities with *commenda* goods up to the point when the merchandise is converted into cash; at that point the *commenda* is considered to be dissolved. The *commenda* can be ended and the agent's activities restricted by the investor only while the investment is in the form of cash; once the agent has made a purchase, and the *commenda* has become effective, any interference by the investor in *commenda* affairs must await the completion of whatever transactions the agent is involved in and the conversion of the capital back into cash.[161]

Only in exceptional circumstances can the investor effectively intervene in the conduct of *commenda* affairs while the investment is in the form of goods. If the value of the merchandise bought by the agent is equivalent to the cash value of the investment, there being no apparent profit, the investor can insist and compel the agent to sell the goods and then retrieve his capital. This is so even if the agent wishes to wait in the hope of selling the merchandise at a profit. However, if there is an apparent profit, e.g., if the investment was 1000 dirhams and the goods acquired by the agent are worth 1500 dirhams, then the investor cannot force a total sale. By virtue of his share in the profit, the agent has now become a part owner of the merchandise. The investor, therefore, can only

[161] Shaybānī, *Aṣl, Muḍāraba,* fols. 97a–98a; Sarakhsī, *Mabsūṭ,* 22:85–86.

initially invested, the agent becomes a part-owner by virtue of his share in the increase over and above the investment, and his manumission of the slave is valid. The agent then becomes liable to the investor for the difference; e.g., he must repay to him his capital as well as the sum equivalent to the investor's share of the profit.[167]

With respect to the slaves acquired with the capital, the agent's behavior must generally conform to commercial custom and must coincide with the best interests of the contract. Thus he may confer *ma'dhūn* status on a slave, e.g., empower him to participate in trade on his behalf, since "conferring *ma'dhūn* status on a slave is part of trade . . . and by the very nature of the contract, the agent has the absolute right to engage in practices that are part of trade with the *commenda* capital."[168] He may not, however, consort with, caress or fondle the female slaves he acquires, since any benefit this may entail is distinctly "not a part of trade" (*laysa min at-tijāra*).[169] For the same reason, he may not marry off a male slave bought with *commenda* capital.

> Marrying off a male slave constitutes a handicap; there is no advantage to the *commenda* in such an action. . . . The agent was entrusted with this capital for the purposes of trade, and marrying off a slave is not a feature of trade, nor is it one which the merchants customarily practice. We know of no place in any country having a market devoted to marrying off slaves! And with respect to practices which are not normally part of trade, the agent, like any other person, is a stranger with reference to the *commenda* capital.[170]

Two Agents

The basic model for a *commenda* contract is an arrangement between one investor and one agent. There is no barrier, however, to a multiplicity either of investors or of agents in the same contract. In the latter case, the agents are considered as

[167] *Ibid.*, fol. 116a.

[168] Sarakhsī, *Mabsūṭ*, 22:124; cf., also, Shaybānī, *Aṣl*, *Muḍāraba*, fols. 124a–124b.

[169] *Ibid.*, fols. 125b–126a, and Sarakhsī, *Mabsūṭ*, 22:126 (top).

[170] Sarakhsī, *Mabsūṭ*, 22:122.

one with respect to the conduct of *commenda* business. If an investor hands over an investment to two agents instructing them "to act with it according to their judgment," the agents may act only in concert and with mutual agreement and approval. If either agent acts independently without his colleagues' permission, he becomes liable to the investor for any ensuing loss. The rationale underlying this rule is that the investor, in choosing two or more agents, entrusted his capital to their joint discretion, and since the "opinion of one is not like the opinion of two,"[171] no independent unauthorized action on the part of either agent is permissible.[172] The only circumstances in which one agent can act without his colleague's permission are if he obtains the investor's approval, for "the permission of the investor in this regard and the permission of the other agent are the same."[173]

If he sees fit, an investor may enter into two separate *commendas* with the same agent with the same or with different profit sharing provisions;[174] or, he may invest separately with two agents who may then pool the capital entrusted to them in a *commenda* between themselves. This could result in a rather complex network of commercial relationships as is exemplified by the following passage:

> If a man gives another one thousand dirhams as a *commenda* on a half profit basis on the condition that the latter work with it according to his discretion, and he works and profits a thousand. Then the original investor gives another man one thousand in a *commenda* on a half profit basis and instructs him to work with it as he sees fit. The first agent gives the two thousand to the second agent as a *commenda* on the basis of one-third of the profit going to the latter and on the condition that he work with it as he sees fit. The latter mixes the thousand with the two thousand. There is no liability on him for doing this, and whatever he profits is to be divided in three, and whatever

171 Sarakhsī, *Mabsūṭ*, 22:44 (top).
172 Shaybānī, *Aṣl, Muḍāraba*, fol. 62b; Sarakhsī, *Mabsūṭ*, 22:45–46.
173 Shaybānī, *Aṣl, Muḍāraba*, fol. 66b.
174 Shaybānī, *Aṣl, Muḍāraba*, fol. 130b.

he loses is to be divided in three. If he loses five hundred, the first agent takes 1,666 2/3 and the second agent retains 833 1/3. If he profits one thousand, he withholds one-third himself, and the remaining two-thirds are divided into three. The investor of the two thousand (i.e., the first agent) takes two-thirds of this. Then the division is made with the investor. His capital of one thousand is returned to him; from what remains, the investor gets half of the profit of the first agent in the capital which is the five hundred on the original thousand and three-quarters of the second profit. For the profit that the first agent gives the second agent is from the former's portion. The remainder of the profit goes to the first agent and this is one-half of the first thousand and one-quarter of that which comes to him from the second *commenda.* And the other agent takes one-third from the first agent; then the second agent makes a division with the investor. He returns his capital to him, and what remains is divided between them as follow: three-quarters to the investor, and for the agent one-quarter.[175]

The various possibilities considered in the preceding passage probably do not reflect any actual case, and is very likely simply an involved exercise of legal deduction and casuistry. Nevertheless, nothing would theoretically exclude the possibility of weaving such a complex network of commercial interconnections. Even if commercial operations never became quite as involved as the hypothetical example treated in the preceding quotation, there is no reason to doubt that the exigencies of long-distance trade often required *commenda* agents to reinvest and consolidate the capital entrusted to them with third and fourth parties with varying provisions for profit sharing in order to ensure a profitable trading venture.

Interdenominational *Commenda*

That differences in religious affiliation were no barrier to economic collaboration is amply documented by the Geniza papers which are replete with examples of business relations

[175] Shaybānī, *Aṣl, Muḍāraba,* fols. 131b–132a.

between the Jewish merchants, who left us these letters and contracts, and their Christian and Muslim neighbors. Among these, are several instances of interdenominational partnerships and *commendas*.[176] The views of Muslim law on this point are not unequivocal. Even the Ḥanafīs, who, as usual, are the most lenient on this question, took a dim view of certain types of Muslim–non-Muslim joint ventures. In an interdenominational *commenda* (i.e., between a Muslim and a non-Muslim, be he Christian, Jew, or whatever), the pleasure or displeasure of the Ḥanafī authorities turns on the religious affiliation of the agent. If the agent is a Muslim, the contract is permissible and valid like any other between two Muslims; if, however, the agent is a Christian, the agreement, while not invalid, is disapproved and considered reprehensible (*makrūh*). The reasons are summarized by Sarakhsī as follows:

> There is nothing wrong with a Muslim accepting capital from a Christian as a *commenda*, since doing this is a category of trade and of commercial activity, Or, it can be considered as a mandate (*tawkīl*) from the investor to the Muslim for him to work with the capital. There is nothing wrong with a Muslim overseeing sales and purchases on behalf of a Christian as his agent.
>
> Even though it is judicially permissible, it is reprehensible for a Muslim to entrust capital as a *commenda* to a Christian, just as it is reprehensible for a Muslim to mandate a Christian to work with his capital. This is so, because in the latter case the person directly overseeing the transactions is the Christian who will not guard against usury, nor will he be aware of the factors which invalidate the contract, nor will he, because of his faith, guard against them. Similarly, he will deal in wine and pork, and it is reprehensible for a Muslim to deputize another person to deal in these commodities. However, this disapproval does not affect the es-

176 Goitein, *Mediterranean Society*, pp. 172–173.

sence of the *commenda* or of the mandate, nor does it obviate its judicial validity.[177]

Mālikī doctrine is generally in accord with the Ḥanafī position on this problem. Mālik went a step further, and even disapproved of a *commenda* between a Muslim agent and a Christian investor, or anyone "according to whose religion the eating of prohibited things is permissible," and frowned upon entrusting funds to a non-observant Muslim agent, one "who makes permissible that which is prohibited in matters of buying and selling."[178]

Underlying the preceding discussion was the assumption that the non-Muslim trading partner was a resident of the *dār al-Islām*—the territories subject to the hegemony of Muslim rulers. In the case of an association with a foreign merchant hailing from the *dār al-ḥarb* (literally: domain of war)—the lands outside Muslim domination—there was a further complicating factor. A foreigner could enter into and trade within the Islamic domain only if he was granted an *amān*, a guarantee of safe conduct which ensured the safety of his life, limb, and property during his sojourn in the territory of Islam.[179] There is no barrier to a Muslim accepting or giving capital as a *commenda* to a *ḥarbī*; and should all the transactions and trading activity take place within the *dār al-Islām*, the agreement is valid and all its stipulations are to be honored. A serious difficulty arises when the foreign merchant, while the *commenda* is still in force, returns to the *dār al ḥarb*. Crossing the political-denominational boundary of the *dār al-Islām* automatically voids the *commenda* contract.[180] This would seemingly rule out any approved joint means of international trade, since even if a *ḥarbī* agent carries the investment to non-Muslim territory with the express approval and permission of the Muslim investor, the contract, on

177 Sarakhsī, *Mabsūṭ*, 22:125. Cf. also, pp. 60–61, and Shaybānī, *Aṣl, Muḍāraba*, fols. 74b–75b, and 125a–125b.

178 Saḥnūn, *Mudawwana*, 12:107ff.

179 Cf. W. Heffening, *Das islamische Fremdenrecht bis zu den islamisch-fränkischen Staatsvertragen*, Hanover, 1925; and *EI*², *s.v.*, *amān*.

180 Shaybānī, *Aṣl, Muḍāraba*, fol. 128b; Sarakhsī, *Mabsūṭ*, 22:129.

the basis of legal analogy, is void. Whether in response to an economic reality, or as an outgrowth of their lenient attitude toward commercial matters, the Ḥanafī jurists came to the rescue by exercising juristic preference (*istiḥsān*), and recognized the validity of this latter type of arrangement.[181] The way was thus kept opened for licit international commercial collaboration. Whether it was exploited, and how extensively, we do not as yet know; but the possibility existed.

Expenses

Since a *commenda* investment generally entailed travel on the part of the agent, often to distant parts and for extended periods, the question of his expenses, both personal and business, assumed paramount importance. By definition, profit from a *commenda* venture was the sum remaining at the time of its dissolution after the repayment of the invested capital to the investor and the deduction of the agent's expenses. Thus the elaboration of clear and definitive guidelines for the agent's expenditure of *commenda* funds on the various ancillary aspects of trade, i.e., on all operations and services other than the direct acquisition of goods and merchandise, was also necessary from an accounting point of view.

Regardless of whether or not the agent undertakes travels with the *commenda* investment, he may deduct all legitimate business expenses from the capital entrusted to him. As indicated above, the limits of this freedom are defined by its conformity to the twin criteria of customary commercial practice and the pursuit of profit.[182] Essentially the same considerations, although somewhat modified, govern the agent's expenditures on his personal needs while engaged in *commenda* business.

If the agent does not travel with the investment, but stays in his native town or with his family, he is not entitled to cover any of his personal expenses from *commenda* funds. The entire discussion of an agent's personal expenses assumes that the agent will in fact travel on behalf of the *commenda*.

[181] Shaybānī, *Aṣl, Muḍāraba*, fols. 128b–129a; Sarakhsī, *Mabsūṭ*, 22:130.
[182] Cf. above, "Conduct of the *Commenda*."

If a man entrusts to another ten thousand dirhams as a *commenda* investment on the basis of one-half, or one-third or one-fourth of the profit, or more, or less, and the agent trades with it while in his own town or while remaining with his family, then the agent's expenses for his food, clothing, and all his needs are to be borne by himself. None of his expenses are to be borne by the investor or the *commenda,* because he does not travel with the capital and does not depart from the town with it. Since he does not travel with it, his expenses are to be borne by himself.

If, however, he departs with the capital to any other town in order to make purchases with it, or to sell some of the merchandise he has already purchased, then his expenses while travelling and while in the town to which he is heading are to be borne by the capital. This includes his clothing, food, ointment, the cost of his mount while traveling and during his sojourn in the city to which he has come, in the customary manner commensurate with the expenses of somebody of his status.[183]

In the preceding passage, Shaybānī merely asserted the general procedure governing expenses in the *commenda.* Sarakhsī, as he so often does, probes somewhat deeper and offers us a valuable insight into the rationale behind this procedure.

If the agent departs with the capital to another place for the purpose of trading with it, then his expenses on the road and while in the city to which he is travelling are to be taken from the *commenda* capital. This is so, because of custom; for his departure and travel are on behalf of the *commenda* capital. A person does not normally undertake this kind of hardship for the sake of an uncertain profit which he may or may not achieve, and then pay his expenses from his own money. However, he is willing to undertake such hardship with a view to the benefit that might accrue to him; and this will not come about except by taking the expenses sufficient

[183] Shaybānī, *Aṣl, Muḍāraba,* fols. 76a l. 10–76b l. 1.

> for his upkeep from the money at hand (i.e., the *commenda* investment).[184]

Sarakhsī then goes on to compare the *commenda* agent with a wife:

> Because he has freed himself from all other work for the sake of the *commenda* capital, he is in this respect like a wife who has freed herself from all other things for the sake of her husband by staying in his house.[185]

This explanation of the agent's right to personal expense from the *commenda* capital reflects one of the basic features of the contract which made it a practical and efficient instrument for profitable long-distance trade. In a paradigmatic *commenda* agreement, the investor contributed his capital but no time and effort, and the agent contributed his time and effort but no capital. By joining these two investment components, the work of one and the capital of the other, both parties hoped to share in a profitable venture; but both also shared the risk of losing their respective contributions in the event of a misfortune or business reverse. If, in addition to his time and effort, the agent's own funds while engaged in travel and trade on behalf of the *commenda* investment were also subject to risk, the distribution of risks between the parties would have become less equitable and the *commenda*, as a result, a less attractive and practical instrument for combining the capital and skills necessary for the successful prosecution of trade.

The Islamic lawyers were thoroughly consistent in their view of the division of risks and investments in the *commenda* and carried it to its ultimate conclusion. Thus, even if the agent completed a journey on behalf of the *commenda* but did not buy any goods or otherwise invest the capital, his travel and personal expenses were nevertheless covered from the capital.[186]

> The agent is not liable for the amount of his expenses because he spends it by virtue of a right to which he is entitled.

184 Sarakhsī, *Mabsūṭ*, 22:62–63.
185 *Ibid.*, p. 63.
186 Shaybānī, *Aṣl*, *Muḍāraba*, fol. 80b.

> For his travel is on behalf of the *commenda*, and the fact that he does not buy anything does not prove that his travel is not on behalf of the *commenda*. A merchant certainly does not use his capital to make purchases in every place to which he comes for the purposes of trade. He buys only if he finds something on which he can make a profit; if not, he returns with the capital, the latter being the most congenial of the two alternatives facing him.[187]

The extent of the agents' expenses is determined by commercial custom; their quality, however, is determined by his social status. While every *commenda* agent is entitled to have his expenses for food, clothing and travel covered by the capital by virtue of commercial custom, the quality of his food and clothing and the comfort with which he travels are determined by his social status. Just as the agent's business expenses are governed by the customs of the locale within which he is trading, so too are his personal expenses. Among the items to which he is entitled, the legal sources mention ointment. However, this is restricted by some as applying only to travel in the regions of the Ḥijāz and Iraq where the use of ointments is customary, but not to areas in which this is not the case.[188] Adjusting personal expenses to local standards and practices presumably made good economic sense, as well. One could assume that in order to succeed in his affairs in the marketplace the agent would have to be presentable, and meet certain personal and social standards. Examples of exactly how the agent's social status affected his expenses are not elaborated in the legal texts. Nevertheless, the social and commercial standing of the agent must have been of considerable practical importance *vis à vis* his expenses. From the Geniza texts we know that the social and economic backgrounds of those engaged in trade, and more specifically those who were involved in partnerships and *commenda* agreements, were varied indeed. A *commenda* agent may have been an apprentice from a

[187] Sarakhsī, *Mabsūṭ*, 22:67. Cf. also, Saḥnūn, *Mudawwana*, 12:92–94. The Mālikī view of the agent's expenses is almost identical with that of the Ḥanafīs.

[188] Sarakhsī, *Mabsūṭ*, 22:63.

humble family, a novice of limited means and even more limited experience just starting out on his commercial career, or a well-established, experienced merchant of considerable wealth and of semi-aristocratic standing in the community.[189] As far as I know, we have no data to document exactly how the difference in status and background affected their expenses while traveling; however, since social position affected their general standard of living, it must have been of considerable importance, too, in regard to their expenses when undertaking a *commenda* investment involving travel. It is in this social context that we should place the gradation of the agents' personal expenses which are covered from the *commenda* capital.

Extra-Commercial Expenses

It is rare indeed to encounter an instance in which later legal authorities explicitly depart from a point of law unequivocally fixed by the founding fathers of Islamic law without seeking recourse to *istiḥsān* (juristic preference) or some other recognized source of legal interpretation. One clear case of a development of this kind occurs with respect to the status of expenditure by the *commenda* agent for unusual but often necessary services, as for example, the favors of rapacious government officials. According to Abū Ḥanīfa and Shaybānī, funds used by the *commenda* agent to bribe a tax collector or other government official, even for the purpose of protecting the investment from confiscation or a similarly unprofitable fate, is not to be covered from the *commenda* capital, but from the private funds of the agent.[190] Between the eighth and eleventh centuries, the Ḥanafī position on this point underwent a complete about face. Sarakhsī unabashedly attributes this change to the deteriorated moral quality of political rule. He argues that exclusion of bribes as an appropriate business expense may have been appropriate at the time of Abū Ḥanīfa and Shaybānī when the power of political authority was exercised justly; however, in his own time (eleventh cen-

189 Cf. Goitein, *Mediterranean Society*, pp. 165 and 173–175.

190 Shaybānī, fol. 81a; for the attribution of this opinion to Abū Ḥanīfa, cf. Sarakhsī, *Mabsūṭ*, 22:67.

tury), a bribe should be considered a legitimate expense since it is intended to benefit the investment by paying out part of it in order to protect the rest from harm.[191] No legal theory underlies this change of legal opinion; it is due quite explicitly to the pressure of historical and political circumstances.

Local and Short-Distance *Commenda* Expenses

The discussion concerning the *commenda* agent's expenses provides some interesting incidental information on the various uses to which the *commenda* could be put in trade. In addition to extended journeys which may have lasted from six months to several years, for which the *commenda* was an ideal form of commercial endeavor, and for which it was undoubtedly the predominant instrument of trade, it could also be employed for ventures of a more limited scope. It could be used for short-distance trade. A frequently discussed example of this kind is an expedition by the *commenda* agent in the urban hinterlands for the purpose of purchasing quantities of food supplies and staples for the city markets. Even though the duration of such journeys might only be from one to three days, an agent was entitled to receive his personal expenses from the capital.[192] Even more restricted, and indeed probably more unlikely in practice, was a *commenda* which entailed no travelling at all, i.e., one in which the investment and trading activities all took place within the confines of one city. Even if the city was a large one, and the agent's trading activities took him to the opposite end of town from his home and involved spending nights away from home, his personal expenses are not covered from the capital.[193] While the *commenda* had the potential flexibility for use in local and short-distance trade, and was probably occasionally employed in this way, other commercial techniques were far more efficient for these purposes. Its most prominent role was undoubtedly in long-distance trade.

[191] Sarakhsī, *Mabsūṭ*, 22. The Mālikīs equate any extortion by officials with robbery, and therefore absolve the agent from any responsibility; cf. Saḥnūn, *Mudawwana*, 12:101.

[192] Shaybānī, *Aṣl*, *Muḍāraba*, fol. 77a; Sarakhsī, *Mabsūṭ*, 22:64.

[193] *Ibid.*

Problematic Expenses

If the agent mixes his private fund with that of the investment, or if he trades separately with his funds while traveling, his personal expenses are to be covered by the *commenda* in a direct ratio of the investment to the total amount of money being traded with.[194] If, with regard to the quantity and quality of his personal expenses, the agent exceeds the customary level, the excess is to be covered from his own funds. These two provisions reinforce the supposition that the agent was required to keep fairly detailed records of his expenses while traveling.

Only those business and personal expenses incurred directly or indirectly by the agent are covered from the investment capital. Should the investor, for example, insist on providing his own slaves or animals to facilitate the agent's work, the upkeep and expenses to cover these items are borne by the investor, and their cost does not affect the total profit nor the agent's share of it.[195] However, expense for any slaves of the agent that accompany him on his travels are taken from the capital since "he (the slave) stands in the place of his master in this regard."[196] This is but another manifestation of the wide measure of freedom and independence vested in the *commenda* agent in all his trading activities.

The status of expenses of parties outside the *commenda* to whom the agent may entrust the capital depends on the conditions in which this takes place. If it is given as an *ibḍāʿ*, then the expenses, if any, are borne by the *mustabḍiʿ*, since this arrangement is in the nature of favor among trading colleagues.[197] On the other hand, if the agent is operating in an unlimited mandate *commenda*, and entrusts the investment to another agent on a *commenda* basis, the latter's expenses are borne by the capital because "in this situation he (i.e., the first agent) stands in the investor's stead; and just as the first

194 Shaybānī, *Aṣl*, *Muḍāraba*, fols. 79b–80a; Sarakhsī, *Mabsūṭ*, 22:67.

195 Shaybānī, *Aṣl*, *Muḍāraba*, fols. 78a–78b, also 79b; Sarakhsī, 22:65–66.

196 Shaybānī, *Aṣl*, *Muḍāraba*, fol. 78b; Sarakhsī, *Mabsūṭ*, 22:66.

197 Shaybānī, *Aṣl*, *Muḍāraba*, fols. 79a–79b; Sarakhsī, *Mabsūṭ*, 22:66. Re: *ibḍāʿ*, cf. above, Chapter 3, "Ibḍāʿ in the Mufāwaḍa Partnership."

agent's expenses are borne by the capital, so too are the second agent's."[198]

Any distinction between the treatment of personal and business expenses occurs only in very special circumstances. Such is the case, for example, in the event that the investment is entirely lost. Normally, the responsibility of the investor extends only up to the amount of the investment. If the agent's expenses exceeded this amount, he can claim reimbursement only for his business expenses from the investor; the money expended on his own needs are his loss.[199] This apparent inconsistency is not fully explained, but is justified by simply pointing to the fact that under the circumstances the two categories of expenses are not alike; those expended on the care, transportation, etc., of the investment were incurred, as it were, on behalf of the investor who is therefore expected to cover them, whereas this is not the case with the agent's personal expenses.

Commercial Accounting

Implicit in the entire discussion of the agent's business and personal expenses is the existence of some form of commercial accounting. Since the exact amount of the expenses had to be known in order to determine each party's share of the profits, the agent had to keep track of the various items of business and personal expenditure while he was traveling. We have no way of knowing whether such records took the form of random and hurried scribbles on a scrap of paper or parchment, or whether a more formalized and systematic form of accounting prevailed. Whatever the form, the legal discussions of this problem leave us with the strong impression that such accounts were quite detailed. This impression is reinforced by documents from the Geniza containing detailed accounts of the expenses involved in the shipment, handling and ultimate sale of merchandise from one city to another. The number of individual expense items recorded in such accounts

[198] Sarakhsī, *Mabsūṭ*, 22:66.

[199] Shaybānī, *Aṣl*, *Muḍāraba*, fols. 82b–83a; Sarakhsī, *Mabsūṭ*, 22:71–72.

reaches as high as eighty.[200] While the accounts and ledgers found in the Geniza were by no means as orderly and systematic as the commercial bookkeeping records of late medieval European enterprises, they were sufficiently detailed to enable the merchants to keep track and control of their farflung and diversified operations. Prominent among the types of accounts preserved are seasonal reports to associates about sales and purchases made, balances outstanding from the preceding trading season or from the preceding year's or years' business activities, as well as accounts of specific transactions concerning goods held in partnership or as a *commenda* investment.[201] Moreover, the overall circumstances of trade—the prevalence of credit transactions, the prominence of trade associations as the social instruments of commerce, the fact that these associations extended beyond the members of a family—required the existence of some form of accounting.[202] Nor should we be unmindful of the advice offered to merchants in an early Islamic work of belles lettres: "For kings the study of genealogy and histories, for warriors the study of battles and biography, and for merchants the study of writing and arithmetic."[203]

Methods and techniques of commerce—especially long-distance commerce—remained generally the same between the eighth and eleventh centuries. We may justifiably assume that records and accounts approximating those kept by the eleventh and twelfth century Geniza merchants already existed in the eighth century Near East.

Distribution of Liability

The most innovative feature of the *commenda* contract and the aspect that distinguished it most clearly from other forms of commercial association known and practiced in the

200 Goitein, *Mediterranean Society*, pp. 339–343.

201 *Ibid.*, pp. 204–209.

202 Re: the importance of these factors in the development of Western accounting and bookkeeping procedures, cf. Max Weber, *General Economic History*, New York, 1961, pp. 170–174.

203 Ibn 'Abd Rabbihi, *Al-'iqd al-farīd*, Cairo, 1293 A. H., 1:198; quoted in P. K. Hitti, *The Origins of the Islamic State*, New York, 1916, p. 2.

medieval Islamic world was its treatment of the distribution of liability between the parties to the contract. Absent from this "partnership in profit," as some legal writers designated it, was the formation of any social capital; consequently, one party, the agent, was not liable for any part of the investment in case of loss, and the other party, the investor, except under exceptional circumstances, did not become jointly liable with the agent in transactions with third parties who need not even have known of the investor's existence. Since we can assume that the *commenda* found its most frequent employment in long-distance trade, which of necessity geographically separated the two parties for most of the contract's duration, this distribution of liability between the parties would appear to have been ideal. With their customary thoroughness, the Islamic lawyers probed all aspects of the principles governing liability distribution in the *commenda* by confronting them with numerous hypothetical situations. While the specific cases constructed by the lawyers may have had little, or no significance in actual commercial practice, they are noteworthy for the light they shed on the relationship between the agent and outside third parties as well as between the agent and investor to each other.

> If a man entrusts to another a thousand dirhams as a *commenda* on a half-profit basis, and the latter uses it to purchase wheat, or a slave-girl, or any other goods, and the thousand dirhams are lost before the agent pays them to the seller, then the agent has recourse to the investor for another thousand dirhams to deliver them to the seller. If the agent takes possession from the investor of the thousand in order to pay the seller, and these are also lost, he has recourse to the investor for another thousand until he delivers them to the seller. A similar procedure is to be followed if this last thousand is also lost.[204]

There are a number of points to be noted in this passage. First, the entire problem arises only after the agent has made a purchase on behalf of the *commenda*. This contract, like that

[204] Shaybānī, *Aṣl, Muḍāraba*, fol. 161a, l. 16–161b, l. 5.

of partnership, goes into full effect only after employment of the capital in some commercial transaction. Had the money, for example, been lost prior to any purchase by the agent on behalf of the *commenda* the contract would have simply lapsed and the *commenda* ended.[205] Second, the separation between the investor and outside third parties is strictly maintained. Third, in spite of the repeated hypothetical losses, the agent is in no way liable since these occurred in the normal course of business operations and not as the result of any misconduct on the part of the agent. Shaybānī justifies the agent's lack of liability as follows:

> For everything the agent takes from the investor is part of the *commenda* investment. And since the capital in the agent's possession is part of the *commenda,* he stands in relation to it as a trustworthy party (*amīn*).[206] For *commenda* capital cannot be a source of liability for the agent (*maḍmūnan*);[207] if it is a source of liability to him, the contract will not be a *commenda* and the investor will have no claim for a share in the profit. How can the investor claim a share of the profit while the agent is liable for the capital?[208]

The conception of the agent as an *amīn* ("a trustworthy party") is the cornerstone upon which the entire structure of equity within the *commenda* contract rests. Any arrangement involving the agent's liability for the investment was by definition disqualified as a *commenda* contract. On the other hand, the investor, who does not work with the capital, was entitled to a share of the profit only by virtue of the risk of possible loss which he faced. While the Islamic *commenda* did entail a community of risks, the substance of each party's risk was radically different. The investor risks only his capital; the agent risks only his time and effort.

In the case of the repeated losses alluded to above, each addi-

205 Cf. Sarakhsī, *Mabsūṭ*, 22:169.

206 Re: *amīn*, cf. *Grundzüge*, p. 64 and Schacht, *Introduction*, pp. 147–148.

207 Re: this term cf. *Grundzüge*, p. 55, n. 2.

208 Shaybānī, *Aṣl*, *Muḍāraba*, fol. 161b, ll. 13–17.

tional sum that the investor provides is added to that of the original investment. Thus, if after the agent's initial purchase he lost the original one thousand dirhams invested and received an additional one thousand from the investor to cover his purchase, the investment would then consist of two thousand dirhams. The practical importance of this point lies in the fact that subsequently, the agent could not realize any profit until these two thousand dirhams were restored to the investor. The investor's greater risk as represented by the increased extent of his financial involvement is paralleled by the increased time and effort required from the agent before he could hope to realize any profit.

The Mālikī resolution of these problems is less favorable to the agent in some respects and less favorable to the investor in others. If the capital should be lost after a purchase is made, the investor has the option of either providing the agent with additional funds to cover the obligation incurred, or of ending the *commenda*. In the latter case, the agent is required to make good the debt, and the goods belong to him. If the investor does provide the additional capital, the *commenda* continues on the same basis as originally contracted. Rather surprisingly, however, the amount of the investment is not increased (as is the case in Ḥanafī law) to comprehend both sums paid by the investor; only the last sum forms the investment.[209]

If the loss of the capital took place after the agent had succeeded in parlaying the original investment into a larger sum, the procedure of distributing the liability would be somewhat different.

> A man entrusts another with a *commenda* of one thousand dirhams on a half-profit basis. With them, the agent buys a slave worth two thousand dirhams and takes possession of him. He then sells the slave for two thousand dirhams and with them buys a slave girl. Before he pays for the slave girl, the two thousand dirhams are lost. The agent has recourse to the investor, and takes from him one thousand five hun-

[209] Saḥnūn, *Mudawwana*, 12:102.

> dred dirhams. One thousand of these are instead of the thousand which were his investment, and five hundred of these represent the investor's share of the profit. From his own funds the agent pays five hundred dirhams which represents his share of the profit.[210]

Once the original investment has increased as a result of the agent's activities, the latter is considered a part-owner of the capital even if the *commenda* is still ongoing. His ownership consists of that sum which would constitute his share of the profit were the *commenda* to be concluded at that moment. Consequently, in the event of loss, the agent, and not the investor, would be liable for that share.

> For the agent only pays (i.e., is liable) to the extent that he has a share in the profit. If he has no profit, the investor is liable for everything that the agent undertakes with regard to all sellers.[211]

In spite of the fact that the investor might, under certain exceptional circumstances, become liable for a sum larger than his original investment, his relationship with outside third parties always took place through the mediation of the agent. The principle emerging from the discussion of the *commenda*'s conduct and operations, and particularly from the treatment of the distribution of liability between the parties, is as follows: The responsibility for all contact with third parties resides in the agent.[212] The agent, however, not being personally liable for any loss involving obligations toward third parties, has recourse in such instances to the investor for the sum involved, and then treats with the third parties as required. Except in rare and exceptional circumstances,[213] the investor is never a litigant with outside third parties as a result of the agent's actions.

210 Shaybānī, *Aṣl, Muḍāraba*, fol. 162b, ll. 5–11.

211 Shaybānī, *Aṣl, Muḍāraba*, fol. 168b.

212 Cf. for example, Shaybānī, *Aṣl, Muḍāraba*, fols. 71a–71b, 82a–82b; Sarakhsī, *Mabsūṭ*, 22:55 and 71.

213 The most notable exception would be if the investment was entrusted to a minor or to a slave with no trading rights (*'abd maḥjūr*); cf. Shaybānī, *Aṣl, Muḍāraba*, fol. 74a (bottom).

Istidāna

It was only under unusual circumstances such as those outlined in the preceding pages that the investor could become liable for more than his original investment. Normally, the limit of his risk was the sum he entrusted to the agent and no more. To protect the investor's interests in this regard, one absolute restriction was placed on the agent's trading activities. He was not permitted to engage the *commenda* for any sum greater than the capital in hand. If he exceeded these bounds in any way, the agent became liable for any sum in excess of the *commenda* capital.

> A man gives to another one thousand dirhams as a *commenda* on a half-profit basis. With the thousand, the agent purchases a slave girl on a year's credit extended by the seller. The slave girl is worth a thousand dirhams, and the agent purchases her for the *commenda*. This is permissible, and the slave girl belongs to the *commenda*. If the agent then takes possession of the slave girl and uses her to purchase a slave or something else, then the latter is also *commenda* property. However, if he does not use the slave girl to buy anything, but uses the one thousand dirhams in his possession to make this purchase, then the object of his purchase does not belong to the *commenda*, but belongs solely to the agent. This is so, because the thousand dirhams which he uses to make the purchase are already beyond the bounds of the *commenda*, since the thousand is already committed for the credit purchase. For if I permit the agent to use this money for additional purchases, he will be able to acquire the slave girl with the one thousand dirhams. Then, even though the *commenda* investment is one thousand, he can make purchases for ten thousand. This would not be proper.[214]

Thus within the framework of the *commenda* agreement, the area in which the agent could function freely and with relatively few restrictions was delimited absolutely by the ex-

[214] Shaybānī, *Aṣl*, *Muḍāraba*, fol. 163b, ll. 6–14.

tent of the *commenda* investment. Once he stepped beyond this boundary in his commercial dealings, he was, so to speak, on his own, himself eligible for all the profits from his extra-*commenda* commitments and also solely liable for them in case of loss. This prohibition against *istidāna*—the commercial commitment of the *commenda* by the agent in excess of its capital—carried along with it several corollary restrictions on the agent's activity. For example, he was not permitted to augment his working capital by negotiating a loan for the *commenda*.[215] Nor could he, at the *commenda*'s expense, alter or improve any of the goods he purchased if their acquisition alone had required all the available capital. If, for example, he invested the entire amount of the capital in cloth, he was not permitted to have it dyed or otherwise altered at the *commenda*'s expense.[216] Of course, if only part of the capital was used for procuring the cloth, he could use the remainder to have it dyed, fulled, or subject to any other process he deemed appropriate "because this is the practice current among the merchants."[217]

One final point concerning the problem of *istidāna* within the *commenda*: If expressly authorized to do so by the investor, the agent may incur debts in excess of the amount of the *commenda*. However, there is a difference in the status of the goods bought with the actual *commenda* investment and those procured over and above that amount.

> That which the agent purchases with the *commenda* capital is not comparable to that which he purchases on credit beyond that sum; it belongs to them both in equality between them.[218]

What we find described here is actually a conjunction between two separate Islamic forms of commercial association

[215] Shaybānī, *Aṣl*, *Muḍāraba*, fol. 192b.

[216] *Ibid.*, fol. 193a–193b. Although it differs in some details, the Mālikī position on the agent's commitments in excess of the *commenda* capital resembles that of the Ḥanafīs; cf. Saḥnūn, *Mudawwana*, 12:94–97, 120–121.

[217] Sarakhsī, *Mabsūṭ*, 22:75.

[218] Shaybānī, *Aṣl, Muḍāraba*, fol. 175b, ll. 9ff.

—the *commenda* and the credit partnership. Goods acquired by the agent on credit above and beyond the amount of *commenda* capital are not subject to the principles of ownership and liability obtaining in a *commenda* agreement. The ownership, risk, and profit are shared jointly by the agent and the investor, thus in practice constituting a credit partnership. The combination of contracts provided for a considerable extension in the scope of the *commenda*'s commercial effectiveness. Armed with the investor's authorization to engage in *istidāna*, the agent would be in a position to take advantage of various promising commercial opportunities that might require a larger volume of capital than that furnished by the investor. By using the actual *commenda* investment as a base, he would probably find himself in a more favorable position to obtain credit and thus to increase the profitable returns of the venture.

Invalid *Commenda*

Any invalid *commenda* is treated as a hire contract (*ijāra*); all profits accrue to the investor and all losses are borne by him. The agent's personal expenses, but not his business expenses, are borne solely by the agent, who in turn, as an employee, is entitled to an equitable wage.[219]

The grounds for declaring a *commenda* invalid are numerous and can be connected with almost any aspect of the contract. These include: provisions for a non-proportional division of profit; non-alienation of the investment on the part of the investor; the agent's violation of a legitimate restriction placed on him by the investor; as well as many other circumstances which have been alluded to throughout the preceding discussion. In all such cases, the nature of the contract is transformed, as is the relationship of the parties to each other. The investor's position becomes that of an employer, responsible for his goods and property and fully entitled to all profit from it; the agent's role is changed to that of a simple employee, entitled

[219] Shaybānī, *Aṣl, Muḍāraba*, fols. 80a–80b; Sarakhsī, *Mabsūṭ*, 22:67.

to remuneration for his time and effort regardless of whether his exertions on behalf of his employer are successful.[220]

Division of Profit

Although the *commenda* could be terminated by the will of either party at any point, no time limit for the duration of the agreement could be stipulated at the outset.[221] It was envisaged that the *commenda* would normally be concluded when the agent returned from his travels, or when he completed his series of transactions profitably. At that time, he returned the capital to the investor, and the remainder, i.e., the profit, would be divided between them according to the proportions agreed upon at the initiation of the contract. The *commenda* was then considered as dissolved.

The return of the capital to the investor was crucial. In this respect, there is a kind of symmetry at both temporal poles of the contract. Just as the *commenda* could not begin without the investor relinquishing control over his capital and handing it over to the agent, so too, did its conclusion depend on the agent's restoring it in full to the physical possession of the investor. If, for some reason, the agent and investor divided only the profit, while the amount equivalent to the investment remained in the agent's hands and the latter continued to trade with it, the original *commenda* was considered as continuing in force. Were the agent subsequently to suffer any business reverses, he would be required to return part, or even the entire amount, of his share of the profit until the amount of the original capital was entirely made good to the investor.

> A man gives to another one thousand dirhams as a *commenda* on a half-profit basis, and the agent makes a profit of an additional thousand. The two then divide the profit between themselves, with each taking five hundred dirhams while the capital of the *commenda* remains as it is in the pos-

220 Shaybānī, *Aṣl, Muḍāraba*, fols. 81a, 108–109a. On the relationship, both historical and structural, of the *commenda* to the hire contract, cf. above, note 51.

221 Shirbīnī, *Mughnī al-muḥtāj*, 2:312; Ghazzālī, *Al-wajīz*, 1:221–222.

session of the agent. If the capital is then immediately destroyed, or if the agent trades with it unsuccessfully, or if it is lost after he trades with it, their division is void; the five hundred that the investor took is to be considered as part of his capital, and the agent owes him the five hundred which he took for himself, which is also to go to the investor as part of his capital. The money which was lost is from the profit; because the profit does not emerge until the capital is delivered to the investor. He (Muḥammad) said, God's peace and blessing upon him, "The believer is likened unto the merchant. Just as the merchant's profit is not complete until his capital is restored, so too are the believer's supererogatory works incomplete until his prescribed duties have been fulfilled."[222]

After the investment is restored and the remaining profit divided, the investor is perfectly free to immediately reinvest the original sum with the original agent according to the provisions of their previous agreement. This, however, is viewed as a completely independent and new contract; and, in spite of the identical *mis en scène*, any subsequent financial reverses would not in any way affect or undermine the finality of the earlier division of profits.[223]

Apparently animated by a desire to minimize disagreements and litigations among merchants and to constantly keep the nature of their relationships clear and uncomplicated, the Ḥanafī jurists indicate an unequivocal preference that the profit-division be accompanied by the return of the investment and the termination of the *commenda*.[224] That is, they conceived of this contract primarily as an instrument of single-venture commerce. It was, indeed, ideally suited for this purpose and was extensively used in this way. It was not however exclusively employed in this manner, as is made apparent by the seasonal and other accounts preserved in the

[222] Sarakhsī, *Mabsūṭ*, 22:105; also, Shaybānī, *Aṣl, Muḍāraba*, fols. 112a–112b.

[223] Sarakhsī, *Mabsūṭ*, 22:106; Shaybānī, *Aṣl, Muḍāraba*, fol. 112b, ll. 11–15.

[224] *Ibid.*

Geniza,[225] as well as by the explicit testimony of Sarakhsī. In connection with the problem of profit-division in the *commenda,* he states that: "There is a prevailing custom among the merchants of periodic accounting (*al-muḥāsaba fī kull waqt*), at which time each of the two parties withdraws his share of the profit, while the investment remains as it was (i.e., in the hands of the agent).[226]

It therefore seems clear that in addition to single-venture commerce, the *commenda* also served as a vehicle for more enduring, ongoing associations, associations whose existence spanned as much as a decade, as is attested by the legal texts and the Geniza documents.[227]

Conclusion of the *Commenda*

In the legal sources, very little attention is paid to the manner in which the *commenda* agreement is to be concluded. If all went well, the agent and the investor would, at the appropriate, but not predetermined time, presumably settle their accounts, divide their profit and happily conclude their association. In case of an unsuccessful venture, the agent would return to the investor his capital, or whatever portion of it that was not lost, and both would presumably hope for better fortune in their future endeavors.

Other than by means of its "natural" conclusion, there are a number of occurrences which automatically and instantaneously put an end to the *commenda* agreement. Among these are: the decision of either party to the agreement to withdraw; the death, insanity, or apostasy from Islam of either party. Aside from apostasy, which is governed by its own rules, the terminated *commenda* is to be dissolved by immediately converting all its assets into cash form, by restoring the capital to the investor (or his heirs), and dividing the remainder, if any, among the parties according to their agreement.[228]

225 Cf. Goitein, *Mediterranean Society*, pp. 172, 178.

226 Sarakhsī, *Mabsūṭ*, 22:107.

227 E.g., Goitein, *Mediterranean Society*, pp. 169ff. and Shaybānī, *Aṣl, Muḍāraba*, fols. 42b–43a, and Sarakhsī, *Mabsūṭ*, 22:20–21.

228 Shaybānī, *Aṣl, Muḍāraba*, fols. 134b–135a.

VII

Islamic Law: Theory and Practice

"The grandeur and significance of the medieval merchant is that he creates his own law out of his own needs and his own views." Thus the great nineteenth century historian of commercial law, Levin Goldschmidt, epitomized the development of the major institutions of European commercial law.[1] In the context of the history of Western law, this statement would go unchallenged. The independent jurisdiction of medieval fairs and trading towns contributed toward the creation in every commercial country in Europe of a body of rules and legal doctrines for merchants and mercantile transactions. These rules were regarded by merchants and jurists alike as distinct from the common law of the land. They constituted a practical law adapted to the requirements of commerce. When, at a later period, these were absorbed by state legislation, it was by way of confirmation, or at most, slight modification, of rules that had long before been established by commercial custom. The charters of medieval European fairs, the statutes of medieval towns, the records of commercial courts and the archives of medieval European merchant companies combine to provide ample evidence to show the legislators copied, and did not dictate, in most important matters relating to commerce.[2]

Because of the nature of our source material for the first three centuries of the Islamic Middle Ages, the structure and methodology of this inquiry are almost the exact reverse of parallel studies of medieval European commercial institutions. For Europe, scholars extrapolated the general outlines of major commercial institutions from the actual practice of the merchants as recorded in archives, documents, and contracts. In the absence of archival and similar sources, we are of necessity reduced to attempting a reconstruction of actual commer-

[1] Quoted in W. Mitchell, *An Essay on the Early History of the Law Merchant*, Cambridge, 1904, p. 10.

[2] Cf. *ibid.*, pp. 1–21.

cial practices primarily from the theoretical formulations found in the appropriate sections of the legal writings emanating from the early Islamic period. Having in the preceding chapters outlined and described the two major institutions of medieval Islamic commercial cooperation as they appear in the legal texts, it is now appropriate to inquire whether these texts justify the confidence which our procedure has placed in them. The issues are these: Can these theoretical texts, in fact, serve as a guide to the qualitative aspects of the trade of the early medieval Muslim world? Did the institutions of *commenda* and partnership as they emerge from their legal description, in fact, reflect actual business practice?

With minor qualifications, and with particular reference to the Ḥanafī school, I believe that we can clearly answer in the affirmative. From internal evidence, and by comparison with later documentary sources, the Ḥanafī formulation of the partnership and *commenda* contracts emerges as a segment of the Law Merchant of the medieval Islamic World—a law essentially created by the merchants, meeting their needs, and according to which their trade relations were carried out.

The Ḥanafī jurists' consciousness of their economic environment is repeatedly demonstrated in their discussion of various aspects of partnership and *commenda* law. Although their primary concerns in elaborating the *sharī'a* were of a more lofty nature, they were certainly neither oblivious nor unsympathetic to the mundane operations and requirements of the marketplace. In discussing the permissibility of the *commenda* contract, Sarakhsī, in addition to citing a number of traditions attributing to the Prophet and his companions the use of this contract in trade, goes on to justify it on the practical grounds of its economic function in commerce—a function which he summarizes with admirable accuracy and lucidity. The attentiveness of Ḥanafī law to the needs of commerce is perhaps most pointedly exemplified in its treatment of the problems arising out of an association between a craftsman and a stall-owner. As we recall, the normal application of legal analogy would rule out such a partnership. In justifying the suspension of traditional legal considerations and in exercising juristic preference in order to permit this partnership, Sarakhsī goes beyond a general appeal to the needs of commerce. He illustrates his argument by detailing the particular economic disadvantages which the prohibition of this arrangement would entail both for the individuals involved and for the community, thus revealing a fairly intimate knowledge and concern for the smooth conduct of economic life.[3]

"In relation to this contract, the requirements of the law yielded in face of the people's need for it."[4] This summary of the case referred to in the preceding paragraph can be said to characterize the Ḥanafī approach to conflicts between legal analogy and economic necessity. The restricting consequences of analogical reasoning are by no means unique to medieval Islamic law. Sir Henry Maine, in his study of ancient law, has observed that the application of analogy tends to infuse customs which may in their inception have been rational with non-rational elements. In his words:

> A process commences which may be shortly described by saying that usage which is reasonable generates usage which is unreasonable. Analogy, the most valuable of instruments, in the maturity of jurisprudence, is the most dangerous of snares in its infancy. Prohibitions and ordinances, originally confined, for good reasons, to a single description of acts, are made to apply to all acts of the same class.[5]

However, Ḥanafī commercial law seems largely to have escaped this pitfall. Whenever the application of analogy threatened to confine the range of permitted commercial practices, the early Ḥanafī lawyers were quick to exercise the prerogative of *istiḥsān* (juristic preference). By appealing to the needs of trade or the established practice of the merchants, they justified the suspension of the application of strict analogy and thus preserved the vitality and flexibility of these institutions within the framework of Islamic sacred law. Indeed it was via the route of *istiḥsān* that large segments of the customary

[3] Cf. above, Chapter 3, "Labor as Partnership Investment."
[4] Sarakhsī, *Mabsūṭ*, 30 vols., Cairo, 1324/1906–1331/1912, 11:159.
[5] Sir Henry Maine, *Ancient Law*, New York, 1887, p. 18.

Law Merchant of the medieval Near East found their way into Ḥanafī law.

Another route by which commercial practice was absorbed into Ḥanafī law was that of the *ḥiyal,* or legal devices. Certain restrictions in the area of trade and exchange, based on analogy or other formal legal considerations, and which could not be resolved by the exercise of juristic preference, placed some aspects of practice on an inevitable collision course with legal theory. In partnership and *commenda* law, one of the most burdensome restrictions imposed by Islamic law was the exclusion of goods and merchandise as an acceptable form of investment. Ḥanafī lawyers were quick to construct a fairly simple but effective legal device to circumvent this prohibition. One is already found in Shaybānī's treatise on *ḥiyal,*[6] and it was subsequently incorporated into the very body of the legal codes and is usually presented immediately following the prohibition.[7] The assimilation of this legal fiction into the body of Ḥanafī law was so complete that in several codes and in the early *shurūṭ* handbooks it is outlined without the designation of *ḥīla*, and appears an accepted feature of positive law.[8] Other legal devices, concerned with a variety of restrictions on the operations of the partnership and *commenda* fulfilled an analogous function; i.e., they increased the options available to the trader, thus making it less likely that his activities would conflict with the explicit injunctions of the *sharīʿa.*

In their treatment of the multifarious operations involved in the conduct of partnership and *commenda* business, the early Ḥanafī jurists identified in a large measure with the commercial ethos of their day. The profit motive as a driving force underlying commercial endeavor found a prominent place in their thinking. They epitomized the chief purpose of partnership and *commenda* simply as "the attainment of profit." The attainment of profit is the touchstone by which the actions of

[6] Shaybānī, *Kitāb al-makhārij fil-ḥiyal*, ed. J. Schacht, Leipzig, 1930, p. 58; cf. also, al-Khaṣṣāf, *Kitāb al-ḥiyal wal-makhārij*, ed. J. Schacht, Hanover, 1923, p. 67.

[7] E.g., *Kāsānī*, 7 vols., Cairo, 1328/1910, 6:59.

[8] E.g., Sarakhsī, *Mabsūṭ*, 11:179; and Ṭaḥāwī, *Kitāb ash-shurūṭ, aṣ-ṣaghir*, ms. Istanbul, *Bayazit*, 18905, fol. 95.

all parties to a commercial association are judged. Those actions which promote the attainment of profit are permitted, and those which are extraneous or inimical to this goal are excluded. Concomitant with the "profit" criterion in evaluating the legitimacy of any party's actions, is its adherence to the practice and customs of the merchants. If the business conduct of the partners conformed to either of these standards, i.e., if it was conducive to profit, or was a recognized feature of customary mercantile usage, it was allowed even if it necessitated the suspension of legal analogy, or the compromise of some religious-ethical consideration. The remarkable consistency with which these twin criteria were applied endowed the *commenda* agent and members of commercial associations with great flexibility, and extended their freedom of action to the commercial horizons in which they functioned.

The prominence of custom in the Ḥanafī elaboration of *commenda* and partnership law is reminiscent of its equally decisive role in Western medieval commercial law where it has been described as "alike the ruling principle, and the originating force of the Law Merchant."[9] Yet, paradoxically, Islamic legal theory officially rejected custom as a valid source of law. Even though the *sharī'a*, in its early stages, absorbed in large measures the customs and legal practices of the territories over which Islam had attained hegemony, this raw material was in the course of its absorption transformed by a thorough-going Islamizing process. As Schacht has expressed it:

> The essential contribution that Islam made toward the formation of its sacred law was not material but formal. . . . Over those elements of varied provenance that were retained, the central core exerted a strong attracting and assimilating power, permeating them with what was felt to be the Islamic spirit, until their foreign origin, short of a searching historical analysis, became well-nigh unrecognizable.[10]

[9] Mitchell, *An Essay on the Early History of the Law Merchant*, p. 12.

[10] J. Schacht, "The Law," in G. E. von Grunebaum, ed., *Unity and Variety in Muslim Civilization*, Chicago, 1955, p. 65.

This, however, must be qualified by the fact that within the *sharī'a*, the impact of Islamization varied considerably among its various segments—some being completely transformed, and others being only lightly affected. While the "spiritual ascendancy of the sacred law of Islam as a religious ideal over the practice"[11] created a tension between these two elements leading ultimately in many areas to a separation between them, it also resulted in an equilibrium between religious ideal and actual practice and created "a stratification with variant shades in each stratum."[12] I believe that in those areas of Ḥanafī commercial law with which we are here concerned, the shades and hues of customary practice were more prominent, and determined the coloring of the law to a much larger extent than has hitherto been thought. The Islamic modification of the positive legal contents of this material is sporadic, uneven, and in many cases, minimal. Islam's formal contribution was very much conditioned by the underlying raw material. The only overall formal Islamizing elements are represented by the opposition to unjustified enrichment, which includes the prohibition against usury, and the exclusion of any element of chance in contractual relations, i.e., any undefined or unknown element.[13] While religious-ethical considerations affected the way the law was formulated, in the case of the Ḥanafīs, it had slight impact on its positive contents. The customs and practices of commerce formed and fashioned the legal institutions of *commenda* and partnership. Furthermore, the jurisdiction of custom was not relegated or confined merely to marginal details, but was given free reign over the most important and substantive components of these institutions.

The customary usages adopted by Ḥanafī commercial law exhibit the same classic characteristics of custom as a source of law that have been found to be present in almost all legal

[11] *Ibid.*

[12] R. Brunschvig, "Perspectives," *Unity and Variety*, pp. 48ff.

[13] For a succinct summary of these prohibitions as they affect the Islamic law of obligations, cf. J. Schacht, *An Introduction to Islamic Law*, Oxford, 1959, 1964, pp. 144–147.

systems from that of the Barotse tribesmen in Rhodesia[14] to the Roman *Corpus Juris*.[15] Emphasis is constantly placed on the antiquity and continuity of practice of a custom. Customs are viewed as inveterate, existing, to use a phrase from the common law, from "time whereof the memory of man runneth not to the contrary."[16] In Ḥanafī law we have already seen examples of corresponding appeals made to the antiquity of a custom in order to justify its permissibility. "This arrangement is permitted because of its continuous use in the affairs of men without any disapproving voice being raised against it," says Sarakhsī in arguing for the validity of the partnership between a stall-owner and an artisan.[17] This phrase, and others like it occur frequently in early Ḥanafī literature in order to bring within the pale of licitness practices which on the basis of strict legal and analogical reasoning should be excluded.

Commercial custom as manifested in Ḥanafī law shares in another universal feature of custom as observed in many other legal systems, namely that of reasonableness. Custom is seen as answering to a reasonable social or economic need. Such is the case, for example, in regard to the justification of the *commenda*,[18] where the jurist's view of the economic need that these institutions fulfill is epitomized in a particularly succinct and relevant manner. Similar examples drawn from early Ḥanafī legal writings are not lacking.[19] Ḥanafī literature justifies an even broader generalization. We often encounter detailed and involved discussions of problems connected with conduct of partnership and *commenda* contracts in which the economic or social rationale is not made explicit, and appears to be entirely absent. Our initial inclination might be to consider these as purely casuistic and hairsplitting legal

[14] Max Gluckman, *The Judicial Process Among the Barotse of Northern Rhodesia*, Manchester, 1955, pp. 236ff.

[15] C. K. Allen, *Law in the Making*, Oxford, 1961, pp. 76ff.

[16] *Ibid.*, p. 130.

[17] Cf. Sarakhsī, *Mabsūṭ*, 11:159 and also 155.

[18] Cf. Sarakhsī, *Mabsūṭ*, 22:19, and cf. also *Kāsānī* 6:79.

[19] E.g., in connection with the use of credit and credit partnerships, for which cf., A. Udovitch, "Credit as a Means of Investment in Medieval Islamic Trade," *Journal of the American Oriental Society* (*JAOS*) 87 (1967): 60–64.

exercises. However, a careful scrutiny of the resultant legal opinions, particularly with a view to the medieval commercial context, will almost always make apparent a compelling practical reason for what at first sight might have seemed entirely arbitrary and fortuitous.[20]

In its recognition of particular customs, that is, customs affecting only a particular geographic region, Ḥanafī law implicitly adheres to a further feature commonly encountered in customary law.[21] The European Law Merchant, even though its major institutions were the common and largely uniform patrimony of merchants all over Europe, nevertheless recognized that on certain matters custom varied from one locale to another and made provisions for such variations.[22] The identical recognition is reflected in Ḥanafī law, which on certain questions, such as the freedom of action of a partner or *commenda*-agent, relinquished its jurisdiction and relegated their determination to purely local and particular standards.[23]

Any lingering doubt concerning the close relationship of Ḥanafī *commenda* and partnership law to the commercial practice of the medieval Islamic world is largely dispelled by the evidence from the Geniza documents. In the Geniza material of the eleventh and twelfth centuries bearing on partnership and *commenda* that has so far been published,[24] there is scarcely a legal aspect which is not touched upon and anticipated in the Ḥanafī legal discussions of the late eighth century. Indeed, the theoretical legal discussions can often serve as a guide to the intricate and occasionally baffling mercantile arrangements portrayed in the Geniza.

When compared, a remarkable symmetry becomes evident between the legal formulations of the late eighth century on

[20] As, for example, in the case of *ibḍāʿ*, or, in regard to the extensive treatment of profit division.

[21] Cf. Allen, *Law in the Making*, pp. 69–70.

[22] Mitchell, *An Essay on the Early History of the Law Merchant*, pp. 6–10.

[23] On this point cf. Y. Linant de Bellefonds, *Traité de droit musulman comparé*, Paris and The Hague, 1965, p. 26.

[24] Cf. S. D. Goitein, "Commercial and Family Partnerships in the Countries of Medieval Islam," *Islamic Studies* 3 (1964):318–319; *idem.*, *A Mediterranean Society*, pp. 169–183.

the one hand, and the documented commercial practices of the eleventh and twelfth century Geniza merchants on the other. The types of partnership contracts described by the lawyers—such as universal partnerships, credit and labor partnerships, are found actualized in the Geniza records. There is an almost one to one relationship between the importance of problems as reflected in the Geniza papers, and the amount of space and attention they receive in the law books. Those aspects of commerce which loomed large for the Geniza merchants are exactly those to which the legal texts devote lengthy and detailed discussions. Such is the case, for example, with the question of the relationship of each party's investment to his share in the profit and risk in any given undertaking. The basis of one's claim to share in the profit of a venture and the circumstances governing one's liability in case of loss is the subject of careful scrutiny and detailed attention in all early Ḥanafī writings. Numerous hypothetical examples of varying combinations of investment ratio to profit and loss are worked out in detail; at times tediously so. In the light of the information contained in the Geniza documents, these seemingly casuistic discussions assume a new relevance. Few were the commercial associations which followed the simplest and most elementary paradigm of only two parties contributing equal investments and sharing equally in the profits and risks. Most arrangements were much less symmetrical, and involved complex patterns of distribution of investments, work, risks, and profits among the parties to a partnership or *commenda*—often entailing such clumsy fractions as 9/84 or 59/150. Uneven arrangements of this kind were not arbitrary, or the result of happenstance, but were the expression of numerous factors known and recognized by merchants as contributing in different ways to the success and efficiency of a commercial undertaking. Included were such qualities as skill and expertise in trade generally, or with reference to certain commodities of trade; also included were reputation, and business and family connections. These are qualitative and not quantitative considerations, yet they found their expression, as they had to, in quantitative terms in commercial usage and in

Further parallels between the Geniza practices and the cases described in the legal texts can easily be multiplied. While in some matters of detail, we find the Geniza merchants diverging from the prescriptions contained in the law books; the areas of correspondence, both in the general outlines of their associations and in the detailed execution of their transactions, are overwhelming. This identity between the theoretical formulations of the late eighth century and the actual commercial practice of the eleventh through thirteenth centuries corroborates the thesis that the earliest Ḥanafī law treating partnership and *commenda* contracts is to be viewed, with minor qualifications, as a veritable Law Merchant.

Of course, not every detail in the sections of Ḥanafī law examined here constituted the practice of the merchants; nor did every commercial practice find an echo in Ḥanafī law. It was not the lawyers' intention to construct an efficient commercial code; their primary concern was with the more elevated endeavor of elaborating God's commands into a comprehensive system of religious duties according to which every Muslim was to conduct his life. The Law Merchant character of these chapters of Ḥanafī law is not self-conscious; it is incidental. This fact, however, does not at all diminish the relevance of the early legal material for the daily practices of the marketplace. Its significance is rather to reclaim portions of these texts for a wide range of historical inquiries, and to enhance their eligibility as primary sources for the reconstruction of the quality of social and economic life during the early Islamic Middle Ages.

When viewed in their fullness, the Ḥanafī institutions of partnership and *commenda* emerge as versatile legal commercial instruments, capable of fulfilling a variety of functions in the economic life of the medieval Muslim world. They could be adapted to the needs of local as well as long-distance trade. In local trade and industry these forms of association to a large extent performed the tasks normally associated with the hire contract, which, because of the social stigma attached to it, was infrequently employed except for menial tasks. They were also of importance in the industrial sector, permitting workers in similar, complementary, or even disparate trades to combine their efforts. The versatility of these legal techniques was further extended by permitting the inclusion of workers and entrepreneurs in the framework of one association, thus combining the production and distributive aspects of manufacture.

In long-distance trade, these contracts effectively provided what Weber termed "an organized community of risk"[29] to meet the requirements of the venturing nature of medieval trade. The range of permissible combinations of risks and gains was sufficiently broad, and the provisions allowing for both diversification and specialization in trade sufficiently flexible to offer both a protection against the instability of market conditions as well as the instruments for the exploitation of profitable opportunities. Endowing the parties to these associations with considerable freedom of action enabled them to take advantage of any promising business situation that might arise, and to invest and otherwise dispose of the social capital in any manner intended to benefit the association. Medieval Islamic trade was multifocal; i.e., there were numerous urban centers from which trade radiated in many directions. The problems of business organizations which this reality posed—such as delegation of authority and control over the conduct of business—were efficiently solved by Islamic law by means of a fully developed law of agency (*wakāla*) and by means of such practices as *ibḍāʿ* and deposit. In most cases partners and *commenda* agents were empowered to delegate their authority and control not only to associates and colleagues, but even to strangers, if the commercial circumstances demanded it. This fact, incidentally, reinforces the impression that Islamic entrepreneurial activity had already, by the late eighth century, moved beyond purely family associations. As important as family associations continued to be throughout the Islamic Middle Ages, the earliest legal sources already recognized that traders were likely to place commercial success ahead of family ties.

[29] Max Weber, *General Economic History,* Collier Books, 1961, pp. 157–158.

By recognizing credit as a valid form of commercial investment, and by placing a premium on any special skills of partners and agents, the Ḥanafī partnership and *commenda* served as a means of financing and, to some extent, insuring commercial ventures, as well as of providing the combination of necessary skills and services for their satisfactory execution. Not only the travelling merchants who accompanied their wares, but also the sedentary merchants, urban notables, and others who preferred to stay put could effectively make use of these arrangements and their variations by investing their surplus capital with those who did travel and thereby enjoy the profits of long-distance trade while providing the capital necessary to finance it.

The prominence of the Muslim world in the trade of the early Middle Ages, if not attributable to, was certainly reinforced by the superiority and flexibility of the commercial techniques available to its merchants. Some of the institutions, practices and concepts already found fully developed in the Islamic legal sources of the late eighth century did not emerge in Europe until several centuries later. The efficacy and vitality of these legal-commercial institutions endured, I believe, for most of the Islamic Middle Ages.

Bibliography

Abū Yūsuf. *Kitāb al-athār*. Cairo, 1355/1936.

———. *Ikhtilāf Abī Ḥanīfa wa-Ibn Abī Laylā*. Cairo, 1357/1938.

Aghnides, Nicolas P. *Mohammedan Theories of Finance*. 2nd impression. Lahore, 1961.

al-'Alī, Sāliḥ. *at-Tanẓīmāt al-ijtimā'iyya wal-iqtiṣadiyya fil-Baṣra fil-qarn al-awwal al-hijri*. Baghdad, 1953.

Allen, C. K. *Law in the Making*. Oxford, 1961.

Andersen, Neils J. *Studier Over Hovedprincipperne I Den Islamiske Handelsret*. Copenhagen, 1961.

Arberry, A. J. *The Seven Odes: The First Chapter in Arabic Literature*. New York, 1957.

Asaf, A., ed. *Gaonic Responsa*. Jerusalem, 1928.

———. *Gaonica*. Jerusalem, 1933.

Aṣl. See Shaybānī. *Kitāb al-aṣl*.

Astuti, G. *Origini e svolgimento della commenda fino al secolo XIII*. Turin, 1933.

Balādhurī. *Ansāb al-ashrāf*. Edited by S. D. Goitein. Vol. 5. Jerusalem, 1936.

Bergsträsser, G. "Zur Methode der *fiqh*-Forschung." *Islamica*. 4 (1931) :283–294.

Black, Henry Campbell. *Black's Dictionary of Law*. 3rd edition. St. Paul, 1933.

Bousquet, G.-H. "La Moudawwana (Recension de Sah'noun)," *Annales de l'Institute d'Études Orientales d'Alger*. 16 (1958/9) :175–206; 17 (1959) :169–211; 18–1 (1960–1961) :73–165.

Brockelmann, C. *Geschichte der arabischen Litteratur*. 2 vols.; *Supplement*, 3 vols. Leiden, 1937–1943.

Brunschvig, R. "Considérations sociologiques sur le droit musulman," *Studia Islamica*. 3 (1955) :61–73.

———. "Perspectives," *Unity and Variety in Islamic Culture*, Edited by G. E. von Grunebaum. Chicago, 1955, pp. 47–62.

———. "Conceptions monétaires chez les juristes musulmans (VIIIe-XIIIe siècles)," *ARABICA*. 14 (1967) :113–143.

Buckland, W. W. *A Text Book of Roman Law*. 2nd edition. Cambridge, 1932.

Buckland, W. W. and McNair, Arnold D. *Roman Law and Common Law*. 2nd edition. Cambridge, 1952.

Cahen, Claude. "A propos et autour d'Ein arabischen Handbuch der Handelswissenschaft," *Oriens*. 15 (1962): 160–171.

———. "Quelques problèmes concernant l'expansion économique musulman jusqu'au XIIe siècle," *L'Occidente e l'Islam nell'alto medioevo*. Spoleto, 1965. 1:391–432.

Chehata, Chafik T. *Essai d'une théorie générale de l'obligation en droit musulman*. Vol. 1. Cairo, 1936.

Cipolla, C. *Money, Prices and Civilization in the Mediterranean World*. Princeton, 1956.

Corpus juris civilis. Digesta. 17.2. *Pro Socio*. Edited and translated by C. H. Monro. Cambridge, 1902.

Coulson, N. J. *A History of Islamic Law*. Edinburgh, 1964.

Dietrich, Albert. *Arabische Briefe aus der Papyrussammlung der Hamburger Staats-und Universitätsbibliothek*. Hamburg, 1955.

———. *Arabische Papyri aus der Hamburger Staats-und Universitätsbibliothek*. Leipzig, 1937.

ad-Dimashqī, Abū al-Faḍl Ja'far b. 'Alī, *Kitāb maḥāsin at-tijāra*. Cairo, 1318.

Dozy, R. *Supplément aux dictionnaires arabes*. 2nd edition. 2 vols. Leiden, 1927.

Dūrī, 'Abd al-'Aziz. *Ta'rīkh al-'irāq al-iqtiṣādī fil-qarn ar-rābi' al-hijrī*. Baghdad, 1948.

Ehrenkreuz, Andrew. "Studies in the Monetary History of the Near East in the Middle Ages," *JESHO*. 2 (1959): 128–161; 6 (1963): 243–277.

EI. *Encyclopaedia of Islam*. 1st edition. 4 vols.; and *Supplement*. Leiden, 1913–1934. Second edition, in the course of publication.

Eilers, W. *Gesellschaftsformen im altbabylonischen Recht*. Leipzig, 1931.

Fischel, W. J. *Jews in the Economic and Political Life of Mediaeval Islam*. London, 1937.

Frezzia, Paolo. "Il *Consortium Ercto Non Cito* E I Nuovi Frammenti Di Gaio," *Revista Di Filologia e D'Istruzione Classica.* N.S., 12 (1934): 27–46.

Gaiani, Alberto. "The Judicial Nature of the Moslem *Qirāḍ,*" *East and West.* 4 (July, 1953) : 81–86.

GAL. See Brockelmann, *Geschichte der arabischen Litteratur.*

Ghazzālī. *Iḥyā' 'ulūm ad-dīn.* 4 vols. Cairo, 1957.

———. *al-Wajīz fī fiqh al-imām ash-Shāfi'ī.* 2 vols. Cairo, 1317.

Gluckman, Max. *The Judicial Process Among the Barotse of Northern Nigeria.* Manchester, 1955.

Goitein, S. D. "The Cairo Geniza as a Source for the History of Muslim Civilization," *Studia Islamica.* 3 (1955): 168–197.

———. *Jewish Education in Muslim Countries, Based on Records of the Cairo Geniza* (Hebrew). Jerusalem, 1962.

———. "The Main Industries of the Mediterranean Area as Reflected in the Records of the Cairo Geniza," *JESHO.* 4 (1961): 168–197.

———. "From the Mediterranean to India," *SPECULUM.* 29 (1954): 181–197.

———. "Slaves and Slavegirls in the Cairo Geniza Records," *Arabica.* 20 (1962): 1–20.

———, and Ben Shemesh, A. *Muslim Law in Israel* (Hebrew). Jerusalem, 1957.

———. "Commercial and Family Partnerships in the Countries of Medieval Islam," *Islamic Studies.* 3 (1964): 315–337.

———. *A Mediterranean Society, The Jewish Communities of the Arab World as Portrayed in the Documents of the Cairo Geniza.* Vol. 1. *Economic Foundations,* Berkeley and Los Angeles, 1967.

Goldziher, I. "Muhammedanisches Recht in Theorie und Wirklichkeit," *Zeitschrift für vergleichende Rechtswissenschaft.* 8 (1889): 406–423.

———. "The Principles of Law in Islam," in *The Historians History of the World.* Edited by Henry Smith Williams. Vol. 8. New York, 1904, pp. 294–304.

———. *Vorlesungen über den Islam.* Heidelberg, 1910.

Gottheil, R., and Worrell, Wm. H., eds. *Fragments from the Cairo Geniza in the Freer Collection*. New York, 1927.

Grasshoff, Richard. *Das Wechselrecht der Araber*. Berlin, 1899.

Grohmann, A. *Arabic Papyri in the Egyptian Library*. 6 vols. Cairo, 1934ff.

———. *Einführung und Chrestomathie zur arabischen Papyruskunde*. Prague, 1955.

Grundzüge. Cf. Schacht, J., ed. *G. Bergsträsser's Grundzüge des Islamischen Recht*.

Guidi, I., and Santillana, D., trans. *Il "Muḫtasar" o Sommario del Diritto Malechita di Ḫalil ibn Isḥaq*. 2 vols. Milan, 1919.

Heyada. See Marghīnānī.

Heffening, W. *Das islamische Fremdenrecht*. Hanover, 1925.

Hildesheimer, E. E. *Das jüdische Gesellschaftsrecht*. Leipzig, 1930.

———. *Rekonstruktion eines Responsums des R. Saadje Gaon zum jüdischen Gesellschaftsrechts*. Frankfurt A. M., 1926.

Hurgronje, C. Snouck. *Selected Works*. Edited by G.-H. Bousquet and J. Schacht. Leiden, 1957.

Ibn 'Abd Rabbihi, *Al-'iqd al-farīd*. Cairo, 1293.

Ibn Khaldūn. *The Muqaddima*. 3 vols. Trans. Franz Rosenthal. New York, 1958.

Ibn Manẓūr. *Lisān al-'arab*. 15 vols. Beirut, 1955–56.

Ibn Qudāma. *Al-mughnī*. Cairo, 1367/1947.

Ibn Qutlūbughā. *Tāj at-tarājim fī ṭabaqāt al-ḥanafiyya*. Baghdad, 1962.

Ibn Rushd (Averroes). *Bidāyat al-mujtahid wa-nihāyat al-muqtaṣid*. 2 vols. Cairo, 1952.

Ibn Sa'd. *Kitāb aṭ-ṭabaqāt al-kabīr*. Vol. 3, pt. 1. Edited by E. Sachau. Leiden, 1904.

Idris, H. R. *La Berbérie orientale sous les Zīrīdes, Xe-XIIe siècles*. 2 vols. Paris, 1959.

Institutes. See Moyle, J. B., trans. *The Institutes of Justinan*.

Jāḥiẓ. *Kitāb at-tabaṣṣur bit-tijāra*. Edited by Ḥ. Ḥ. 'Abd al-Wahhāb. Cairo, 1935. French translation by Charles Pellat in *ARABICA*. 1 (1954): 151–165.

JE. *Jewish Encyclopaedia.* 12 vols. New York, 1906.

JESHO. Journal of the Economic and Social History of the Orient.

Juynboll, Th. W. *Handbuch des islamischen Gesetzes.* Leiden, 1910.

Kāsānī. See Kāsānī.

Kāsānī. *Badā'i' aṣ-ṣanā'i' fī tartīb ash-sharā'i'.* 7 vols. Cairo, 1328/1910.

Khadduri, M., and Liebesny, H. J., eds. *Law in the Middle East.* Vol. 1. Washington, D. C., 1955.

Khalīl ibn Isḥāq. *Mukhtaṣar.* Cairo, n.d.

Khaṣṣāf. *Kitāb al-ḥiyal wal-makhārij.* Edited by J. Schacht. Hanover, 1923.

al-Khaṭīb al-Baghdādī. *Ta'rīkh Baghdād.* 14 vols. Cairo, 1349/1931.

Kister, M. J. "Mecca and Tamīm," *JESHO.* 8 (1965): 113–163.

Kohler, J. "Die Wirklichkeit und Unwirklichkeit des islamitischen Rechts," *Zeitschrift für vergleichende Rechtswissenschaft.* 8 (1889) : 424–432.

——, and Wenger, L. *Allgemeine Rechtsgeschichte, Orientalisches Recht und Recht der Griechen und Römer.* Berlin, 1914.

Labib, S. "Geld und Kredit, Studien zur Wirtschaftsgeschichte Aegyptens im Mittelalter," *JESHO.* 2 (1959):225-246.

Lammens, H. *La Mecque à la veille de l'Hégire.* Beirut. 1924.

Lane, E. W. *An Arabic-English Lexicon.* 8 parts. London, 1863–93.

Law in the Middle East. See Khadduri, M.

Lieber, Alfred E. "Eastern Business Practice and Medieval European Commerce," *Economic History Review.* 2nd series. 21 (1968): 230–243.

Linant de Bellefonds, Y. *Traité de droit musulman comparé.* Paris, 1965.

Lopez, Robert S. "The Dollar of the Middle Ages," *Journal of Economic History.* 11 (1951): 209–234.

——. "The Trade of Medieval Europe: The South," *The*

Cambridge Economic History of Europe. Vol. 2. Cambridge, 1952, pp. 257–354.

———, and Raymond, I. W. *Medieval Trade in the Mediterranean World*. New York, 1955.

Mabsūṭ. See Sarakhsī. *Kitāb al-mabsūṭ*.

Mahmassani, S. *The General Theory of the Law of Obligations and Contracts under Muhammadan Jurisprudence* (Arabic). 2 vols. Beirut, 1948.

———. *Falsafat at-tashrī' fil-Islām*. Beirut, 1961; English translation by Farhat J. Ziadeh, with subtitle: *The Philosophy of Jurisprudence in Islam*. Leiden, 1961.

———. "Transactions in the Sharī'a," *Law in the Middle East*, 1:179–202.

Maimonides. *The Code of Maimonides*. Book 12. *The Book of Acquisition*. Translated by Isaac Klein. Yale Judaica Series. Vol. 5. New Haven, 1951.

Maine, Sir Henry. *Ancient Law*. New York, 1887.

Mālik b. Anas. *Al-muwaṭṭa'*. Edited by M. Fu'ād 'Abd al-Bāqī. Cairo, 1951. (Cf. also, Zurqānī. *Sharḥ 'alā al-Muwaṭṭa'*.)

Marghīnānī. *Hedaya, or Guide*; *A Commentary on the Mussulman Laws*. Translated by Charles Hamilton. 4 vols. London, 1791.

———. *The Hidayah with Its Commentary Called the Kifaya*. 4 vols. Calcuatta (?), 1834.

———. *Al-Hidāya*. 4 vols. Cairo, n.d.

Merx, A. *Paléographie Hebraique et Arabe*. Leiden, 1894.

Mez, A. *The Renaissance of Islam*. Translated by S. Khuda Bukhsh and D. S. Margoliouth. Patna, 1937.

Minhāj. See Nawawī.

Miskimin, H. A. *Money, Prices, and Foreign Exchange in Fourteenth Century France*. New Haven, 1963.

Mitchell, W. *An Essay on the Early History of the Law Merchant*. Cambridge, 1904.

Moyle, J. B., trans. *The Institutes of Justinian*. 4th edition. Oxford, 1906.

Mudawwana. See Saḥnūn.

Muzanī, *Mukhtaṣar*, on margin of Shāfi'ī's *Kitāb al-umm*. Vols. 1–4. Cairo, 1321/1903–1325/1907.

Nasā'ī. *Sunan*. 8 vols. Cairo, 1930.
Nawawī. *Minhāj aṭ-ṭālibīn* (with commentary of Shirbīnī, *Mughnī al-muḥtāj*). 4 vols. Cairo, 1374/1955.

Popper, W. *Egypt and Syria under the Circassian Sultans, University of California Publications in Semitic Philology*. Vol. 16. Berkeley and Los Angeles, 1957.
Postan, M. M. "Credit in Medieval Trade," *Economic History Review*. 1 (1927–1928) : 234–261.
———. "Partnership in English Medieval Commerce," *Studi in Onore Di A. Sapori*. Vol. 1. Milan, 1957, pp. 521–549.

Qudūrī. *Mukhtaṣar*. Istanbul, 1319–1901.

Ritter, H. "Ein Arabische Handbuch der Handelswissenschaft," *Der Islam*. 7 (1917) : 1–91.
Rodinson, Maxime. *Islam et Capitalisme*. Paris, 1966.
Rosenthal, F. *The Muslim Concept of Freedom*. Leiden, 1960.
Ruxton, F. H. *Mālikī Law*. London, 1916.

Sachau, E., ed. *Muhammedanisches Recht nach Schafiitischer Lehre*. Berlin, 1897.
Saḥnūn. *Al-mudawwana al-kubrā*. 16 vols. Damascus, n.d.
Santillana, D. *Istituzioni di diritto musulmano malichita con ruguardo anche al sistema sciafiita*. 2 vols. Rome, 1925–1938.
Sarakhsī. *Al-mabsūṭ*. 30 vols. Cairo, 1324/1906–1331/1912.
Schacht, J. "Die arabische ḥijal-Literatur. Ein Beitrag zur Erforschung der islamischen Rechtspraxis," *Der Islam*. 15 (1926) : 211–232.
———. *Esquisse d'une histoire du droit musulman*. Paris, 1955.
———. "Foreign Elements in Ancient Islamic Law," *The Journal of Comparative Legislation and International Law*. 3rd series. Vol. 32, nos. 3–4 (1950) : 9–17.
———. "The Law," *Unity and Variety in Islamic Culture*. Edited by G. E. von Grunebaum. Chicago, 1955, pp. 65–86.
———. *An Introduction to Islamic Law*. Oxford, 1959, 1964.
———. *Origins of Muhammadan Jurisprudence*. Oxford, 1959.
———. "Pre-Islamic Background and Early Development of Jurisprudence," *Law in the Middle East*. 1 : 28–56.

Schacht, J. "The Schools of Law and Later Developments of Jurisprudence," *Law in the Middle East.* 1:57–84.

———. (ed.) *G. Bergsträsser's Grundzüge des Islamischen Rechts.* Berlin, 1935.

Shāfi'ī. *Kitāb al-umm.* 7 vols. Cairo, 1321/1903–1325/1907.

Shaybānī. *Al-amālī.* Hyderabad, 1360/1941.

———. *Al-jāmi' al-kabīr.* Cairo, 1356/1937.

———. *Al-jāmi' aṣ-ṣaghīr,* on the margin of Abū Yūsuf, *Kitāb al-kharāj.* Cairo, 1302/1884.

———. *Kitāb al-aṣl, Kitāb al-buyū' was-salam.* Edited by Shafīq Shiḥāta. Cairo, 1954.

———. *Kitāb al-aṣl, Kitāb ash-sharika,* manuscript *Dār al-Kutub al-Miṣriyya, Fiqh Ḥanafī* 34, folios 57b–77b.

———. *Kitāb al-aṣl, Kitāb al-muḍāraba,* manuscript *Dār al-Kutub al-Miṣriyya. Fiqh Ḥanafī* 491, folios, 42–198.

———. *Kitāb al-makhārij fil-ḥiyal.* Edited by J. Schacht. Leipzig, 1930.

Spies, O. "Das Depositum nach islamischem Recht," *Zeitschrift für vergleichende Rechtswissenschaft.* 45 (1930): 241–300.

Supp. Supplement (Vols. 1–3) to *GAL.*

Taḥāwī. *Kitāb adhkār al-ḥuqūq war-ruhūn min al-jāmi' al-kabīr fish-shurūṭ, Sitzungsberichte der Heidelberger Akademie der Wissenschaften, Philosophisch-historische Klasse.* 1926–1927.

———. *Kitāb ash-shuf'a min al-jāmi' al-kabīr fish-shurūṭ, Sitzungsberichte der Heidelberger Akademie der Wissenschaften, Philosophisch-historische Klasse,* 1929–1930.

———. *Kitāb ash-shurūṭ aṣ-ṣaghīr,* manuscripts. Istanbul. *Bayazit* 18905, *Murad Mollah* 997 and 998.

Tyan, E. *Le notariat et le régime de la preuve par écrit dans la pratique du droit musulman.* 2nd edition. Beirut, n.d.

Udovitch, A. "At the Origins of the Western *Commenda*: Islam, Israel, Byzantium?" *SPECULUM.* 37 (1962): 198–207.

———. "Credit as a Means of Investment in Medieval Islamic Trade," *JAOS.* 87 (1967): 260–264.

———. "Labor Partnerships in Medieval Islamic Law," *JESHO*. 10 (1967) :64–80.

Umm. See Shāfi'ī.

Vesey-Fitzgerald, S. G. "Nature and Sources of the Shari'a," *Law in the Middle East*. 1: 85–112.

Wakin, Jeanette A. *Islamic Law in Practice: Two Chapters From Ṭaḥāwī's Kitāb Al-Shurūṭ Al-Kabīr*. Dissertation (unpublished). Columbia University, 1968.

al-Wanscharīsī. *La Pierre de Touche des Fetwas*. Summary translations by E. Amar. *Archives Marocaines*. 12 (1908), 13 (1909).

Weber, Max. *Zur Geschichte der Handelgesellschaften im Mittelalter*. Stuttgart, 1889.

———. *General Economic History*. N.Y., 1961.

Zurqānī. *Sharḥ 'alā muwaṭṭa' al-imām Mālik*. 4 vols. Cairo, 1961–1962.

Glossary

amāna	Trust, fiduciary relationship
'āriyya	Loan for use; putting another temporarily and gratuitously in possession of the use of a thing, the substance of which is not consumed by its use
biḍā'a	See *ibḍā'*
commenda	Arrangement in which one party invests capital and another party trades with it on the understanding that they share the profits in an agreed upon ratio, and that any loss resulting from normal trading activity is borne by the investing party
dinar	Gold unit of currency in early Islam
dirham	Silver unit of the Arab monetary system during most of the Islamic middle ages
fals (pl. *fulūs*)	Designation of the copper coin current in the early centuries of the Islamic era
fatāwā (pl. of *fatwā*)	Opinions, or *responsa* on a point of Islamic law issued by a competent authority
fiqh	Science of the *sharī'a*; Islamic jurisprudence
ḥawāla	Transfer of debt
ḥiyal	Legal devices; evasions for the purpose of circumventing, not violating, provisions of Islamic law
ibḍā'	Type of informal commercial collaboration in which one party entrusts his goods to the care of another, usually to be sold, after which the latter, without any compensation, commission, or profit, returns the proceeds of the transaction to the first party
ījāb wa-qabūl	Offer and acceptance—the two essential formal elements required for a contract in Islamic law
ijāra	Hire or lease contract

ijmāʿ	Consensus of Islamic scholars on a point of Islamic law
ʿinān	In Ḥanafī law, a partial investment partnership involving only mutual agency and not mutual suretyship in the relations between the partners; in Mālikī law, a partnership limited either to a single commodity or a single transaction
istidāna	Commercial commitment of the *commenda* by the agent in excess of the capital invested
istiḥsān	Juristic preference; in Ḥanafī law, an exercise of discretionary opinion in breach of strict analogy
istiṣlāḥ	Literally: "having regard for the public interest"; a concept in Mālikī law functionally akin to that of *istiḥsān* in Ḥanafī law
kafāla	Suretyship
maʾdhūn	Slave whose owner has granted him permission to engage in trade
māl ḥāḍir	Ready cash
maʿlūm	Known, certain, determined; particularly in reference to the object or objects of a contract
mudabbar	Slave whose manumission is to take effect upon the death of his owner
muḍāraba	Ḥanafī designation of a *commenda*
mufāwaḍa	In Ḥanafī law, a partnership embracing all the resources of the parties to the contract, and involving mutual agency and suretyship in the relationship between the partners; in Mālikī law, a partnership in which each partner confers upon his colleague full authority to dispose of their joint capital in any manner intended to benefit their association

mukātab	Slave who acquires his freedom against a future payment, or installment payments to his owner
muqāraḍa	Mālikī and Shāfi'ī designation of a *commenda*
murābaḥa	Resale of goods with the addition of a fixed surcharge to the stated original cost
musāwama	Sale of goods at any price mutually agreed upon by the buyer and the seller
qarḍ	Loan of money or other fungible objects intended to be consumed
qirāḍ	Mālikī and Shāfi'ī designation of a *commenda*
ra'y	Opinion, with the significance of independent reasoning as applied to the legal method of the Ḥanafī school
salam	Form of sale entailing advance payment for future delivery
sharī'a	Sacred law of Islam
sharika (also *shirka*)	Partnership
sharikat al-'aqd	Contractual partnership
sharikat al-milk	Proprietary partnership
shurūṭ	Legal formularies
suftaja	Bill of exchange
takafu'	Principle of proportionality in Mālikī partnership law requiring the distribution of profit and liability in a partnership to correspond to the distribution of the various components constituting the investment
tawliya	Resale of goods at the stated original cost
waḍī'a	Resale of goods with a discount from the original stated cost
wakāla	Agency
wakīl	Agent

Index